Too Bold for the Box Office

Too Bold for the Box Office

The Mockumentary from Big Screen to Small

Edited by
Cynthia J. Miller

THE SCARECROW PRESS, INC.
Lanham • Toronto • Plymouth, UK
2012

Published by Scarecrow Press, Inc.
A wholly owned subsidary of The Rowman & Littlefield Publishing Group, Inc.
4501 Forbes Boulevard, Suite 200, Lanham, Maryland 20706
www.rowman.com

10 Thornbury Road, Plymouth PL6 7PP, United Kingdom

British Library Cataloguing in Publication Information Available

Library of Congress Cataloging-in-Publication Data

Too bold for the box office : the mockumentary from big screen to small /
edited by Cynthia J. Miller.
    p. cm.
  Includes bibliographical references and index.
  ISBN 978-0-8108-8518-9 (cloth : alk. paper) — ISBN 978-0-8108-8519-6 (ebook)
  1. Documentary-style films—History and criticism. 2. Documentary-style
television programs—History and criticism. I. Miller, Cynthia J.
  PN1995.9.D62T66 2012
  070.1'8—dc23
                                                              2012011326

Printed in the United States of America

*For my mom, who loved to laugh,
and my dad, who usually gave her a reason.*

Contents

Acknowledgments

Who are you that you can't be laughed at?

I heard those words decades ago and have carried them with me all this time. They were hurled in challenge to a classroom full of anthropology students who were too clever by half and oh so serious about their efforts to make their mark in academia. The professor had passed off some outrageous story about the reproductive practices of some long-forgotten group, and we'd all furiously scribbled down every word. He laughed long and hard, and we flared in response—collectively furious at the joke made at our expense. The professor, whom I would come to affectionately think of as "Big B," was indeed mocking us, and we certainly needed it. We needed the challenge, the shock, the righteous indignation, and the reflection that followed. We needed to have our certainty about the way the world worked called into question, to be hauled up short for our uncritical acceptance of authority, and to learn to see the humor in our fumblings to "get it right."

I found myself thinking about those lessons time and again as this project came together—about the inestimable value of being challenged and infuriated by, and ultimately learning from, humor—and so, my deepest thanks to Bob Dryfoos—"Big B"—for what may well be one of the most valuable lessons of my education and for fostering the turn of mind that led me to this book.

As with any project like this, there are countless people to thank for their influence, their caring, their good humor, and their patience. First and foremost, thanks to my father, who passed on without seeing this volume reach publication, for his love and support of all the academic projects that left him shaking his head; and to Bow Van Riper, for being my editorial wingman, my technological guru, and the best partner in crime that I could have asked for on this project. His support and encouragement have been without equal. Thank you to Peter Rollins, for organizing the conference from which this work arose; to John Tibbetts, for his enthusiasm and encouragement when the volume was little more than an idea and for his thoughtfulness and help all along the way; to Stephen Ryan, who believed in the project and gave it an excellent home with Scarecrow Press; and to the fifteen gifted contributors whose thoughts, hard work, and good cheer fill these pages. Thank you, one and all.

Introduction

Despite the etymology of the genre's label, mockumentaries have always been about more than just cynical laughs purchased at the expense of the people, events, and ideas that animate our worlds.[1] They exist in a place where social commentary, cultural critique, and the crisis of representation collide, where humor—whether in the form of blatant laughter or simply rueful shakes of the head—meets reflection. We look for truth, and they offer us a map to a falsehood; we cling to our notions of the past, and they call forth long-lost chronicles; we believe that we can trust our eyes, and they testify with images of reality stolen from other times and places. And buried deep within the lie is, in fact, a kind of truth: just not the truth we were after.

One part humor and two parts transgression, the many forms and variations of the mockumentary genre hold a mirror to our flaws, poke fun at our assumptions, and refuse to let us look away from our most cherished notions about reality and the taken-for-granteds about everyday life, laying bare the audacities, frailties, and well-guarded fantasies that bring them into being. Mockumentaries play with our inner worlds, as well as our social lives—at times, gently; at others, drawing blood. They make no apologies, they take no prisoners, and they laugh at our discomfort in the process.

Ranging from parody to hoax to active critique of documentary aesthetics, each with multiple nuances, the mockumentary genre holds that discomfort as central to its mission—for it is through that discomfort that we, as both audience and subject, reflect on our norms, values, ideologies, and ways of being. Mockumentary's cinematic roots run deeper in Western culture than in the cinematic traditions of other nations, with British and American traditions being the most prolific, but recent additions to the genre have originated in Germany, Russia, Sweden, and Iran. Ties can certainly be made between mockumentary and early theatrical social commentary, as well as other forms of transgressive performance, such as the parodies of class and gender found in turn-of-the-century burlesque, but as film historian and producer Jerome Kuehl reveals in his prologue, "Nothing New under the Sun—Or on Film," the mockumentary has links to other forms of image fakery as well. Though far from the first instance of such fakery, its contemporary form is most often traced back to a three-minute April Fool's Day hoax, "The Swiss Spaghetti Harvest," aired on the BBC's current affairs program *Panorama* in 1957. The program featured broadcaster Richard Dimbleby reporting that, due to a mild winter and the eradication of the spaghetti weevil, Switzerland was experiencing a bumper crop of spaghetti. The spot, which featured mock-documentary footage of the annual Harvest Festival, elicited hundreds of calls, seeking to verify the story's authenticity and obtain instructions for cultivating spaghetti trees in England.

In the fifty-four years that have passed since "The Swiss Spaghetti Harvest" aired, the mockumentary genre has exploded, training its lens on historical figures and discoveries (*Forgotten Silver*, 1995; *Forbidden Quest*, 1993), icons of popular culture (*Drop Dead Gorgeous*, 1999; *Elvis Meets Nixon*, 1997), nationalism and intercultural relations (*Talking to Americans*, 2001; *F**kland*, 2000), religion (*Enlightenment Guaranteed,* 1999; *The Proper Care and Feeding of an American Messiah*, 2006), race and ethnicity (*The History of White People in America*, 1985; *Born in the Wrong Body*, 1995), the horrors of death (*Cannibal Holocaust*, 1980; *Faces of Death*, 1978), and the horrors of suburbia (*G-Sale*, 2003; *Human Remains*, 2000), along with numerous send-ups of the culture industries, from television to music (*This Is Spinal Tap*, 1984; *CNNNN: Chaser Non-stop News Network*, 2002–2003). While a number of these films have mocked their way into first-run theaters and the hearts of mainstream audiences as the mischievous brainchildren of notable filmmakers such as Christopher Guest, Woody Allen, and Rob Reiner, others have been relegated to art house theaters, direct-to-video releases, Internet-only sales, and new media formats such as YouTube. As a body of moving image literature, they speak volumes about the traditions and trappings of the human condition. Likewise, as a body of moving image literature, they have only recently begun to receive scholarly attention.[2]

As several of the chapters in this volume illustrate, a key issue in the analysis of the mockumentary is, first and foremost, what qualifies? Are there degrees of mocking, and how do we understand them? Do different styles function differently or require different contexts to function—styles such as parody, with its focus on humor derived from the contrast between the rational and the irrational; hoax, which reflexively sets up a fictive documentary text as a means of commentary; or active documentary critique, with its open confrontation of documentary aesthetics? In what ways are the moving-image texts created by those various styles received differently by audiences? When a fiction film contains actual documentary footage imported to its narrative, how is its mockumentary status assessed? At the outset, mockumentaries may be thought of comprising a range, or continuum, of hybrid fictional texts that borrow from documentary modes to achieve their own ends. While scholarly examination sometimes differentiates strongly between "parody" and "fake" within the genre (often framed as the distinction between "mockumentary" and "fake documentary"), there are a number of common elements employed in their analysis. Jane Roscoe and Craig Hight emphasize appropriation, mimicry, confusion, and subversion of documentary modes as key determinants of a film's status as a mockumentary.[3] Gary Rhodes and John Parris Springer expand these evaluative criteria to include elements of parody, pastiche, and self-referential irony.[4] All of these criteria are useful in constructing a fluid, contextually dependent framework for considering mockumentary films, and within that framework lies a key, much-agreed point: the mockumentary owes its lifeblood to the documentary form that it references.

Like other film genres, however, each filmmaker tends to use these elements to focus the lens of narrative commentary a bit differently. As John Kenneth Muir points out, while many mockumentaries, such as Larry Charles's controversial *Borat: Cultural Learnings of America for Make Benefit Glorious Nation of Kazakhstan* (2006), employ elements such as satire, irony, and parody to create embarrassment and suffering for their characters, Christopher Guest, the filmmaker behind the mockumentary trilogy *Waiting for Guffman* (1996), *Best in Show* (2000), and *A Mighty Wind* (2003), combines his parody with an element of naiveté to produce what critic David Denby has called "affectionate satire." Guest insists that no one in his films is ever "mocked" in the hostile, disparaging sense: "I call it comedy that's done in a documentary style."[5] In the hands of filmmaker Chris Hansen, that sort of gentle comic affection, while still very much present, develops teeth and a somewhat sharper "bite" in its

treatment of blue-collar self-proclaimed "local, regional messiah" Brian in
The Proper Care and Feeding of an American Messiah (2006).

As Jesse Lerner points out in his introduction to *F Is for Phony*, though,
complications remain, complications focused not on the nature of mocking but on the active use of nonfiction—perceived "truth"—in the service
of fiction and on "the varieties of fictional narratives that incorporate
documentary tropes . . . the host of strategies practiced in the murky bor-
derlands of documentary, fiction, and fake."[6] Cinematic history is brimming with films that variously fake, duplicate, and blend fiction and nonfiction images and tropes and challenge the creation of tidy categories and
definitions. Hybrid films since the silent era have created admixtures of
fiction and nonfiction footage that blurs genre boundaries—on one hand,
newsreels pieced together with representative but inauthentic documentary footage added for narrative support; on the other, newsreel footage
added to fiction films to heighten impact. The 1939 film *Hitler: Beast of
Berlin*, for example, dovetailed newsreel footage of Nazi troops parading
through the streets of Berlin with cutaway shots of scripted onlookers in
support of the film's narrative. Far from parody or satire, with no subversion or irony intended, hybrid techniques such as this create "fakes" that
challenge and complicate our notion of the "truth," yet they may also
be seen as lacking criteria of intentionality necessary for inclusion in the
range of fictional texts considered mockumentary.

Still, that intentionality—whether parody, hoax, pastiche, or active
critique—relies on the status of the documentary and on its audience's
familiarity with documentary codes, formats, and objective authority to
do its social and cultural work. For the "truth" to be subverted, parodied,
or otherwise taken out to play, audiences must first believe that a format
exists for reliably delivering that truth. While audiences of films, television, and new media are increasingly aware that documentary truth is
"relative" truth—authenticity that begs interrogation—that truth still
functions to lend a degree of ontological stability to audiences' beliefs, experiences, and identities.[7] Mockumentaries, then, in degrees correspond-
ing to their style, reach out and pull the cushion of certainty out from
under audiences as they sit.

Too Bold for the Box Office is a compilation of chapters by scholars, by
filmmakers, and by individuals who wear both hats with equal comfort.
Reflections by filmmakers Kevin Brownlow (*It Happened Here*), Chris
Hansen (*The Proper Care and Feeding of an American Messiah*), and Spencer
Schaffner (*The Urban Literacy Center Manifesto*) add valued perspective
that is often unavailable in scholarly anthologies and that significantly
deepens the discussions in the pages that follow. The chapters included
here spotlight the parody, cultural critique, and interrogation of "truth"
found in mockumentaries, fakes, speculative histories, and docufictions,

as they demonstrate just how tenuous and problematic our collective understandings of our social worlds can be.

Writing from—and about—national film, television, and new media traditions as diverse as their backgrounds, the volume's contributors explore and theorize the workings of mockumentaries, as well as the strategies and motivations of the writers and filmmakers who brought them into being, to better understand the larger cultural truths artfully woven into their deception. Individually, each chapter looks at a given instance of mockumentary parody and subversion, examining in depth the ways in which each calls into question our assumptions, pleasures, beliefs, and even our very senses. Taken together, this collection on films, television programming, and new media from Canada, the United States, Germany, New Zealand, the Netherlands, and the United Kingdom illustrates common threads running across cultures and eras, as individuals, social groups, and entire nations negotiate identities, cope with social tensions, acknowledge fears, make peace with ideologies, and attempt to answer sweeping existential questions about the nature of social life and the human condition.

* * *

Opening the volume is a special introductory prologue, "Nothing New under the Sun—Or On Film," by film historian Jerome Kuehl, which provides unique contextualization not often available to analyses of mockumentaries. A long-time archival researcher, writer, adviser for the BBC, and producer for Thames Television, Kuehl takes a journey through the extensive history of "fakes" and misuses of documentary imagery not ordinarily attributed to authoritative, "factual" media, such as newspapers, news broadcasts, and historical programming. Narrated by Kuehl's alter ego, "The Office Cat" (a bit of mockery itself?), the prologue is extensively illustrated by archival materials that demonstrate the ties between "found footage" and "lost history" mockumentaries, such as the BBC's "Swiss Spaghetti Harvest" hoax, and their more revered, factual counterparts. Kuehl situates those that follow in the larger context of documentary truth telling, asking us to consider the murky heritage of our understandings of mediated history.

LOST HISTORIES

With this framework as background and touchstone, the volume's first segment focuses on "lost histories." Each contributor looks at the ways in which mockumentary draws on history's silenced voices and salvaged stories to comment on our understandings of the past. Eve Allegra Raimon's "Making Up Mammy: Reenacting Historical Erasure and Recasting Authenticity in Cheryl Dunye's *The Watermelon Woman*" examines Cheryl Dunye's mock reconstruction of a fictional lost history. In its chronicle of a young black lesbian filmmaker's attempts to recover the life and career of "Fae Richards"—a black character actor in the tradition of Hattie MacDaniel and Butterfly McQueen—the film dramatizes historical absence and takes on, as Raimon points out, the long-standing scholarly quandary of how to engage in historical research when there are few surviving artifacts. Raimon demonstrates the multiple ways in which Dunye's multilayered fake confounds authenticity in both the documentary form and history itself.

The volume's next chapter moves from the exploration of space to the intersection of "lost" histories and race with Cynthia J. Miller and A. Bowdoin Van Riper's "Mercury's on the Launch Pad, but Cadillac's on the Moon: *The Old Negro Space Program*." The most forthright of this segment's lost histories, filmmaker Andy Bobrow's parody of Ken Burns, *The Old Negro Space Program* (2003), was one of the first Internet-based short films to go viral. Miller and Van Riper discuss the ways in which Bobrow's historical invention comments not only on the black experience in the mid-twentieth-century United States but also on the reification of the historical canon, as it celebrates some histories, leaving others untold (such as the real-life African American actresses who inspired Dunye's *Watermelon Woman*).

For the next contribution, we move from lost artifacts to the exploration of the Antarctic regions. In "Peter Delpeut's *The Forbidden Quest*: History and Truth in Fiction," Robert G. Weiner investigates another lost history fake: the *Hollandia* expedition. Supported by found footage from actual Arctic expeditions, Delpeut's tale of the *Hollandia* is a true fake, containing only the subtlest of clues about its status as a fictionalized reconstruction. Weiner argues that the film goes beyond mere fakery to become an artifact of found-footage art. Echoing Kuehl's exposé of recontextualized imagery—and validating his greatest fears about its eventual attainment of historical acceptance—Weiner demonstrates the complex interweaving of fiction and multiple realities drawn on and *created* by the film as it attains its own truth status.

POPULAR CULTURE AS COMMENTARY

Each chapter in the volume's next segment examines "popular culture as commentary"—the diverse ways in which the mockumentary genre uses our media as both vehicle for and object of its cultural critiques. Leading off the segment is Linda Kornasky's "Polka Settles the Score in *The Schmenges: The Last Polka*," which moves the discussion of culture and the mockumentary from race to ethnicity, as she examines Eugene Levy and John Candy's 1984 parody of Martin Scorsese's *The Last Waltz* (1978) in *The Schmenges: The Last Polka*. Kornasky contends that the film offers a uniquely critical perspective on mainstream American popular culture—explicitly and implicitly—through its transgressive and carnivalesque treatment of ethnic stereotypes and prejudices, as well as through its creative engagement with the mockumentary form. Kornasky argues that it is precisely in this complex approach that *The Last Polka* offers its sharpest cultural commentary.

Craig Hight next examines a cluster of comic productions in "Experiments in Parody and Satire: Short-Form Mockumentary Series." While the chapters in the volume thus far have drawn on cinematic and Internet film, Hight's is the first to explore the ways that mockumentary's popular-culture parodies engage with television. Looking at three mock-documentary series produced by the BBC and Australia's Channel Seven—*Posh Nosh*, *Marion and Geoff*, and *Double Take*—Hight discusses the unique ways in which televised mockumentaries take advantage of not only the domestic medium's more intimate form of address but also its capacities for intertextuality and self-reference. With the ever-increasing demand for reality television, Hight argues that television's opportunities to develop the short-form mockumentary will continue to expand.

As the volume's look at mockumentary's interplay with popular culture continues, Gary D. Rhodes's "Commando Raids on the Nature of Reality" disentangles notions of reality and representation in Norman Mailer's experimental film *Maidstone* (1970). The film, often said to be one of Mailer's boldest gambits, stars the filmmaker as his own alter ego and namesake—at least, when he remains in character. Rhodes painstakingly traces the film's trajectory from mockery to catastrophe as the film increasingly blurs the lines between fiction and reality. In analyzing the filmmaker's "assault on reality," Rhodes concludes that Mailer's true target is not reality but its cinematic representations.

DARING TO BELIEVE

The next segment of the volume, "Daring to Believe," creates a conversation about how mockumentaries engage with notions of faith, hope, and the need to believe in something that transcends the human condition. Scott Wilson's analysis of New Zealand's *Forgotten Silver* (1995), in "Aching to Believe: The Heresy of *Forgotten Silver*," begins the discussion with a look at the way that the hoax perpetrated by the televised mockumentary struck a bitter chord with much of its audience, who were all too ready to embrace the lost history of the film's fictional filmmaker and momentary national hero. Wilson's careful analysis offers not only insights into filmmakers Costa Botes and Peter Jackson's crafting of a successful mockumentary hoax but also a rare glimpse at the most important component of any good hoax: its reception.

Faith takes a double mockumentary hit in Heather Merle Benbow's "'That's Not Zen!' Mocking Ethnographic Film in Doris Dörrie's *Enlightenment Guaranteed*." Benbow's analysis demonstrates that while Dörrie's film enacts its first layer of parody on the contemporary search for enlightenment and peace in the midst of chaos, its second layer of cultural commentary is aimed at the truth status of ethnographic film—the subgenre of documentary that is the trademark of anthropological inquiry. Benbow's own inquiry reveals that in *Enlightenment Guaranteed* (1999), the "truth," much like "enlightenment," can be elusive, even in those places where it is most expected to be found.

This segment's critical commentary on the fragility of faith concludes with "The Mind behind the Mockumentary: *The Proper Care and Feeding of an American Messiah*," by Chris Hansen. Hansen provides the volume's first filmmaker's reflection on the genre, as well as discussing the making of his film, which is now achieving cult status. In the tradition of *Man Bites Dog* (1992) and *The Magician* (2005), Hansen uses the mockumentary form to construct an intimate chronicle of a would-be "local messiah" and deliver a palatably humorous critique of the cultural thrusts that produce billionaire televangelists or spur national attention when the image of the Virgin Mary is claimed to appear on a ten-year-old piece of toast.[8]

THE WAR THAT WASN'T

The horrors of war have been well represented in the mockumentary genre over the past half century of films. In "The War That Wasn't," the discussion turns to some of these "speculative histories"—battles reconfigured in a blend of the real and the imagined—as this segment examines the social and moral anxieties surrounding some of the great military conflicts of the Western world and debates the genre status of the fake documentary. This segment of the volume begins and ends with chapters focused on the influential 1966 film *It Happened Here*. John C. Tibbetts's "It (Might Have) Happened Here: How Nazi Germany Won the War" provides a critical analysis of the film *It Happened Here*, framing it in historian Niall Ferguson's rhetoric of "counterfactuals"—plausible outcomes of historical moments, culled from seemingly infinite variety, to better understand the course of human events. Tibbetts argues that these "what if?" questions of history demand to be answered, and he cites the counterfactual nature of *It Happened Here* not as an example of creative mocking of history but, rather, as one of responsible historiography.

Thomas Prasch continues this analysis of counterfactuals in "Between What Is and What If: Kevin Willmott's *CSA*," demonstrating that counterfactuals—"what if's?"—have a long and rich history in the search for meaning, despite generations of historians dismissing counterfactual arguments as "parlor games" and "unhistorical shit." Willmott's film *CSA: The Confederate States of America* (2004) is a double-level parody in which a British documentary on American history since the southern victory in the Civil War is aired on CSA-controlled television. Much like Willmott's film, Prasch's analysis takes place on dual levels. On the first, he examines the "plausibility" and "utility" of the film as axes for evaluating its effectiveness. He then clears these aside to expose the film's central thesis: that in some significant ways, the South *did* win the war.

Countering these analyses that find productive engagement between counterfactual history and the mockumentary genre, James M. Welsh mounts an argument against the inclusion of these speculative histories and fake documentaries under the genre's mantle in his discussion of Peter Watkins's films *Culloden* (1964) and *The War Game* (1965): "The 'Serious' Mockumentary: The Trivialization of Disaster? The Case of Peter Watkins." Here, Welsh questions whether, in fact, a "serious" category of mockumentary exists or whether the broad boundaries of the genre risk what he terms "the trivialization of disaster," through the conflation of parody and speculative history. In this, Welsh raises significant questions about genre ethics and—harkening back to Kuehl's prologue—the permeability of the boundaries between "fake" documentaries and the crisis of authenticity among those that are trusted to be "real."

Returning once again to *It Happened Here*, filmmaker Kevin Brownlow offers a look at the film's making. In his chronicling of the film's origins and production, Brownlow provides keen insights into the interconnections among film, formal history, and the lived realities of people's social and political worlds. Of course, "mockumentary" was a nonexistent concept during Brownlow's early career, applied retroactively to *It Happened Here*, just like what occurred with Watkins's films, as Welsh observes. But in the filmmaker's reflections, there is a certain . . . delight . . . in his part in the ongoing evolution of the mockumentary tradition.

EPILOGUE

The volume's discussion of mockumentaries closes with a look at the ways in which new media have affected the creation, production, and dissemination of the genre. Spencer Schaffner's epilogue, "Mockumentaries Meet New Media," offers a filmmaker's-eye view of the impact of Web technologies, including a discussion of his two Internet-based mockumentaries, *9Interviews.com* (2004) and *The Urban Literacy Center Manifesto* (2007). Schaffner brings the mockumentary into the twenty-first century, where YouTube, Twitter, Facebook, and countless file-sharing sites for images, music, text, and video all bleed into one another to create endless-seeming possibilities for intertextuality. The increased ability to appropriate still and moving images (as recounted by Brownlow and illustrated by Kuehl) and combine them in complex, experimental ways, along with the comparative ease of creating online productions, allows new media mockumentarians a creative freedom unfamiliar to their predecessors. Similarly, as Schaffner points out, the Internet's broad and almost instantaneous connection with audiences, along with the potential for audience interaction (in the form of participatory viewing, fan editing, and other manners of active feedback), works to shift and complicate the roles of viewers/users in ways not previously experienced—creating the potential for exceptionally media-savvy audiences at one pole and even deeper and more complex hoaxes at the other.

The volume concludes with an annotated filmography of selected mockumentaries. The list, while not intended to be comprehensive, offers an extensive array of various mockumentary forms—fakes, docufictions, mock documentaries, and fiction-newsreel hybrids—selected from a wide range of nations and perspectives. From the earliest examples ("The Swiss Spaghetti Harvest") to the most recent additions (*All You Need Is Brains,* 2009), the filmography provides an overview of cinematic work in the genre. Included in this list are well-known first-run film parodies, such as Christopher Guest's *A Mighty Wind* and *Best in Show*, Woody Allen's *Zelig* (1983) and *Sweet and Lowdown* (1999), and, of course, Rob Reiner's classic *This Is Spinal Tap*; but the list also extends its reach well beyond to include numerous lesser-known films, from Russia's first mockumentary, *First on the Moon* (2005), to the Argentinean *F**kland* (2000). While not citing single-episode mocks found in continuing series (such as those found in *M*A*S*H*, *ER*, and others), television programming is found in this gathering of mockumentary offerings, such as the Canadian parody *Talking to Americans* (2001). Additionally, the list includes Internet short-film mockumentaries, such as *The Old Negro Space Program*, further demonstrating the depth and breadth of this underexamined genre.

NOTES

1. An earlier version of segments of this introduction appeared in *Post Script* (summer 2009).

2. See Jane Roscoe and Craig Hight, *Faking It: Mock-Documentary and the Subversion of Factuality* (Manchester: Manchester University Press, 2001); Gary Rhodes and John Parris Springer, *Docufictions: Essays on the Intersection of Documentary and Fictional Filmmaking* (Jefferson, NC: McFarland, 2006); Alexandra Juhasz and Jesse Lerner, eds., *F Is for Phony: Fake Documentary and Truth's Undoing* (Minneapolis: University of Minnesota Press, 2006).

3. Roscoe and Hight, *Faking It*, 1.

4. Rhodes and Springer, *Docufictions*, 5.

5. John Kenneth Muir, *"Best in Show": The Films of Christopher Guest and Company* (Milwaukee, WI: Leonard, 2004), 4.

6. Juhasz and Lerner, *F Is for Phony*, 19.

7. Robert F. Reid-Pharr, "Makes Me Feel Mighty Real: *The Watermelon Woman* and the Critique of Black Visuality," in Juhasz and Lerner, *F Is for Phony*, 130–40.

8. The toast, auctioned on eBay, ultimately netted $28,000 in 2004. These urges are also parodied in Mark Pellington's 2008 comedy-drama *Henry Poole Is Here*.

Prologue: Nothing New under the Sun—Or on Film

Jerome Kuehl

We all know that films can record things as they really are, but we also know that cinema has relied on tricks and fakery from its very beginning. In 1895, when films were first shown to a paying audience, the Lumière brothers showed an episode of a team of workmen demolishing a wall and then ran the sequence backward.[1] This was the very first of the many deceptions that continue to this day.

The Lumières' falling wall.

The wall collapsing, then miraculously being rebuilt, could also be seen as the first of the cinema's jokes. The Lumières and their great colleague and rival Georges Méliès enjoyed visual pranks, and audiences never complained that Méliès's *Voyage dans la Lune*, with its prancing moon maidens, was scientifically impossible or demanded their money back.

Preparations for launch in *Voyage dans la Lune* (1902).

One cinematic joke, which still has the power to make viewers misty-eyed with nostalgia, was the April Fool's Day BBC *Panorama* "hoax" in 1957, "The Swiss Spaghetti Harvest," which showed spaghetti harvested from trees in Switzerland. The item was presented with a perfectly straight narration by Richard Dimbleby, who explained that the year's unusually mild winter had resulted in an "exceptionally heavy" crop—a boon to the small family farmers whose spaghetti crops often fell victim to late-season frosts or the destructive "spaghetti weevil," leaving them unable to compete with the "vast spaghetti plantations" of Italy. Newsreel footage illustrates the spaghetti's journey, from tree to table, as it is picked by young women, laid out to dry in the sun, then cooked and served to celebrate the successful harvest, while Dimbleby observes, "For those who love this dish, there's nothing like real home-grown spaghetti." At the time of the hoax segment's airing, rationing in

Britain had ended only three years previously, and pasta was relatively unknown. Even today, many consumers are ignorant of the sources of the processed food they eat and might also fall victim to such a parody. The hoax generated a combination of curiosity and criticism, but even the many viewers who got the joke hardly felt that the BBC's reputation for probity had been sullied.

A bountiful "spaghetti harvest" in Switzerland.

It's been claimed that this was the first mockumentary, but in film, as the book of Ecclesiastes observes, there is no new thing under the sun, and Georges Méliès did get there first.

In 1896, Francis Doublier, a sixteen-year-old cameraman whom the Lumière brothers sent to Russia, found himself in a Ukrainian community with a large Jewish population where he cobbled together a story—a kind of newsreel *avant la lettre*—showing scenes of the Dreyfus affair. In 1894, Captain Alfred Dreyfus, the first Jew appointed to the French General Staff, was accused of spying for the Germans. He was arrested, court-martialed, and sent to Devil's Island, off the coast of French Guiana. Doublier calculated that these scenes would be of more interest to Dreyfus's coreligionists than the miscellaneous collection of travelogues, street scenes, and parades, which he usually showed. What he in fact exhibited was a collection of episodes, each no more than a minute in length, of a French officer accompanied by troops, a public building in Paris, a Finnish tug with a seagoing barge, and film of a delta on the Nile. He described the anonymous officer as Captain Alfred Dreyfus, the building as the Palais de Justice, the tug and barge as the vessels that transported Dreyfus to Devil's Island, and the Nile delta as the island itself. As Doublier tells the story, spectators were enthralled, except for one skeptic, who asked how the court-martial in 1894 could have been filmed by a device that had not yet been invented. Doublier does not record his answer.[2]

However, there is another account by Doublier of how he came to create this collection of images:

> The Dreyfus affair was still a source of great interest in those days, and out of it I worked up a little film story, which made me quite a bit of money. Piecing together a shot of some soldiers, one of a battleship, one of the Palais de Justice, and one of a tall grey-haired man, I called it "L'affaire Dreyfus." People actually believed that this was a filming of the famous case.

The resolution of the second account also differs, with Doublier describing how he was forced to admit to the "little old man" who questioned the veracity of the film that it was indeed a fake. "Suffice to say," Doublier concludes, "I never showed 'L'affaire Dreyfus' again."[3]

Even in confessing (or boasting about) his feats as a young man, Doublier was not only giving two versions of events, only one of which might be veridical—the privilege of autobiographers throughout the ages—but also placing himself firmly within an ancient tradition of deception, which goes back as far as St. Paul's *Epistle to the Laodicians*. The truth is that, so far as moving images are concerned, every foot of film is exposed at a particular time, in a particular place, and by a particular person. Automatic cameras—whether strapped to the outside of submarines, moon-bound rockets, or the wingtips or bomb bays of aircraft—or, for that matter, surveillance cameras or closed-circuit televisions don't need people except to activate them, but even so, the provenance of all such moving images is certain.

That Ukrainian skeptic who wondered how films could be made by an apparatus that had not yet been invented was the spiritual ancestor of the Office Cat, a creature who has been embarrassing slovenly producers and directors since it first saw the light of day in the pages of the *History Workshop Journal*, an avowedly left-wing British scholarly publication. It was born in 1976, in the course of a polemic between a colleague and me, in which I complained that a filmed excerpt was overcranked—and it didn't matter whether the deed was perpetrated by the labs, the holders of the archive, or the Office Cat—it was totally unacceptable. That is why the Office Cat has such a Sisyphean task: No sooner has it rolled one bit of faked, misused, or dishonestly employed film to the top of the mountain than another takes its place.

The Office Cat is not an ordinary cat—it's a film researcher. Unlike human researchers, it never takes "no" for an answer. One of its ancestors found film of the Wright Brothers' first flight; another found film of the Battle of Jutland; and a third unearthed shots of Adolf Hitler marrying Eva Braun in the Führerbunker. In other words, the Cat is an expert at finding film that doesn't actually exist, or that does exist, but not in the way that producers and directors would like it to. (To be clear: the first film of a Wright Brothers' aircraft was taken in France, on the outskirts of Le Mans in 1908; no one filmed the Battle of Jutland, because the British Admiralty wouldn't allow cameramen on board their ships; and the only film of Hitler's last days was taken by his personal cameraman, Walter Frentz, who recorded him issuing medals to Hitler Youth outside the Führerbunker on March 20. The images were shown in Berlin in the *Deutsche Wochenschau* (No. 755) two days later, a remarkable feat.)

The Cat swipes its paw at both feature films and documentaries. It would certainly have noticed *The King's Speech*, a feature film that won four Oscars in 2011, including Best Picture, and gave Tom Hooper the Best Director award. It would have pointed out that the film depicts events during the 1930s in which women wore seam-free stockings but that seamless stockings, though common in medieval England, fell out of favor and were not much used until the 1960s. It would have been astonished to learn that during the royal family's viewing of newsreels, the images were projected at a ratio of 16:9, which, like seamless stockings, wasn't used until the 1960s. Newsreels until then were projected at a 4:3 aspect ratio.[4] The Cat certainly would have also noted that Lionel Logue, the Australian speech therapist who did his best to alleviate the Duke of York's—later, King George VI's—stutter did not live in a tiny house surrounded by grubby street urchins but in a substantial dwelling in the Boltons—the London equivalent of Central Park West.[5]

The Office Cat generally finds dealing with features unrewarding. It's like discovering that bare-armed extras in Cecil B. DeMille's biblical blockbusters sometimes wear watches. Alert audiences can see that fictional films and even drama documentaries can't really make serious truth claims, and so the Cat devotes itself to documentaries, which do make such claims. Fictional accounts may certainly be lifelike, even though they cannot pretend to be true, but historical documentaries use film, narration, and the interviews that accompany them to tell true things about past events. Needless to say, the Office Cat has never been popular with producers, directors, commissioning editors, or distributors.

Consider the Windsor Hotel fire of 1899. Raymond Fielding, in his book on the American newsreel, described how the fire broke out in New York on March 17, 1899, and cost the lives of forty-five people. The tragedy was notable for what Terry Ramsaye, a prolific but gullible historian of silent cinema, hailed as probably "the first time the motion picture camera pictured news in the process of happening." The fire was filmed by J. Stuart Blackton and Albert E. Smith, who according to Ramsaye "had covered the fire with their camera, getting short bits of film of the burning ruins."[6]

The trouble was that Smith had written this in his journal: "March 30, 1899: Filmed miniature of Windsor Hotel fire with little rubber figures jumping out of windows of cardboard model. Ignited gunpowder for fire and smoke. Used toy squirt guns for streams of water. Film very successful." Audiences need not necessarily have been culpably gullible for having been deceived. Four years after the invention of the Lumière brothers' *cinématographe*, few had ever seen fires in large hotels, and fewer still had much of an idea about how they might appear on a flickering screen. But Blackton and Smith certainly knew what they were doing, and they put themselves in the Office Cat's black book forever.

A more striking instance was the first flight of the Wright Brothers, of which YouTube contains 1,250 examples. Wilbur and Orville made their first flight on December 17, 1903, with Orville at the controls. A still photograph by John T. Daniels, one of the five people present, records the event, but no one filmed it.

Orville Wright wrote this in his diary:

> When we got up, a wind of between 20 and 25 miles was blowing from the north.
>
> We got the machine out early and put out the signal for the men at the station. Before we were quite ready, John T. Daniels, W. S. Dough, A. D. Etheridge, W. C. Brinkley of Manteo, and Johnny Moore of Nags Head arrived.
>
> After running the engine and propellers a few minutes to get them in working order, I got on the machine at 10:35 for the first trial. The wind, according to our anemometers at this time, was blowing a little over 20 miles (corrected) 27 miles according to the Government anemometer at Kitty Hawk. On slipping the rope the machine started off increasing in speed to probably 7 or 8 miles. The machine lifted from the truck just as it was entering on the fourth rail. Mr. Daniels took a picture just as it left the tracks.[7]

The first time that the Wright Brothers' flights were filmed was in 1908, when cameras captured Wilbur's demonstration flights near Le Mans, France, in August and Orville's at Fort Myer, Virginia, in September.[8]

The Wright Brothers prepare for a 1908 flight.

So where do the 1,250 instances of the "Wright Brothers' first flight" on YouTube come from? Some are of the Le Mans flights, some of the Fort Myer episode; some are of flights at Huffman Prairie near the brothers' hometown of Dayton, Ohio, where they established a flying school; and some are simply commemorations of the first flight and don't purport to be of the flight itself. It's ironic that none of these 1,250 flights show the original aircraft, which—damaged on December 17 and never flown again—now hangs (restored) in the National Air and Space Museum in Washington, DC. One lesson that the Office Cat learned from this episode is to be very skeptical about film that purports to illustrate events at which no motion picture cameras were known to have been present. Even today, when so many people in the world use camcorders, such events are far from rare—which is one reason for the continuing popularity of dramatized documentaries. They have no difficulty in showing things at which film cameras are not present, but they pay a heavy price by forfeiting any claims they may make to presenting a veridical picture of events.

Between the last decade of the nineteenth century and the 1960s, moving images were principally made by newsreel and television cameramen and camerawomen, scientists, explorers, and home movie enthusiasts—probably no more than fifty thousand in all. Political events and personalities, spectacular accidents, pretty girls, sports, and natural disasters were all popular subjects among such professionals, but they could never film when they were prevented by censorship (or self-censorship), when it would have been too foolhardy to do so, or when they simply weren't present.

The absence of cameramen has had a dramatic effect on the visual history of the twentieth century. Among the most striking episodes of which no film exists is the maiden voyage of the *Titanic* in April 1912 (though YouTube has a staggering five thousand entries depicting the event). Two cameramen—an American, William Harbeck, and a Frenchman, Noel Malachard, from *Pathé-Journal*—doubtless filmed its departure and life on board, though both went down with the ship and their film has never been recovered.[9] The assassination of Archduke Franz Ferdinand of Austria in 1914, which prompted the First World War, wasn't filmed (though YouTube has 363 entries), nor was the sinking of the *Lusitania* by a German U-boat in May 1915 (YouTube has 398 entries). Other episodes that weren't filmed included the Battle of Jutland—or *Die Skaggerakschlacht*, depending on one's point of view—on May 31–June 1, 1915 (YouTube has 181 entries for the Battle of Jutland and only 10 for the *Skaggerakschlacht*, though it was the same battle), and the storming of the former tsar's Winter Palace by the Bolsheviks in October 1917 (YouTube has twenty-two entries).

Closer to our own time, though spectacular accidents were eminently newsworthy, no film exists of the destruction of the dirigibles *R38* (1921), *Shenandoah* (1925), *R101* (1930), *Akron* (1933), *Macon* (1935), or even the Soviet Union's *OSOAVIAKhlM* (1938). While five newsreel companies filmed the *Hindenburg* disaster, none of them caught the exact moment it burst into flame. It was already alight by the time they began filming.

Dirigible passengers observe landing preparations.

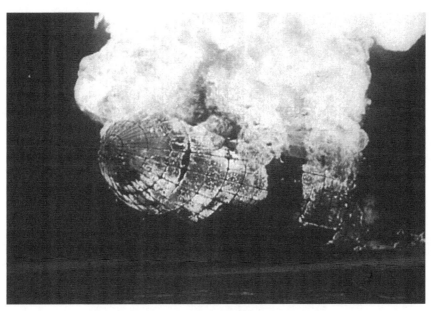

The Hindenburg burns at Lakehurst, NJ, in 1937.

No one filmed passengers in their cabin, though their images appeared in newsreel stories.

Charles Lindbergh's flight from New York to Paris in May 1927—both its heart-stopping beginning (as Lindbergh cleared the telephone wires at the end of the runway by a few feet) and its triumphant conclusion—was certainly filmed: a 20th Century Fox newsreel cameraman and sound recordist provided one of the first instances of a newsreel with direct recorded sound.[10] Lindbergh had no camera on board, however, and even his landfall over Ireland went unrecorded.

There is no film of the assassination of the American president William McKinley in September 1901, nor of the American demagogue Huey Long in September 1935, nor any of the communist Leon Trotsky in 1940, or the Nazi Reinhard Heydrich in 1942, or the pacifist Mahatma Gandhi in 1948.

There is no film of the German Condor Legion's aerial assault on Guernica, a Basque town attacked on April 26, 1937, during the Spanish Civil War, though YouTube has 150 entries. The first newsreel cameraman to arrive in the city was Raymond Méjat, a stringer for the Hearst-Metrotone newsreel who arrived on April 29, 1937, three days after the aerial attack and so only filmed rubble and ruins.[11]

The ruins of Guernica.

No one filmed any of the speeches that announced the outbreak of the Second World War in September 1939, and the filmed record doesn't exist of such actions during its course as the commando raid during which the HMS *Campbeltown* rammed the dry dock at St. Nazaire, France, on March 28, 1942. The raid severely damaged the ability of the Germans to harass Allied ships in the Atlantic, and YouTube has thirty-four entries chronicling it.[12] In fact, of the fifty-seven raids against Europe, only one, a raid against the Norwegian Lofoten islands, was ever filmed.[13]

British commandos storm the Lofoten Islands in 1941.

Hitler's announcement of the invasion of the Soviet Union on June 22, 1941, wasn't filmed, though a radio broadcast by Josef Goebbels reading his proclamation was.

Goebbels announces the invasion of the USSR.

Hitler's Bunkers Revealed, produced by Richard Belfield, directed by George Pagliero for Fulcrum Productions, and transmitted by the National Geographic Channel on November 7, 2008, used this image of the announcement of the invasion of the Soviet Union in June 1941 to illustrate Dr. Goebbels's last broadcasts from the ruins of the Third Reich in April 1945. Likewise, Stalin's defiant speech to the Russian people as his armies paraded on November 7, 1941, while the German forces were poised at the gates of Moscow wasn't filmed, because the parade began early to avoid possible *Luftwaffe* attacks and the newsreels weren't ready to record sound. The speech was mocked up later in the great hall of the Kremlin.

Stalin recreates, indoors, his speech during the siege of Moscow.

That's why Stalin has no snow on his greatcoat, nor does his breath condense, though it was bitingly cold when the parade took place.

No Germans filmed the D-Day invasion on June 6, 1944, or the attempt on Hitler's life on July 20, 1944, while, from the point of view of the Western allies, no one filmed the work of Bletchley Park, where German codes were broken, or the loss of the British capital ships *Prince of Wales* and *Repulse*, sunk by a Japanese aerial attack in December 1941, or the efforts of the American 32nd division as it fought the Japanese Army in New Guinea in July 1942.

German civilians (not Polish Jews) in 1945.

More important was the fact that no filmed records of what went on in Nazi extermination camps have survived, though it's possible that some were made. Films of death squads—the so-called Einsatzgruppen—concentration camps, and antipartisan warfare with their accompanying atrocities were filmed, and the liberation of Majdanek and Auschwitz by the Red Army, of Bergen-Belsen by the British, and of Dachau, Mauthausen-Gusen, and Buchenwald by the Americans was also filmed.

This has led to two quite distinct kinds of confusion and muddle. The first is to mix up films of the liberation of camps by the Red Army with those liberated by the British and Americans and, indeed, to confuse Dachau with Buchenwald or Mauthausen-Gusen with either. The second is a question of nomenclature. The sole purpose of an extermination camp was to put its inmates to death, but concentration camps had other functions as well. They imprisoned those whose enthusiasm for the regime was defective—Social Democrats, Communists, Seventh Day Adventists, Jehovah's Witnesses, and what the Nazis described as Zigeuners— Gypsies: Roma and Sinta. Bergen-Belsen, for example, was used to incarcerate prisoners whose prominence might be used as bargaining chips in dealing with Germany's adversaries. Auschwitz was a labor, concentration, and extermination camp, and this has led to further confusion when scriptwriters have an imperfect understanding of what is involved in this brutal, complex world.[14]

One problem is that in historical documentaries, narration is often the last element to be incorporated. Only when the visual elements are set in place does the producer or director turn his or her mind to the text, and by that time, it may well be too late to provide any but the most cursory investigation into what needs to be said. Professional filmmakers have a name for this state of affairs: KBS, or *kick, bollock, and scramble*, and it's not a pretty sight. No wonder text can stray so wildly from images. A sad example can be found in the last program of *Civilization and the Jews*, a PBS production released in 1984, directed by Alan Rosenthal and narrated by the former Israeli foreign minister Abba Eban. The narration speaks of Polish Jews returning to their homeland, as what is shown on the screen are German civilians who have attached themselves to the Waffen SS division Das Reich surrendering to elements of the American Third Army.[15]

So far as the period of the Cold War is concerned, there is no point in looking for footage of Nikita Khrushchev banging his shoe (or moccasin or slipper) on the table at the United Nations General Assembly meeting on October 12, 1960 (though YouTube offers 146 versions), because he never did so. He certainly waved a slipper or moccasin, and some still photographs show him doing this, though their authenticity has been questioned.[16] Neither newsreel nor television cameramen recorded the episode, since both were on strike that day.

Even today, in an age of ubiquitous coverage by camcorders, mobile telephones, smartphones, blogs, and Facebook, newsworthy stories can still be missed. The revolt against the Ben Ali regime in Tunisia was sparked by the self-immolation of Mohamed Bouzizi in Sidi Bouzid, on December 17, 2010, and though YouTube offers several views of the police repression that followed the event, there is no record of the act itself. Mohamed's cousin, Ali, arrived too late to either save Mohamed's life or film his sacrifice.

Pretending that events or persons that were never filmed were recorded is only one class of deception. There are other kinds as well, though this list is far from exhaustive:

1. Film that is claimed to be of one event, which is in fact of another event. Much of this prologue is devoted to this kind of deception.
2. Film shot in one place, which purports to have been shot somewhere else.
3. Feature film masquerading as factual film. The classic instance of this is *The Great War*, a twenty-six-part series transmitted by the BBC in 1964. One of the executive producers, Tony Essex, deliberately mixed the two to give the programs more zip and zing, but the result was such a confusing potpourri of material that the BBC did not dare rebroadcast the series for almost forty years because the documentation on the copyright holders was so inadequate. The programs were made at a time when, since time codes had not been invented, it was impossible to determine the provenance of material shot by shot. That meant that all the PSB (Programme as Broadcast) records ever indicated was that, for example, so many feet came from the West German Archives, so many feet from the Imperial War Museum, and so many feet from the American National Archive and Records Agency.
4. Film of an event that was never filmed at all, such as the maiden and final voyage of the *Titanic* or the first flight by the Wright brothers.
5. Film made before the invention of motion picture cameras, such as Columbus discovering America or the Battle of Waterloo—though even if cameras had existed, the thick black smoke would have made the battlefield virtually invisible after the first volley. One of the Office Cat's human film researcher friends was asked for film of Columbus's landing at Santa Domingo, "preferably in black and white but color will do." The producer didn't specify whether the film should be shot from on board the ship or from the native peoples' point of view.

The Office Cat has many worries but is principally concerned about the kind of deception that involves wilfully using material shot in one place and at a particular time to represent events or personalities from a different time and from a different place. There are countless examples, but one of the earliest and most spectacular was the sinking of the battleship *St. Stephen* or, to give it the name under which it sailed when it was part of the Austro-Hungarian navy, the SMS *Szent István*. Toward the end of the First World War, on June 10, 1918, the *Szent István* participated in a raid against the allied blockade at Otranto in the Adriatic Sea. The vessel was struck by two torpedoes fired from the Italian torpedo boat MAS 15, and it sank off the coast of Premuda Island near Zadar in Croatia. The torpedo boat, one of two, escaped, while the twenty-one-thousand-ton *Szent István* (which did not have watertight bulkheads) turned turtle and went to the bottom in under three hours. The crew milled around on deck because the captain refused to give the order to abandon ship. The loss of life was remarkably small: 89 dead. The episode was filmed from a fixed camera position on board a sister ship, the SMS *Tegetthoff*.

Sinking of the SMS *Svent István* in 1918.

These shots do not seem to have been used until 1934, when they were incorporated into a compilation film, *The First World War*, produced by Truman Talley, managing director of Fox newsreels, with a script by Laurence Stallings, who had written a stage production of Ernest Hemingway's *A Farewell to Arms* and was to later write the screenplay for John Ford's *She Wore a Yellow Ribbon*. The first instance of the misuse of this unfortunate ship came from the BBC, which transmitted *Nautilus: To War in Iron Coffins*, shown on September 12, 1995, and produced by Alan Lowenstein. It's supposed to be the HMS *Hogue*, a British cruiser sunk in the North Sea by a U-boat on September 22, 1914, and her sister ships, the *Aboukir* and the *Cressy*.

The *Szent István* surfaced in Jonathan Martin's "Battleship," a program in the *Weapons of World War II* series shown on March 17, 2004, where it was sunk to illustrate Major Gordon Corrigan's point about battleships during the Second World War being seriously vulnerable to attack from the air. The Cat guessed that if a torpedo strikes you, you don't really care where it came from or even which war you're fighting.

Adolf Hitler became chancellor of Germany on January 30, 1933, and lost no time in pursuing his animosity toward German Jews. In this, he was enthusiastically supported by Dr. Josef Goebbels, his minister for public enlightenment and propaganda—Volksaufklärung und Propaganda. Goebbels inspired an anti-Jewish boycott on April 1, 1933. The boycott was filmed by at least two newsreel companies: Deulig Tonwoche (No. 66) and Fox Tönende Wochenschau (No. 2600).[17] Sound was in its infancy, yet both companies dispatched recording trucks to the scene, and versions of what their cameramen saw and heard are available on YouTube.

Sign from the Nazi anti-Jewish boycott of April 1, 1933.

One scene shows two youths on bicycles, hitching a ride on the back of a lorry.

A truckload of Nazi Party stormtroopers during the April 1933 boycott.

In another, passersby were more interested in the camera and its bulky recording gear than the storm troopers chanting or barring the way to Jewish shops.

One storm trooper even succumbed to the temptation to sneak a peek—something he would hardly have dared to do later on when the regime organized its demonstrations more effectively.

In the period before the outbreak of the Second World War, Nazi-controlled newsreels and documentaries did not emphasize the persecution of Jews: there is, for example, no filmed record of *Kristallnacht*, the so-called Night of Broken Glass on November 9 and 10, 1938—except for a few meters of film of synagogues burning in Bielefeld and Buehl—and this has always posed a grave problem for subsequent filmmakers. How *are* they to show the plight of Germany's Jews during that dark period without any film? The easy solution is to use the April 1933 boycott footage, even though viewers may be puzzled by the presence of carefully lettered placards written in German and English, protesting against the Jewish boycott of German goods.

Stormtroopers orchestrate the April 1933 boycott.

Media-savvy poster designed to build support for the boycott.

In March 1933, some Jewish organizations in England and the United States had indeed called for a boycott against German goods and services, and the one-day boycott of Jewish professions, shops, and department stores—though ignored by many—was in the view of Dr. Goebbels simply a retaliatory move designed to bring to the world's attention the iniquity of the Jewish action. Hence, the signs are in English—a language that the organizers correctly thought would reach a far larger audience than a bilingual sign in Spanish or French, never mind Norwegian, Flemish, or Hungarian.

That's hardly an excuse. Fiona Cotter Craig, who produced and directed *Hitler's Favourite Royal* (the "favorite royal" was Prince Charles Edward, Queen Victoria's grandson) for Monkey Productions, transmitted by Britain's Channel 4 on December 6, 2007, illustrated *Kristallnacht*, the Night of Broken Glass, in November 1938 with scenes of these anti-Jewish boycotts in April 1933.

A Hand of Peace, produced by Gita Hosek and directed by David Naglieri for Salt and Light Television and transmitted by the Canadian Salt and Light Television ("Your Catholic Channel of Hope") on February 22, 2008, did the same. The scenes—which accompanied the persecution of Catholics after the signing of the Concordat between the Vatican and the Nazi authorities on July 20, 1933—were illustrated by the same anti-Jewish boycott on April 1. The Cat didn't have to be a theologian to wonder how an event can be caused by an event that occurred fourteen weeks after it happened.

An equally striking misuse comes from *The Real Albert Goering*, first transmitted on November 1, 2004, by Channel 4. The program was produced by Daniel Korn and directed by Jill Robinson for 3BM television. Albert was an engineer and the brother of the National Socialist leader Hermann Goering, and he kept out of the limelight so successfully that he seems to have been filmed only during his trial in Czechoslovakia after the Second World War. Therefore, the Cat found it necessary to find shots of Albert being absent from events. He wasn't filmed on *Kristallnacht*, the night of the anti-Jewish pogrom in November 1938. Nor was anyone else in Austria, where he lived, so film of the anti-Jewish boycott in Berlin was used, at which Albert wasn't present either.

Natasha Kaplinski, a newsreader for the BBC, was featured in *Who Do You Think You Are*, a genealogical program that seems to have taken the place of BBC programs about serious history. Directed by Christopher Bruce, the episode was transmitted on September 6, 2007, and it showed Ms. Kaplinski discovering some of her roots in Poland before the Second World War. There was something decidedly odd about the anti-Jewish boycott in Berlin in 1933 providing the images for her evocation of village life in her grandparent's hometown of Slonim following the war's outbreak in September 1939. Perhaps this was something that a news-reader, however highly paid, might not be able to grasp. After all, she read only what was written on the teleprompter. No one ever employed her as a fact-checker. The outbreak of the war offered more scope for mischief and genuinely spectacular misrepresentation. The destruction of HMS *Barham* is a case in point. The battleship was patrolling off the Mediterranean coast near Alexandria on November 25, 1941, when it was struck by three torpedoes fired by *U-331* under the command of Hans Diedrich von Tiesenhausen. A Gaumont-British cameraman, John Turner, was on board the *Barham*'s sister ship, *Valiant*, and in his memoirs reports that he missed the first part of the drama. He was having a cup of tea below decks when the torpedoes hit. He said ruefully, "I was back on the bridge within seconds to see *Barham* listing heavily to port and cursing myself for ignoring all training that if you take a chance inevitably some-thing happens."[18] This is the "something" that happened:

HMS *Barham's* powder magazine explodes in 1941.

The main powder magazine exploded, and the *Barham* sank in three minutes. Of her crew, 396 men survived and 862 were lost. Although the Admiralty announced the sinking in January 1942, the film was sup-pressed and seen only when the images were released in the American *Combat Reports* (No. 66) in 1945. It was not seen in Britain until after the war. It was certainly used in feature films such as *Task Force* (1949) and *Earth vs. the Flying Saucers* (1956), but the Office Cat was more interested in its use in television programs.

A Channel 4 series titled *The Battle between the* Hood *and the* Bismarck was shown on December 11, 2001. Part 1, "The Mighty *Hood*," explains how the battle cruiser *Hood* was dispatched by the German battleship *Bismarck* in 1941. In part 2, "Sink the *Bismarck*," transmitted on December 18, 2001, the *Barham* duly explodes, though her presence may be unexpected in the context of battles in the North Atlantic. In *Blitzkrieg: The Fall of France*, transmitted by the Discovery Channel in March 2003, HMS *Barham* was disguised as the German cruiser *Blücher* sinking during the invasion of Norway in June 1940. Then, in October 2003, for Charles Messanger, who wrote and produced *Gladiators of World War II: The Royal Navy*, it became the HMS *Hood* itself sunk in the same North Atlantic by the same *Bismarck* on May 24, 1941.

Jonathan Martin, who sank the *Szent István*, also made "Battleship," in the same *Weapons of World War II* series, transmitted by Five on March 1, 2004. In it, he dispatched the *Bismarck* in May 1941. He must have thought that the *Bismarck* ought to go down with a bang, even though her own crew scuttled her. It was a simple problem that called for a simple solution. He included a shot of the exploding *Barham*.

It's been the Cat's ambition to send the *Barham* to the bottom in every one of the world's proverbial seven seas. It's already been blown up in the Atlantic, the North Sea, and the Mediterranean. Only four more to go.

Where does this sorry tale leave those of us who care about authenticity and accuracy? And what does it mean for the status of the mockumentary, as "fakes" become more and more part of our "truth"? As budgets are slashed, the first thing to go are likely to be film researchers. Someday, some harassed producer or director, having sacked his or her film researcher, is doubtless going to discover the spaghetti harvest in Switzerland and is going to include it in a reality program about the wacky Swiss. As the chapters in this volume demonstrate, the line between truth and fiction—"real" and "fake"—can be very murky territory, especially in the context of this long history of image misuse, misappropriation, and out-and-out deception. From there, the faux histories of *The Watermelon Woman* and *The War Game*, the repurposed past in *The Forbidden Quest* and *The Old Negro Space Program*, and the reality parodies of *Marion and Geoff* and *The Proper Care and Feeding of an American Messiah* may not be such a far stretch after all. The Office Cat may not be put out of business for a long time.

NOTES

1. Geoff King, *Film Comedy* (Wallflower Press, 2002), 43.
2. His account is reported by Jay Leyda, *Films Beget Films: A Study of the Compilation Film* (Allen & Unwin, 1964), 13–14.

3. Francis Doublier, "Reminiscences of an Early Motion Picture Operator," *IMAGE* 5, no. 6 (1956), 134–35. The text is from a lecture given by Doublier on October 15, 1941, at New York University.

4. Keith Eubank and Phyllis Tortora, *Survey of Historic Costume: A History of Western Dress* (Fairchild, 1998), 402, 440; James Monaco, *How to Read a Film* (Oxford University Press, 2000), 117–18.

5. Ian Jack, "Lionel Logue and the King," *The Guardian,* January 15, 2001, 35.

6. Raymond Fielding, *The American Newsreel: A Complete History, 1911–1967* (McFarland, 2006), 31.

7. Orville Wright, Diary D, entry for December 17, 1903. Marvin W. McFarland and Orville Wright, *The Papers of Wilbur and Orville Wright, Including the Wright-Chanute Correspondence* (McGraw-Hill, 2000), 394–95.

8. The 1908 demonstration flights, which followed four and a half years of obsessive secrecy designed to prevent unauthorized copying of their designs, were the first truly public appearance of the Wright Brothers' aircraft. See Tom D. Crouch, *The Bishop's Boys* (Norton, 1989), 360–78.

9. Jeffrey Richards, *A Night to Remember: The Definitive* Titanic *Film* (I. B. Tauris, 2002), 10; Stephen Bottomore, *The* Titanic *and Silent Cinema* (Projection Box, 2000), 20–21, 38–47.

10. A. Scott Berg, *Lindbergh* (Putnam's, 1998), 15.

11. Ian Patterson, *Guernica and Total War* (Harvard University Press, 2007), 69–70; Herbert Rutledge Southworth, *Guernica! Guernica! A Study of Journalism, Diplomacy, Propaganda, and History* (University of California Press, 1977), 63.

12. James Dorrian, *Storming St. Nazaire: The Dock Busting Raid of 1942* (Pen and Sword, 2001).

13. James Chapman, *The British at War: Cinema, State, and Propaganda, 1939–1945* (I. B. Tauris, 1998).

14. On "liberation footage" and its cultural impact, see, for example, Toby Haggith, "Filming the Liberation of Bergen-Belsen," in *Holocaust and the Moving Image: Representations in Film and Television since 1933*, ed. Toby Haggith and Joanna Newman (Wallflower Press, 2005), 33–49; and Jeffrey Shandler, "The Testimony of Images: The Allied Liberation of Nazi Concentration Camps in American Newsreels," in *Why Didn't the Press Shout? American and International Journalism during the Holocaust*, ed. Robert Moses Shapiro and Marvin Kalb (Ktav, 2003), 109–25. On Holocaust documentaries in general, see Annette Insdorf, *Indelible Shadows: Film and the Holocaust*, 3rd ed. (Cambridge University Press, 2002); Jeffrey Shandler, *While America Watches: Televising the Holocaust* (Oxford University Press, 2000); and Alan L. Mintz, *Popular Culture and the Shaping of Holocaust Memory* (University of Washington Press, 2001).

15. Rosenthal presents his account of the filming of the series in *Jerusalem, Take One! Memoirs of a Jewish Filmmaker* (Southern Illinois University Press, 2000), 235–59.

16. William Taubman, "Did He Bang It? Nikita Krushchev and the Shoe," *New York Times*, July 26, 2003.

17. David Bankier and Israel Gutman, *Nazi Europe and the Final Solution* (Yad Vashem, 2009), 17–21.

18. John Turner, *Filming History: Memoirs of John Turner, Newsreel Cameraman* (Wallflower Press, 2001).

I

LOST HISTORIES

1

Making Up Mammy: Reenacting Historical Erasure and Recasting Authenticity in Cheryl Dunye's *The Watermelon Woman*

Eve Allegra Raimon

When Cheryl Dunye's mockumentary *The Watermelon Woman* was released in 1996, reviewers ran into trouble trying to categorize it. The first feature film written and directed by an African American lesbian was variously called a "queer African-American Hip-Hop Comedy,"[1] a "convincing Black dykUdrama," and a "whimsically funny deconstructive pseudo-documentary pastiche."[2]

The *New York Press* went so far as to ask its readers to "imagine Woody Allen refashioned as an African American lesbian."[3] At the same time, film studies accounts have been fascinated with the way the work "sets up a fictional seduction" in which the audience is "led to interpret the film in the language of non-fiction."[4] Other examinations point to Dunye's efforts to intervene in the problem of black lesbian invisibility on screen. While all these dimensions are certainly at play in this story of a documentarian's search for the life of an imagined filmic mammy, what has remained peripheral to critical analyses is the work's investment in dramatizing historical absence and erasure—the aporia of archival lack as it is represented in the search for the elusive title character. Ultimately, *The Watermelon Woman* endeavors to render visible what is usually considered unrepresentable—the complexity, distance, and partiality immanent in the act of historical reconstruction itself, a task made vastly more problematic when the subject of recovery is a mammy character who, as

One of Dunye's "whimsical" deconstructions of Fae Richards in *The Watermelon Woman.*

was often the case in "real" life, is never listed in film credits and whose history is thereby all but effaced.

The work's multiple diegetic layers help account for its varied reception, especially to the extent that it mimics and parodies realist and documentary modes at once. *The Watermelon Woman* opens in the middle of an action sequence about the act of filming itself. In the first shot we see Tamara, the butch friend of budding filmmaker "Cheryl," played by Dunye herself, setting up equipment to shoot a group scene at a wedding.[5] Even before the film's title appears, we see supposedly random shots of wedding goers of various races and descriptions in both posed scenes and candid shots. When Tamara gets angry after Cheryl keeps a cut of their fee to pay for their camera, Cheryl reminds Tamara that their business videotaping events such as weddings is supposed to be their "ticket to Hollywood." By opening the film with scenes of young photographers shooting a wedding, Dunye foregrounds her interest in the paradoxical importance and artificiality inherent in the very project of filming historical events, whether private or public. The cinemagraphic undertaking both captures and conceals the complexity of an occasion as charged with multiple meanings as a marriage ceremony. Similarly, Cheryl's project to document the life of a neglected filmic mammy is bound to be at least as fragmentary and incomplete. In addition, the opening wedding shots foreground the relative legitimacy of that institution and its subjects as opposed to the comparative illegitimacy, historically, of a white married couple's spectral "other"—the mammy, who offers unlimited domestic servitude that is forever undocumented and so unnoticed by history.

While Tamara (Valerie Walker) amuses herself at the video rental shop where the two also work by ordering porn films and billing them to other customers' accounts, Cheryl, who both is and is not Dunye, is fascinated by "race films" of the 1930s and 1940s and, in particular, by a character whom she describes as "the most beautiful black mammy" she's ever seen. Having already addressed her audience directly to announce that the documentary she is going to produce will be about black women because "too often our stories have never been told," Cheryl settles on a film tribute to the "Watermelon Woman," as the character is designated in the opening credits. The camera then shows Cheryl inserting a tape of a film called "Plantation Memories" into her VCR player, after which the camera moves to the TV screen and a grainy black-and-white image of a mammy, "Elsie," running to comfort a distraught plantation mistress whose son is evidently missing in action from the Confederacy: "Oh, don't cry Missy; Massa's child is comin' back for sure. I know he is," she pleads. Then the camera returns to Cheryl, who declares, "Girlfriend has it going on." She elaborates, "Something in her face, something in the way she looks and moves is serious, is interesting, and I'm going to tell you all about it," in a direct address to the camera that both reproduces and spoofs the authority of the documentary genre's first-person narrative voice. Thus, the central diegesis involving Cheryl, Tamara, and their relationships becomes interwoven into another embedded diegetic narrative of the supposed documentary in the making, which itself doesn't appear as a finished production until the closing credits of the film, though it constitutes the film's supposed raison d'être: a "factual" account of the fictional life of the Watermelon Woman. In between these levels is what Andrea B. Braidt has called an "interdiegetic narrative": the aspiring filmmaker's commentary on the ongoing events occurring on the first level of interpersonal drama. The "extradiegetic" dimension, to draw further from Braidt's lexicon, has the film's director playing the role of Cheryl, the documentarian.[6]

More than that, in each of three scenes in the diegesis, in which the audience views the same film clip from *The Watermelon Woman*, Dunye makes a point to show the would-be filmmaker in spatial proximity to the mammy, an artifact of African American filmic history and historical erasure at once. It is the repetition of a single clip from this film that affords viewers their only real portrait of the stock Watermelon Woman character, who, in the words of Phyllis J. Jackson and Darrell Moore, "serves as a social and visual code for a set of race, gender, and class relationships that presume a subservient status for black women and naturalize not only their socioeconomic oppression but their reduction to a visual cliché as well."[7] The second time, the scene with the plantation mistress is presented in voiceover, with the camera aimed at Cheryl instead of at the screen. The director/protagonist sits next to the TV, adorned in a mammy kerchief, lip-synching the script. Though she mock-sobs into her kerchief on cue, her facial expression remains strikingly enigmatic: Cheryl looks as moved by her subject as she does satiric toward her. The irony in the title of the film within the film is overdetermined: Dunye as Cheryl must create memories from fiction since the historical record of African American women in early film is so illusory.

Indeed, the character to which we are first introduced as the Watermelon Woman and whose identity we later learn is Fae Richards or Faith Richardson is a fiction, an invention, an imaginative amalgamation of such historical actors as Hattie McDaniel, Butterfly McQueen, and Louise Beavers, together with numbers of other neglected black women film artists whose histories have been all but forgotten.[8] Moreover, through the repeated staging of Cheryl next to the Watermelon Woman, Dunye intimates that the aspiring filmmaker character and the actor who plays Elsie in the faux clip are interrelated—even if the former has literally to bring the latter into being. In fact, *The Watermelon Woman* is mediated and infused by the exigencies and the imperatives of the mise-en-scène, Cheryl's present-day world. In this way, the past and the present are in constant relation. Dunye insists on stationing the black woman filmmaker—herself as much as her fictional protagonist—front and center throughout to situate black women in film past and present irrevocably back inside history and historical documentation. At the same time, the director wants to dramatize for us the limitations of that endeavor.

In another parallel that will intensify as the film progresses, Cheryl discovers during the course of her research that her subject is, in her words, "a sapphic sister, a bulldagger, a lesbian." Addressing her absent subject directly, she muses, "I guess we have a thing or two in common, Miss Richards: the movies and women." Mark Winokur has noted that Dunye counters the stock trope of the mammy as overweight and asexual in casting Lisa Marie Bronson as Fae, an actor who "is slim and otherwise physically attractive by Cheryl's standards."[9] In Winokur's psychoanalytic reading, Fae serves as both maternal subject and sexual object of desire for Cheryl, projections that allow the protagonist to recast her personal history. He contends, "In pursuing Fae Richards, Cheryl/Dunye

The classic mammy image.

is attempting to render the mammy as the enabling maternal. In Fae, however, she also discovers a physical object of desire and so an awareness of
her own body as historically desirable. She creates a black lesbian body in
order to recover her own."[10] As important as Dunye's project of psychic
self-recovery is her keen desire to represent the possibilities and barriers
to retrieving the larger history of black lesbian cinematography and to
move that history into futurity through her own work and others like her.

In these ways, Dunye's mockumentary is centrally concerned with the
tension between fact and fiction, with the interstices, the interplay, among
representation and "the Real." Indeed, the film's epilogue—"Sometimes
you have to create your own history"—reveals her acute awareness that
the act of creation is typically in a tense—if not oxymoronic—relation
to the act of historical inquiry. In this case, moreover, that productive
tension is heightened by the fact of the very real elision of many female
black film artists from historical and institutional memory. In her efforts
to dramatize these pressures and excisions Dunye heeds Valerie Smith's
caution against the "documentary impulse" in contemporary African
American film.[11] Smith contends that productions by such directors as
John Singleton and Spike Lee fall victim to a fetishization of black vernacular culture that leads to the depiction of "a monolithic black experience."[12] By contrast, Smith maintains, such filmmakers as Camille Billops

and Marlon T. Riggs "experiment with the artificiality of their medium to defamiliarize assumptions about family, sexuality, gender, race, and identity."[13] While Smith's comments are directed at the filmic strategies of documentarians, they can be applied with equal validity to Dunye's formally ambiguous and multidimensional production.

Throughout *The Watermelon Woman*, then, Dunye "experiments with the artificiality of the medium" to "defamiliarize assumptions" regarding film genres and styles themselves. Furthermore, thematically, the film generates a proliferation of meanings associated with the identities of the characters in the unfolding drama of Cheryl's life and in the ongoing interrogation of the mammy figure, which preoccupies and haunts the work. On the formal level, as other commentators have noted, Dunye works artfully with a pastiche of film, video, and stills to create the semblance of authenticity in the search for the historical record of the fictional Fae Richards. Jackson and Moore have observed that the various formats that Dunye employs correspond to specific sequences of the film: specifically, the scenes shot of Cheryl in "real life" are on 16 mm film; the archival footage is shot in Super 8, while Cheryl records her documentary on videotape. Furthermore, Dunye, together with photographer Zoe Leonard, creates a range of supporting documentary materials, including clips of Richards and her white director and lover, Martha Page, newsreel footage of Richards with period luminaries, and home movies with her longtime black lover, June. Jackson and Moore argue that while the film's complex technical and narrative structure at once "seduces" a segment of the audience into reading the production as authentic documentary, the carefully crafted faux archival documents "comment on the constructed artifice of filmmaking and create parallels to lives rather than truths about lives of historical individuals."[14] In the same vein, Robert F. Reid-Pharr concludes that productions like Dunye's serve to demonstrate that

> the histories that we construct, even at their most lush, are always fashioned from the thinnest of materials: faulty accounts, flimsy documents, and grainy images. Thus we will never come to have a truly complicated or thick conception of black or American history until we begin to seriously consider the frail and ephemeral nature of the evidence that we have at our disposal.[15]

Dunye's project is not just to dramatize this fact but also to convey the consequent necessity of artistic renderings that make the past meaningful to a present-day audience despite the limitations attendant upon its reconstruction. To Dunye, one way to convey such limitations is to represent these renderings tongue-in-cheek.

Thus, in addition to emphasizing "the constructed artifice of filmmaking," the work features repeated scenes of archival parody. In one such episode, comedian Brian Freeman plays the queer, well-meaning, Hollywood-obsessed amateur film historian who turns out not to be much interested in collecting images of women: "Women are not my specialty," he sneers. In another, author Sarah Schulman plays the flighty and anal 1970s lesbian archivist of CLIT—the Center for Lesbian Information and Technology—a clear burlesque of such institutions as the New York Lesbian Herstory Archives. There to research her subject, Cheryl finds photos of Richards and Page that have been segregated and cataloged by race while stored in an absurdly haphazard manner. Schulman, as "M. J.," explains that the black collection on lesbians is "very separate" and that whites have been "crossed out" of photos with interracial images. The protagonist fares no better at the public library, where she is directed toward the offensively segregated and monolithic "black section." In each instance, Cheryl's efforts to gather definitive, tangible information about the life of the Watermelon Woman are thwarted by either well-meaning ineptitude or more overtly hegemonic and racist forces of erasure. Either way, the act of historical recuperation is once again frustrated in the very locales that are designed to preserve and cherish historical truth.

Strangely, as Michele Wallace pointed out in a *Village Voice* review, Dunye leaves all actual commentary about the cultural role of the mammy figure to the bizarrely satiric voice of Camille Paglia. From her Swarthmore office, the controversial Paglia argues that our attitude toward the filmic mammy should be one of veneration rather than shame and that, moreover, such figures remind her of her own bountiful Italian grandmothers. The famously acerbic cultural critic launches into an uncharacteristically wistful paean to her kitchen-bound foremothers and then, ludicrously, likens the colors of the watermelon to the Italian flag, before delivering a more typically venomous attack on feminism: "If the watermelon symbolizes African American culture, rightly so, because look what white middle class feminism stands for: anorexia and bulimia," she proclaims, irrelevantly. The farcical nature of the interview conveys the sense that academic "experts" lead us ineffably back to *their* truths more than to any usable past. Dunye then cuts to a brief interview with a group of white college students who confess ignorance about Fae Richards since their course hasn't yet covered "women in Blaxploitation films." Next, the director jumps back to Paglia, who declares "mind-boggling" the prospect of an interracial relationship between Richards and white director Martha Page, citing as her source the controversial *Guess Who's Coming to Dinner*, the 1967 film with Sidney Poitier and Katharine Hepburn. As Paglia makes this pronouncement, Dunye overlays stills of whites and blacks embracing in club scenes of the 1930s and 1940s.

While the Swarthmore professor is clearly in on the joke of the Watermelon Woman's fictional status, the juxtaposition of the two interview scenes works to convey the extent to which the cultural imaginary of white audiences is often limited to popular and clearly demarcated filmic genres and types. The notion of interracial romance is utterly staggering to Paglia—at least in her role as feminist pedagogue—because she has no evidence for it before the release of a popular Hollywood movie. To Wallace, the selection of Paglia as resident academic expert demonstrates the director's "one woman assault upon most aspects of prevailing gender styles in black film."[16] It's not entirely clear whether that assault, in Wallace's view, is aimed at the stock images of mammies Paglia decries or at Paglia herself. However, Wallace goes further, asserting that *The Watermelon Woman* advances the theme that "mammies have been underestimated, overlooked, and insufficiently showered with love."[17] Here, she would seem to be following Paglia in conflating the representational stereotype with actual black women subjects in lived experience. Rather, it's part of Dunye's project to expose as absurd the degree to which black women in film history were reduced to mammies, a largely fictional construct in the history of cinema. The point is not to celebrate mammies as such—since to do so would mean embracing a figure of abjection and to mistake a Hollywood construction as authentic—but instead to recognize the talent and complexity of the lives of those women who played the role of the mammy on screen and off.

Indeed, this act of critical conflation signifies the degree to which Dunye chooses to proliferate rather than to fix meaning about the "mythic mammy." Such interpretive instability is of a piece with the film's larger project of deconstructing the act of historical recovery even as it foregrounds the constructed nature of representation. In the confusion generated by the Paglia interview, Dunye also upsets notions of authenticity—racial, political, or otherwise. On these various levels, the director accentuates the necessary precariousness and elusiveness of such searches for historical and/or interpretive truth. This multifold operation is also present on the diegetic level of the work, in which Cheryl engages in an interracial romance that coincides with the discovery of Fae's romantic liaison with the white director Page. No aspect of the work has garnered greater attention from both academic and political realms than the cross-racial love affair between Cheryl and Diana (Guinevere Turner). Illustratively, Laura L. Sullivan writes,

> Viewers are treated to tight close-ups of Cheryl and Diana's black and white bodies pressed together in explicit sex scenes. Their hands roam across each other's naked bodies as the women kiss. At one point, the camera zooms in on the interlocked black and white hands of the two characters in bed. In this way, the film not only requires that black lesbians be acknowledged; it also documents the existence of interracial lesbian romances.[18]

Indeed, when the film was released in 1996, the images documenting "the existence of interracial lesbian romances" transfixed the popular press and the political Right as much as they did academic commentators. After only reading a review of the film, which announced that it featured "the hottest dyke sex scene ever recorded on celluloid," Republican representative Peter Hoekstra of Michigan denounced the work on the floor of Congress and attempted to revive efforts to curtail funding of the National Endowment for the Arts. At the time, film critic Frank Rich reported that Hoekstra wrote Jane Alexander, then chair of the endowment, to express his "shock" over the production, which had received a $31,500 grant and went on to win two prestigious awards at lesbian and gay film festivals.[19] According to Rich, the congressman also asked where he could find other examples of similar lesbian films. Predictably but ironically, what got rehearsed in that moment of political theater was the effacement of black female artistry and subjectivity once again, this time for the sake of the titillation offered by the voyeuristic and spectacularized scene of interracial lesbian sex.

Of course, absent from all the political posturing was any discussion of the thematic or formal complexity and significance of the love scene. Interspersed with the racy shots of black-on-white skin, but ignored by many audiences, was another faux period scene, this one resembling an early "race" film, also featuring Fae Richards. As Cheryl and Diana engage in foreplay and start kissing, the audio we hear in the background is from the early movie the two had been watching as part of Cheryl's "film project." In it, Fae and another actor, Irene, are seen arguing in a dressing room over the moral ambiguity presented by the prospect of Irene passing into white society. The viewer sees Fae in her role as defender of the race. She scolds Irene: "Haven't you had enough of that white powder? How could you, Irene? How could you?" As the camera moves disconcertingly from the bed and a tight shot of Cheryl and Diana deep kissing to the race film, we see the disapproving Fae character admonish Irene: "You're a no-good lying tramp; that's what you are. Committing a sin that will surely send you to hell." "Why can't I be happy fitting into their world? God made me this color and he did it for a reason," Irene insists, desperately. The scene ends with Fae slapping Irene's face in disgust. Since the "race" film is intercut with the scene of lovemaking, Dunye surely wants viewers to experience the discordance between the foreground images of interracial passion set against a backdrop of intense racial tension. By interpolating the constructed race film into the cross-racial sex scene, the director accomplishes several objectives simultaneously: most conspicuously, she underscores the multiple complications associated with interraciality historically without passing definitive judgment. Concomitantly, Dunye

Dunye and Turner.

literally allows the past to join the present as the filmic protagonists' fight over passing provides a disjunctive auditory accompaniment to a scene of interracial racial lovemaking, still a charged subject—as the political fallout over it made manifest.

Dunye's initial affirmation of cross-racial relations furthers the film's interest in exposing static notions of black authenticity. At one point, in one of the frequent arguments between herself and Tamara over Diana, Cheryl remarks, "Who's to say that dating somebody white doesn't make me black?" However, this narrative trajectory eventually takes a turn to parallel Cheryl's progress in her search for Fae's past. Cheryl becomes disenchanted with Diana, a diplomat's daughter who lives in a luxury apartment and volunteers for poor black youth, when she realizes the extent to which Diana fetishizes blackness. Diana's notion of pillow talk is to assure Cheryl that she's had three black boyfriends and that her "father's sister's first husband was an ex-panther, Tyrone Washington." "You're such a mess," Cheryl responds under her breath. Here again, Dunye holds up diverse—and even conflicting—possibilities for black identity without definitively privileging one over another. It's the commodification of blackness, not interraciality alone, that bears the brunt of Cheryl's—and Dunye's—derision here.

The dissolution of Cheryl's relationship with her white girlfriend co-incides interdiegetically with the protagonist's breakthrough and subse-quent disappointment over her documentary project, a disappointment also related to issues of racial identity, authenticity, and solidarity. Cheryl discovers the existence of June (Cheryl Clarke), Fae's longtime lover, only to miss interviewing her when June falls ill and lands in the hospital. In-stead, June writes Cheryl a wrenching letter making clear her dismay that Cheryl plans to feature the white exploitative director Martha Page in her filmic tribute. The complex racial hermeneutics in both these scenes allow Dunye, recalling Valerie Smith's formulation, to "experiment with the artificiality of [the] medium to defamiliarize assumptions about family, sexuality, gender, race, and identity."[20] That is to say that a parallel exists between Dunye's depiction of the always already-confounded nature of interracial desire and her ongoing dramatization of the elusive nature of historical truth. Here, the multiple diegetic layers of the production con-verge subtly yet powerfully in their recursive focus on the delineation of multiple styles of lesbian subjectivity. As Sullivan points out in "Chasing Fae: *The Watermelon Woman* and Black Lesbian Possibility," "there is no unified lesbian subject position, either black or white."[21] Butch Tamara's racial essentialism is held up to scrutiny, as is another character's "heavy afro-fem-centrism." Yet both Cheryl and Fae's interdiegetic forays into interraciality end badly. Moreover, representation of the intricacies as-sociated with the interdependent identity categories of race and sexuality occurs concurrently with and parallels the film's interest in representing the equally fraught nature of historical reconstruction, which is rendered as the creative tension between inescapable distance and creative recuper-ation, between ineradicable difference and intergenerational connection.

If the pivotal love scene between Cheryl and Diana is considered in the context of the wider project of the film, it becomes clear that its very physicality and corporeality can be contrasted to the shadowy images and incomplete record that Cheryl is able to collect about the life of this mysterious "Watermelon Woman." Indeed, the closest that Cheryl—and the audience—get to Fae is a phone conversation with June, her partner of twenty years, before she is taken ill, and the letter that June writes Cheryl after that conversation. The latter communication is presented in voiceover under black-and-white stills of the actor and June at home. The letter, read first in Cheryl's voice blending slowly into June's, makes clear the former lover's disappointment that Cheryl chose to include Page in the production at all. She is happy to recognize Cheryl as a sister in the lesbian "family," but to June that "family" is clearly raced:

Why did you even want to include a white woman in a movie on Fae's life? Don't you know she had nothing to do with how people should remember

Fae? . . . She paved the way for kids like you to run around making movies about the past and how we lived then. Please, Cheryl, make our history before we are all dead and gone, but if you are really in the family you better understand that our family will always only have each other.

As before, the convergence of past and present as interdependent and mutable is made manifest in the auditory and visual dimensions of the work, accentuated by present-day shots of Cheryl walking through contemporary urban Philadelphia interposed with home movies of Faith and June in decades gone by. Again in this scene, Dunye brings together the linked issues of racial politics and the challenge of recapturing historical truth. June urges Cheryl to "make our history," an idiosyncratic formulation that underscores that history's status as a transmutable entity to be "made," not discovered. More wrenching for Cheryl, though, is that she is faced with a clear decision at this moment about how both are going to be represented on film and, thus, how individuals' legacies will be shaped *and* what kind of models they will provide for their future sisters "in the family." At this point in the film's diegesis, Cheryl explicitly links the end of her love affair with Diana, the unsteady nature of her friendship with Tamara, and, most important, the conclusion of her project of historical recovery. When she acknowledges, "I thought it was going to be easy. I thought I could use the camera to document my search for Fae, but instead, I'm left empty-handed except for this package from June," Dunye points again to the partiality, the illusory nature of historical recuperation. Of still more import is Cheryl's response to June's letter about Fae: "I know she meant the world to you but she also meant the world to me, and those worlds are very different," Cheryl declares, again facing the camera directly. She concludes,

What she means to me, a 25-year-old black woman means something else. It means hope, it means inspiration, it means possibility: it means history. And most importantly what I understand is that I'm going to be the one who says I am a black lesbian filmmaker who's just beginning, but I'm going to say a lot more and have a lot more work to do.

These lines and the tenor of the film's dénouement have prompted criticism that they work to validate an appropriation more than a commemoration of black lesbian filmic forerunners. For example, in "'Joining the Lesbians': Cinematic Regimes of Black Lesbian Visibility," Kara Keeling points to the shrewd packaging of *The Watermelon Woman* by its distributor, First Run Features, to capitalize on the interracial sexuality the film depicts. To Keeling, Dunye's priority is to use Fae's history to redefine black lesbian subjectivity for a contemporary viewership:

Those who exist on a sheet of the past that might support a narrative that would challenge the construction of "black lesbian" that Cheryl provides are relegated by Cheryl's narrative to a "different" world, one that is incommensurate with that in which "black lesbian" can appear and circulate proudly in films.[22]

Keeling has in mind the conventional documentary narrative of the life of the Watermelon Woman that runs concurrently with the film's closing credits, and she includes certain aspects of Fae's life while excluding others that suggest sexual alterity explicitly. For example, Keeling observes, in the closing "documentary-within-a-film," June Walker is relegated to the status of a "special friend," while no mention is made of the fact that Fae sang for "stone butches" in the black Philadelphia clubs.

However, Keeling fails fully to account for the ironic tone in the narrative and in the placement of the conventional "biography" that ends *The Watermelon Woman*. Interspersed throughout this brief account are not just the credits of the film but also such qualifiers as "I think" and "From what I can tell," phrases that foreground the partiality of historical recovery. As well, with such expressions as "This was a big year for Fae," the chronicle strikes the viewer as mostly a filmic derivative of public television celebrity tributes. Indeed, the conventional account of the Watermelon Woman seems

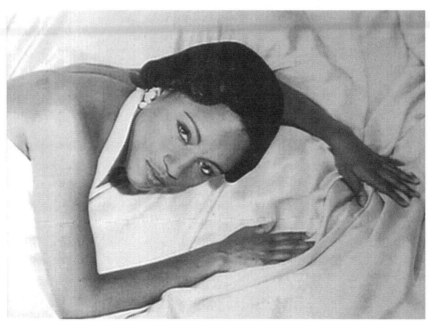

Fae, in a classic glamour shot.

perfunctory since her story—or what we need to know of it—has already been told in the search itself. Of course, the most conspicuous marker of the irony embedded in the biography is the final text to appear in Dunye's work, which reveals definitively that "the Watermelon Woman is fiction." In these lines and in the extended shots of contemporary Philadelphia and the music of political folksinger Toshi Regan playing under the reading of June's letter, Dunye positions history as always already inflected by present contingencies and imperatives. The culmination of Dunye's mockumentary suggests not only that historical recuperation is always elusive but also that history should always be regarded as continuously generative of present agency and the potential for creative and political change. Interviewed about the film, Dunye views her role as a young filmmaker in terms that historicize her own work:

> It's not just to be an actor or a director or a cameraperson or anything like that. There's many other things behind what gay and lesbian cinema is about and I think by really creating an industry with it we'll have a presence that lasts beyond this magical moment in the mid '90s.[23]

More than a decade has now passed since that "magical moment in the mid '90s" in which such films as Dunye's *The Watermelon Woman*, Patricia Rozema's *When Night Is Falling* (1995), and Maria Maggenti's *The Incredibly True Adventures of 2 Girls in Love* (1995)—a film that also explores interracial lesbian romance—were produced. Since then, sadly, an independent, racially self-conscious, and widely circulating "lesbian and gay cinema" has largely suffered from the sharp rightward turn in U.S. political and cultural life in the past decade. Despite such promising exceptions as Alice Wu's *Saving Face* (2004) on the big screen and the increasingly racially integrated Showtime production *The L Word* on the small screen, independent lesbian and gay films seem mired in clichés of early seduction and coming-out dramas. It's distressingly difficult to name a widely distributed film in the new millennium that equals those of Dunye or the late Marlon T. Riggs for its acute sense of its own embeddedness in neglected or transgressive film history and its coterminous sense of play within those strictures. An ever more-impatient queer audience awaits the work of emerging queer film-makers who appreciate—as Dunye does—"the many other things gay and lesbian cinema is about" and the myriad forms that a racially and histori-cally astute queer cinema might take.

NOTES

1. Anne Stockwell, "Color Corrected Film," *Advocate*, March 4, 2007.
2. Peter Keough, "*The Watermelon Woman* Refreshes," *Boston Phoenix*, 1997.

3. Quoted from the back cover of the original VHS version of *The Watermelon Woman*, directed by Cheryl Dunye (1996; New York: First Run Features, 1997).

4. Phyllis J. Jackson and Darrell Moore, "Fictional Seductions," *GLQ* 4, no. 3 (1998): 500. As far as I can tell the phrase "Black dykeUdrama" is Jackson's and Moore's also, although they themselves quote it. Of recent critical work on the film, theirs is most alive to the issue I am predominantly concerned with in this chapter having to do with the absence of any reliable and retrievable past for the mammy. They assert, "Dunye's *The Watermelon Woman* both exploits and undermines the power and authority granted to photographs and films as objective or neutral visual documents" (502).

5. The scare quotes ("Cheryl") signify that the role entails more than the character of Cheryl but not the director as herself either. Mark Winokur contends that Dunye wants to complicate the demarcations between the two. He uses a combination (Cheryl/Dunye) to designate the relation between them: "While Cheryl attempts to establish her identity as a black lesbian filmmaker through an identification with Fae, Dunye is attempting to integrate or reconstitute Cheryl/Dunye—an identity split by the traditional distinction between actor and director—as Cheryl Dunye" (235). See "Body and Soul: Identifying (with) the Black Lesbian Body in Cheryl Dunye's *The Watermelon Woman*," in *Recovering the Black Female Body: Self-Representations by African American Women*, ed. Michael Bennett and Vanessa D. Dickerson (New Brunswick, NJ: Rutgers University Press, 2001).

6. Andrea B. Braidt, "Queering Ethnicity, Queering Sexuality: A Paradigmatic Shift in the Politics of Cinematic Representation in Cheryl Dunye's *The Watermelon Woman*," in *Simulacrum America: The USA and the Popular Culture*, ed. Leisabeth Kraus and Carolin Auer (Rochester, NY: Camden House, 1999).

7. Jackson and Moore, "Fictional Seductions," 503.

8. Dunye uses "Fae Richards" to designate the actor who played the fictional Watermelon Woman most often in the film, though she introduces her in the faux "biography" at the end as "Fae Richards . . . Faith Richardson." In so doing, the director adds another layer of mediation and irony to the work by giving the elusive documentary subject two "real" names.

9. Winokur, "Body and Soul," 245.

10. Winokur, "Body and Soul," 245.

11. Valerie Smith, "The Documentary Impulse in African-American Film," in *Black Popular Culture: A Project by Michelle Wallace*, ed. Gina Dent (Seattle, WA: Bay Press, 1992).

12. Smith, "Documentary Impulse," 58.

13. Smith, "Documentary Impulse," 61.

14. Jackson and Moore, "Fictional Seductions," 502.

15. Robert F. Reid-Pharr, "Makes Me Feel Mighty Real: *The Watermelon Woman* and the Critique of Black Visibility," in *F Is for Phony: Fake Documentary and Truth's Undoing*, ed. Alexandra Juhasz and Jesse Lerner (Minneapolis: University of Minnesota Press, 2006), 139.

16. Michele Wallace, "Sexin' the Watermelon," *Village Voice*, March 4, 1997, 74.

17. Wallace, "Sexin' the Watermelon."

18. Laura L. Sullivan, "Chasing Fae: *The Watermelon Woman* and Black Possibility," *Callalo* 23, no. 1 (2000): 451.

19. Frank Rich, "Lesbian Lookout," *New York Times*, March 13, 1996, A27.

20. Smith, "Documentary Impulse," 61.

21. Sullivan, "Chasing Fae," 451.

22. Kara Keeling, "Joining the Lesbians: Cinematic Regimes of Black Lesbian Visibility," in *Black Queer Studies: A Critical Anthology*, ed. E. Patrick Johnson and Mae G. Henderson (Durham, NC: Duke University Press, 2005), 224.

23. Interview featured in the film.

2

Mercury's on the Launch Pad, but Cadillac's on the Moon: *The Old Negro Space Program*

Cynthia J. Miller and A. Bowdoin Van Riper

It was a different time, you understand. . . . See, in 1957, if you were black, and if you were an astronaut, you were out of work.

With those words, retired astronaut Wallace "Suitcase" Jefferson begins to tell the story of a lost history—the story of NASSA: the Negro American Space Society of Astronauts—as a montage of images, full of the fascination and wonder of space flight, crawls across the screen. "It was a different time, you understand . . . 1957 . . . '58." It is there, in that "different time," that Andy Bobrow's short film *The Old Negro Space Program* (2004) also begins.

It was a different time, indeed, in the late 1950s and early 1960s, when the civil rights movement and the space age took form. The on-screen images, grainy and faded from age, tell the story: In some, grimly determined black faces gaze at signs that mark doorways and water fountains "white" and "colored," while in others, test pilots, sporting crew cuts and flashing confident smiles, dream of space as engineers in crisp white shirts and narrow ties confer over how to get them there. These images, and the people and events they represent, connect instantly with our collective memories of countless pictures and stories that have come before, drawn from the annals of both black history and space history. But, as Bobrow's film reminds us, there are some histories we celebrate and others that never get told.

Bobrow's short mockumentary follows the "blackstronauts" of NASSA as—shut out of jobs with the newly founded, whites-only NASA—they start their own, parallel space program. Outfitting themselves in hand-sewn cloth spacesuits, raising money through barnstorming tours, and welding scavenged NASA rocket engines to Cadillacs and school buses, they rely on "courage and zeal" to make up for their lack of formal engineering skills. Forget the Soviets—Bobrow's film reveals that the real "space race" is here, as images of a NASA think tank expose the agency's "How We'll Beat the Negroes" campaign. NASSA astronauts orbit the earth in the early 1960s and land on the moon in September 1966, nearly three years before Neil Armstrong, but a "black blackout" orchestrated by the federal government suppresses virtually all news of their achievements. Discouraged, the blackstronauts disband NASSA, leaving their exploits, still unknown to most white Americans, to live on only in black folk culture.[1]

The blackstronauts bear little resemblance to the square-jawed, steely eyed, relentlessly serious heroes of the space program pictured in textbooks, newspapers, and newsreels. They conquer the new frontier with a combination of reckless daring and inspired improvisation . . . drinking, swearing, and chasing women along the way. For the ragtag, gritty blackstronauts, space flight is not a romantic adventure; it is a job, as full of hardships as any other done by black men in the 1950s. Two days before his death, blackstronaut Sullivan Carew writes a final letter to his wife:

> Dear Sarah,
>   The indications are very strong that I shall attempt re-entry tomorrow, and lest I shall not be able to write you again, I feel impelled to write a few lines, that they may fall under your eye when I am no more. It sure is fuckin' cold up here. . . . Yessir . . . space is one cold motherfucker.[2]

The history of the blackstronauts' exploits parallels that of the genteel, overprivileged white astronauts whose highly chronicled deeds are familiar to most Americans. Timelines overlap, details interleave, and faded images call forth enough dim memories to lend an air of reality to the blackstronauts' tale, preserved only in scrapbooks and fragments of oral tradition. Bobrow's invented "lost history" implicitly points to other all-but-lost histories in which black Americans were beaten by the racism of the 1950s and 1960s rather than triumphing over it.

CRITIQUING THE CANON

In 1983, Philip Kaufman's film *The Right Stuff* told the story of the Mercury Seven, the original seven astronauts selected by NASA for manned space flight. Their names—Shepard, Grissom, Schirra, Slayton, Cooper, Carpen-

Readying space capsules for the United States of White America. *Courtesy of Andy Bobrow.*

ter, and Glenn—and the missions they flew are indelibly etched into the American experience. The *Old Negro Space Program* is also a film about "the right stuff"—and how it's defined—not only for the space program but also for heroism, national identity, and canonical American history.

Canonical history—the triumphant narratives presented in school textbooks, monuments, and patriotic speeches—emphasizes certainty over ambiguity and inevitability over contingency. Its central figures are flaw-less embodiments of the qualities revered by the society that claims them as heroes, and the tales of their triumphs act as vehicles for the transmis-sion of values, ideals, and cherished beliefs. Images of these foundational figures and stories serve as visual touchstones calling forth pages of nar-rative just as Homeric epithets such as "swift-footed Achilles" and "wise Odysseus" called forth, for classical audiences, reams of shared knowl-edge about the exploits and characters of those legendary heroes. Their time-honored repetition often alleviates the need for the story itself, which remains as only an obstacle between the image and its symbolic message.

The popular history of the U.S. manned space program unfolds as a series of such images. Most recall bold successes; the few that depict fail-ure merely set the stage for triumphs to come. The Soviet Union's launch of *Sputnik* startles the nation in October 1957, and *Vanguard* (meant as an answer to it) collapses in a ball of fire, but the best of America's elite mili-tary pilots—the clean-cut, coolly confident Mercury Seven—emerge to do symbolic battle with the Russians.[3] A series of interchangeable scenes show them honing their already formidable skills—flying jet fighters, fighting gravity in centrifuges, mastering tumbling simulators—and pos-ing, ready for flight, in gleaming silver spacesuits. Alan Shepard rockets into space aboard *Freedom 7*; Wernher von Braun stares at a drawing board; and John F. Kennedy calls for a lunar landing "before this decade is out." John Glenn, ever grinning, orbits the earth in *Friendship 7* and returns to be showered in ticker tape from the windows of Wall Street. The narrative then leaps another five years, hurdling two dozen more manned and unmanned flights to arrive at the disastrous *Apollo 1* fire in 1967, the crew of *Apollo 8* reading from Genesis as they orbit the moon on Christmas Eve 1968, and the final triumph of Neil Armstrong's "one small step" onto the moon in 1969.[4] The camera lingers on the American flag that Armstrong and his moon-walking partner, Buzz Aldrin, plant: tangible proof that America's heroes—backed by American ingenuity and organizational prowess—have made outer space safe for democracy.

Commenting on the Mercury Seven in a 1959 speech, NASA chief T. Keith Glennan described them as exemplary Americans: "happily mar-ried, family men, serious, studious, and highly trained." There was, he continued, "not a daredevil jet jockey—a Buck Rogers type—in the group"; they were expert pilots but also gifted engineers with "a practi-cal, hard-headed approach to the job ahead."[5] The qualities Glennan as-cribed to the astronauts were those cherished by the white, professional, suburban middle class: industry, fidelity, moderation, and seriousness.[6] NASA officials saw the image as vital to continued public support and congressional funding, and they guarded it zealously. New astronauts learned from their more experienced colleagues—as the Mercury Seven had learned from John Glenn—how to project it, and by the mid-1960s, NASA astronauts' status as ideal Americans had become axiomatic.[7]

The Old Negro Space Program turns this carefully burnished image inside out. The blackstronauts of NASSA *are* the "daredevil jet jockeys" that Glennan derided in his speech. Reckless daring is their principal asset, and—far from being carefully choreographed and endlessly practiced—their missions are a blend of improvisation and comic misadventures. "Stinky Pete" Carver catches fire during a failed launch attempt but—briskly extinguished by his ground crew—thinks nothing of flying the next day. "Loopy Louie" Hayes's hotdogging exploits are immortalized in song:

> There goes Loopy Louie;
> Where's he goin', friend?
> If I know Loopy Louie,
> he's shootin' up again!
> Aw, shit . . .

Their equipment, equally improvisational, is shaped by their meager budget. Far from taking decades to design and develop state-of-the-art rockets and confident that money and materials will be available to build them, the blackstronauts design around the materials they can afford: Detroit's relics and white NASA's castoffs. Even the ultimate expression of their skill at make-do engineering—the rocket-powered Cadillac that a pair of blackstronauts park alongside the lunar Sea of Tranquility—echoes an oft-retold urban legend about a hot-rodder who straps a military-surplus rocket to his car and ignites it on an empty stretch of desert highway, with catastrophic results.[8]

Spaceflight is neither a profession nor a patriotic calling for the blackstronauts—it's just a job. "Suitcase" Jefferson applies to work at NASA not because he wants to advance his career or serve his country but because a "sweet little thing" named Alita Monroe tells him that she "couldn't be with a man" who didn't have a job. Rebuffed because of his race, he and his best friend found NASSA. The principal benefit of becoming an astronaut is, for Jefferson, purely carnal: "I got laid that very night." And while the Mercury Seven were propelled forward in the public consciousness by a powerful governmental public relations machine, the men of NASSA become enthusiastic hustlers and skilled self-promoters. A poster for one of their barnstorming tours caters to (presumably white, presumably racist) local crowds by framing the blackstronauts as passive cargo, not bold explorers. "These negroes," it promises, "will be put into rockets and launched before your very eyes. Enjoy cotton candy and beer. See the negroes fly!" A magazine advertisement shows blackstronaut "Rocket" Randall wide-eyed and grinning, holding a rakishly cocked hat atop his space helmet and declaring, "I got mine at the Hat Shack!" Their hustling is like their ball field–style nicknames, and their good-natured coarseness ("Yes, sir," Sullivan Carew writes to his wife, "I about froze my mother-fucking nuts off"), an affront to the qualities that NASA expected their astronauts—as idealized Americans—to embody.

Bobrow's portrayal of NASSA mocks the image that NASA created for its astronauts, but, more significant, it mocks the idea that the image mattered. The blackstronauts, after all, get to the moon first. They beat not only the implacable Russians but also NASA: the best and bright-est that white America has to offer, backed by the full weight of the government and the military-industrial complex. Underfunded, under-equipped, and undertrained, they succeed simply because no one told them they couldn't. They do not represent highly touted mainstream "American values," but they are validated into the most definitively American of ways: They win.

THE TRUTH OF STORIES

One of the primary tasks of the mockumentary is to comment on society's sacred cows—cherished statuses, assumptions, and icons—undermining the notions that fuel our identities and shared "truths." By combining the documentary form with fictional narrative, mockumentaries appropriate the appearance of authenticity in the service of irony and cultural critique. They rely on audience knowledge of the workings of the documentary form to weave a complex tapestry of art and artifice, truth and lies, humor and recrimination.[9] In fact, audience awareness is crucial for the apprecia-tion of the mockumentary's parody and commentary.[10]

Bobrow uses the many codes and conventions that have come to signify the documentary as a distinct screen form, to blur the boundaries between fiction and fact as he creates his parodic "alternate history" of the early space program.[11] Archival and staged historical photographs, commen-tary by an "expert" academic guide, and the voices of witnesses (living and dead) all combine to create a film that draws multiply on the tech-niques of the documentary genre. Together, they create a satirical critique of mid-twentieth-century racism and critically deconstruct the techniques and truth status of contemporary documentaries. Drawing on Nichols's analysis of the documentary form, mockumentary scholars Jane Roscoe and Craig Hight have identified these techniques as key to the effective-ness of the mockumentary's appropriation of that form, as it simultane-ously relies on and critiques audiences' (often passive) acceptance of the authority of nonfiction.[12] For a brief moment, the mockumentary claims the cultural power of the documentary for its own and, in revealing its own ruse, diminishes the authority of both forms.[13]

Working from a palette of slowly panned historical images, Bobrow draws on numerous cultural reference points—from space shuttle launches to Cadillac Coupe de Villes, from John F. Kennedy to Satchel Paige—to reflexively reinterpret history as cultural commentary. In the process, he takes particular aim at the iconic status of documentaries produced by film-maker Ken Burns—his battle cry stamped on the opening credits: "A film not by Ken Burns"—one of the earliest in a cluster of Burns parodies.[14] This appropriation of Burns's "pan and zoom" technique, applied to apparently archival images, suggests the simple label of "fake" for *The Old Negro Space Program*, but the reconstruction of those images—white-coated NASA technicians wearing conical hats symbolizing the Ku Klux Klan, space capsules stamped "United States of White America," and the one-inch news item buried at the bottom of page thirty-four of the *Cincinnati Enquirer*, headlined "Negroes Land on Moon"—gives this "fake" a critical-historical stance rather than a benign comic stance.

The story of the *Old Negro Space Program* eases into being like a back-porch yarn spun on a sunny Sunday afternoon. "It was a different time, you understand, 1957 or '58." "Suitcase" Jefferson's periodic refrain harks back to the traditions of generations of storytellers and narrators of oral

Rocket Randall promotes the Hat Shack. *Courtesy of Andy Bobrow.*

history. It is his "Once upon a time" narrative strategy—a stage-setting device echoed by the off-screen narrator and reinforced throughout the film—backed by the strains of a melancholy fiddle, made familiar in countless mainstream historical documentaries. It *was* a different time: a difference made all the more clear by grainy black-and-white images of the days gone by. The blackstronauts are contextualized by archival photos of roadside America—from "Uncle Tom's Place," boasting "colored" parking and Coca-Cola, to "whites only" sandwich shops—crowds celebrating in Harlem and newspaper headlines warning of riots in Chicago, Boston, and Detroit. Motionless pictures of the unforgettable are marshaled in support of the forgotten, their claim to authenticity made even stronger when juxtaposed against full-color shots of present-day space launches and clips of the film's on-screen personalities. Here, Jefferson is joined by African American studies expert Dr. Warren Fingeroot (played by filmmaker Bobrow), whose vague, jargon-laden commentary and *kufi* cap mark him as the consummate sympathetic liberal academic.

This tension created in Bobrow's film between imitation and authenticity is not new to the documentary genre. It is a contradiction that has troubled the work of photographers and filmmakers for generations, as they struggle with the status of the image as historical record. Prior to the digital age, the photograph was long considered to be an inherently literal medium—one that required no narrator—and yet, even before "Photoshop" became a household word, it was one that lent itself to those who would, following the observations of Miles Orvell, play on the "audience's beliefs in the veracity of the medium, while taking . . . a much more flexible view of the photographic practice . . . in the interest of achieving a rhetorically convincing effect."[15]

Bobrow crafts a parody around these inherent contradictions in the use of imagery, parroting and mocking the techniques that, through films such as *Brooklyn Bridge* (1982), *The Shakers: Hands to Work, Hearts to God* (1985), *The Civil War* (1990), *Baseball* (1994–2010), and *Jazz* (2001), have become synonymous with contemporary historical documentary at the hand of filmmaker Ken Burns. Along with their collages of diary entries, newsreel footage, and the voices of "experts," living and dead, Burns's documentaries showcase collages of daguerreotypes, calotypes, cartes de vistes—still images that seem to stop time, giving testimony to the "truth" of their historical moments—"certificates of presence," as Roland Barthes has called them.[16] The acclaimed filmmaker embraces the task of weaving the "story" into "history" and sees himself serving as a "translator of complex subjects":

> History used to be the great pageant of everything that went before this moment, not some dry and stuffy subject in a curriculum, the word "history"

itself gives away its primary organization. It's mostly made up of the word "story," and we've forgotten to tell stories.[17]

Burns's documentaries reminded audiences of the "power of the single image to communicate"—a power that has been seized on by Bobrow and other mockumentarians.[18] The images that compose *The Old Negro Space Program* bear witness to the "truth" of the story being told, as they chronicle the blackstronauts' barnstorming tours, spectacular feats of aeronautical retrofitting, and fiery disasters. All are part of the film's well-honed "discourses of sobriety": vestments of authority suggesting realism, objectivity, and validity—that refute any suggestions of imaginative storytelling.[19] Yet, these images are also, as poet Donald Hall observes, part of our collective national heritage and cultural identity: "places where memory gathers."[20] And so, Bobrow's narrative imagery zigzags between the poles of audiences' learned interpretive abilities, exploiting, illuminating, and mocking both American cultural nostalgia for the mid-twentieth century and the positioning of the still-image documentary as a form of "transcendent historical discourse,"[21] while also crafting a visual text that reminds us that the nostalgia and canonical history of one community is often created and celebrated at the expense of another.

RETROFITTING HISTORY

Nostalgia for the mid-twentieth century is deeply engrained in the American middle class: classic car "cruise" nights close suburban streets; beds and baths are brightened by *I Love Lucy* accessories; Elvis impersonators abound; reruns from the golden age of television crowd late-night viewing schedules; pin-up art and poodle skirts are familiar sights on college campuses; and phrases such as "One small step for man" and "I have a dream" are indelibly etched in the country's collective memory. To exploit audience's well-reinforced nostalgia for these bygone "happy days," Bobrow uses the elements of documentary popularized by Burns to build a bridge between the present and the halcyon days that never were. Memories of the era marked by civil rights struggles and manned flight are, for many in the twenty-first century, received memories—provisional and unsteady—brimming over with generalities and spaces where ambiguity reigns. Freud notes, "It may indeed be questioned whether we have any memories at all *from* our childhood: memories *relating to* our childhood may be all that we possess. . . . And a number of motives, with no concern for historical accuracy, had a part in forming them, as well as in the selection of the memories themselves."[22]

Into those spaces of ambiguity, Bobrow delivers images and narratives designed to evoke audiences' received memories and then appropriates them for his own critical purposes: The warmly familiar names and faces of Buzz Aldrin and Gordon Cooper bring glimmers of recognition— Mercury . . . Gemini . . . Apollo . . . moon walks . . . solo orbits . . . and, then, the revelation that the pair were blackstronauts, hired away by NASA because they were light enough to "pass." The American flag, planted triumphantly on the lunar surface by a moon-walking astronaut, speaks of a historic moment that captivated the nation . . . until the camera pans away from the image's traditional frame to reveal the blackstronauts' modified "road rocket" parked nearby. Newspapers, unearthed from archives and yellowed with age, quote Deke Slayton, well-known member of the Mercury Seven and chief of the astronaut corps at the height of the U.S.-Russian space race . . . as he offers the government's sole public acknowledgment of NASSA's 1966 lunar landing: "We may want to talk with these Negroes. Their mishap may just help us in our goal to land a man on the Moon by the end of the decade."[23]

Bobrow's deftly manipulated images embed NASA—founded at the height of the civil rights movement and headquartered in the Deep South—in the social realities from which received memory shields it. "Suitcase" Jefferson recalls in voiceover, "To our surprise, NASA wasn't hiring any Negroes" in 1957–1958. On screen, the camera pulls back from an archival photograph of NASA headquarters to reveal two uniformed men: a helmeted soldier and a beefy police officer with a cigar clamped in his teeth . . . reminders of the paratroopers patrolling the streets around Central High School in Little Rock and southern lawmen turning dogs and fire hoses on protestors in Birmingham and Selma. The image underscores the irony in Jefferson's "surprise." Later images show a pair of astronauts in a Gemini spacecraft simulator with the stenciled warning "Whites Only" at the edge of the cockpit, and a Mercury capsule being labeled not with the familiar legend "United States of America" but with "United States of White America," transforming it to an expression of racial, rather than national, pride and achievement. The doctored

The blackstronauts of NASSA. *Courtesy of Andy Bobrow.*

photographs make explicit for modern audiences a truth so obvious in the late fifties and early sixties that no such labels were needed to express it. Lunch counters, water fountains, and theater entrances might be ambiguous territory, needing definition as "colored" and "white" domains, as the film's archival images illustrate, but there was no question of who belonged in the space program.[24]

Bobrow's images of NASSA are created to evoke the Jim Crow–era South. The blackstronauts' "cloth spacesuits"—collarless shirts, belted knickers, calf-high socks, and low shoes—are clearly baseball uniforms. The poses in which they appear—standing or kneeling, shoulder to shoulder—echo dozens of posed portraits of baseball teams from the 1940s and early 1950s. One even includes, incongruously, a man in a black suit and short-billed cap (an umpire?) at the far right of the line. Only the gleaming white space helmets on their heads and the Apollo command modules around which they pose firmly connect them to the space age. A second set of images, purportedly showing the blackstronauts in their role as barnstorming "minor celebrities," shows them in suits, fedoras, and open-necked shirts, posed in chairs or standing around 1940s-vintage buses. This second set of images serves as a different touchstone than the first, evoking the itinerant musicians of Burns's film *Jazz* rather than Negro League ballplayers of *Baseball*, but the underlying message is the same. Bobrow's fictional black astronauts, like their real-world counterparts in sports and entertainment, scramble to earn a living in a world tightly circumscribed by race.

But the troubled racial history of the country is well known and accessible in the many visual and literary texts of the canon. "Lost" histories are increasingly documented and drawn into the public consciousness, and they carry with them a tension between storytelling and history, similar to that discussed earlier. As Reid-Pharr noted, "all of our attempts to recapture the past, to produce narratives of 'forgotten' or 'lost' histories are exercises in fiction."[25] What Bobrow's film brings to the cinematic table is not a cry for the redress of historical wrongs, but through a parody of the "lost" history documentary, he delivers a interlocking set of sharp reminders: first, that all history is constructed from "small fictions" and that the "histories we construct, even at their most lush, are always fashioned from the thinnest of materials: faulty accounts, flimsy documents, grainy images";[26] second, that when set against the diversity, chaos, and individuality of experience of *lived* history, even revisionist histories—our best efforts to remedy the ills of the canon—are pale and myopic.

If we consider the characters in *The Old Negro Space Program*, not only are they a ragtag collection of ne'er-do-wells—consummate underdogs rocketing to space on a shoestring and a prayer—but they are also mid-twentieth-century white caricatures of the African American male. Their "lost" history is populated with hackneyed conceptions of black identity, located somewhere between the icons of minstrelsy and Blaxploitation.[27] "Suitcase" Jefferson is simultaneously hypersexual and lazy—seeking out employment with both the white and the black space programs simply to "get laid." "Loopy Louie" Hayes is cast, at best, as a comic misfit in the tradition of Mantan Moreland, whose missions send his friends and neighbors running for cover and, at worst, as a junkie whose well-known reputation for "shootin' up again" is memorialized in song. "Rocket" Randall tips a dapper hat atop his spaceman's helmet in his ad for the Hat Shack, with a wide-eyed grin made familiar in cinematic and literary illustrations of the naive bumpkin Jim Crow. Unschooled, unrefined, and unemployed, their success owes more to fate and perseverance than to preparation or skill, and the "lost" history narrative that strives to "re-cover" them is shot through with the same social anxieties that lost them in the first place.

Rocket powered and ready to roll. *Courtesy of Andy Bobrow.*

TRUTH SHALL MAKE US FREE

NASA's path to the moon involved dozens of flights, scores of astronauts, and hundreds of rockets and spacecraft. The canonical history reduces this complex story to a handful of highlights: Alan Shepard and John Glenn restoring American pride after *Sputnik*; the sudden tragedy of *Apollo 1* and the averted tragedy of *Apollo 13*; Neil Armstrong planting a flag in the lunar dust; and Buzz Aldrin, in an iconic photograph, raising glove to visor in a silent salute. Between those highlights are gaps where popular memory becomes vague and fuzzy—where missions blur together, astronauts' names are unfamiliar, and the sequence of events is (until the next highlight) unclear. Those gaps have, since the early 1960s, given novelists and filmmakers a place to slip in fictional missions—a multiday Mercury flight in Martin Caidin's *Marooned* (1964), a landing on the far side of the moon in James Michener's *Space* (1980)—or operations such as Project Daedalus in Clint Eastwood's feature film *Space Cowboys* (2000). They also provide a place where, for many, it is easy to imagine secrets being lost or deliberately hidden.

The Old Negro Space Program does both, "discovering" an entire fictional space program in the dark, unknown spaces in audiences' knowledge of space history and in similar spaces in their equally fragmentary knowledge of midcentury black history. Bobrow's telling of the story creates a deliberately awkward fit with both histories. NASA, no different from the rest of white America, shoves the black astronauts of NASSA down as they reach for the moon. Deke Slayton, commenting on Jefferson and Hayes's lunar landing, casually implies that "men" have yet to walk on the moon, and the duo returns home to find that no one cares. "We expected to be heroes," Jefferson remembers, "but when we got back, we were just Negroes."

Bobrow's portrayal of the blackstronauts as the antithesis of the traditional heroes of both space history and black history—they lack the laconic confidence of the former and the enduring vision of the latter—serves as a critique of what is left out of traditional histories: the less-than-perfect individual, the less-than-successful plan, and the less-than-triumphant outcome. The "lost" history that he constructs, chronicles, and interpolates into other histories that we believe we know well is, at the same time, a comment on our willingness to believe that canonical histories *are* incomplete. Convinced that the *real* truth is hidden in the dark corners of history, we are primed to believe that whatever we find there *is* the truth, hidden to prevent us from finding it.

As the film's closing credits roll, this search for the truth is echoed by a well-known verse of "We Shall Overcome"—the unofficial anthem of the civil rights movement. The song is triumphantly rendered in the background by a chorus of black men's voices and a lone guitar intoning, "Truth shall make us free / truth shall make us free / truth shall make us free someday." Associated with church pews and picket lines, images of labor and civil rights protests evoked by the song blend with lingering images of the "lost" history of the blackstronauts, adding an additional layer of authenticity to the film's cluster of cultural commentaries. The trajectory of the song's history and appropriation, however, adds an even additional layer of complexity, as well, to Bobrow's usage. While its origins are found in African American hymns, the song's initial wide-spread popularity was at the hands of two white musicians, folksinger Pete Seeger and musicologist Guy Carawan, the latter of whom is credited with introducing the song into the American civil rights movement. Most recently, however, "Truth shall make us free" has become the touch phrase for another movement—revisionist historians seeking to deny the history of the Holocaust have coined the slogan *Wahrheit Macht Frei* (Truth shall make us free) to parody the *Arbeit Macht Frei* (Work shall make us free) signs that hung over the gates of concentration camps.[28] "Deep in my heart," the triumphant choir concludes, singing a song with a history as complex and culturally fraught as that of Bobrow's fictional space program, "I do believe / truth shall make us free someday." Given all that has gone before, it is the film's final act of mockery.

NOTES

1. Ironically, unbeknownst to NASA, the November 1966 death of Sergei Korolev, the engineering mastermind behind *Sputnik* and subsequent Soviet space exploits, undermined Soviet efforts to reach the moon and virtually ensured an American victory in the space race.

2. Backed by a mournful fiddle tune and mixing declarations of undying love with eloquent profanity, the sequence expertly parodies Ken Burns's most famous work: the "Sullivan Ballou letter" segment that closed part 1 of *The Civil War* (1990).

3. On NASA and the first astronauts as symbols of national competence and vigor, see Walter A. McDougall, *The Heavens and the Earth: A Political History of the Space Age* (New York: Basic Books, 1985), 302–30; and Howard McCurdy, *Space and the American Imagination* (Baltimore: Johns Hopkins University Press, 1997), 84–107.

4. The history of U.S. manned spaceflight from 1958 to 1975 is surveyed—far more comprehensively—in Francis French and Colin Burgess's Outward Odyssey trilogy: *Into That Silent Sea*, *In the Shadow of the Moon*, and *Footprints in the Dust*

(Lincoln: University of Nebraska Press, 2007, 2010); Andrew Chaikin, *A Man on the Moon: The Voyages of the Apollo Astronauts* (New York: Viking, 1994) remains the definitive single-volume history.

5. Quoted in Martin Caidin, *The Astronauts: The Story of Project Mercury, America's Man-in-Space Program* (New York: Dutton, 1960), 89.

6. The reality was frequently far different. Apollo astronaut Walter Cunningham's *The All-American Boys* (New York: Macmillan, 1977) and Tom Wolfe's *The Right Stuff* (Farrar, Straus & Giroux, 1979) demolished the carefully maintained image of astronauts as Boy Scouts, and subsequent astronaut memoirs have made no effort to resurrect it.

7. Glenn's role as the instigator of this process—rooted in the fact that he genuinely embodied the qualities that NASA wished all the astronauts to project—is documented in Wolfe, *The Right Stuff*, 169–77.

8. Jan Harold Brunvand, *Too Good to Be True* (New York: Norton, 1999), 93.

9. See Gary D. Rhodes and John Parris Springer, *Docufictions: Essays on the Intersection of Documentary and Fictional Filmmaking* (Jefferson, NC: McFarland, 2006), 165; and Jane Roscoe and Craig Hight, *Faking It: Mock-documentary and the Subversion of Factuality* (Manchester: Manchester University Press, 2001), 15–21.

10. Gerd Bayer, "Artifice and Artificiality in Mockumentaries" in Rhodes and Springer, *Docufictions*, 165.

11. For more on the documentary form, see Bill Nichols, *Representing Reality: Issues and Concepts in Documentary* (Bloomington: Indiana University Press), 1991; Louise Spence and Vinicius Navarro, *Crafting Truth: Documentary Form and Meaning* (Piscataway Township, NJ: Rutgers University Press), 2011.

12. Roscoe and Hight, *Faking It*, 15–21. See also Nichols, *Representing Reality*.

13. See Alexandra Juhasz and Jesse Lerner's *F Is for Phony: Fake Documentary and Truth's Undoing* (Minneapolis: University of Minnesota Press, 2006) for an extended discussion of this transformation.

14. Including short films such as *The Three Stooges* (2007), *American Industry* (2008), and *Luncheon Meat* (2009), several of which carry the self-conscious "A film not by Ken Burns" label.

15. Miles Orvell, *The Real Thing: Imitation and Authenticity in American Culture, 1880–1940* (Chapel Hill: University of North Carolina Press 1989), 95–96.

16. Roland Barthes, *Camera Lucida: Reflections on Photography* (New York: Hill & Wang, 1981), 87.

17. John C. Tibbetts, "The Incredible Stillness of Being: Motionless Pictures in the Films of Ken Burns," *American Studies* 37, no. 1 (1996): 118.

18. Gary Edgerton, "Ken Burns's America. Style, Authorship, and Cultural Memory," *Journal of Popular Film and Television* 21, no. 2 (1993): 53.

19. Bill Nichols, *Blurred Boundaries: Questions of Meaning in Contemporary Culture* (Bloomington: Indiana University Press, 1995), 67.

20. One of Hall's concluding comments at the introduction of "Something like a War," the "second inning" of Burns's documentary *Baseball*.

21. Timothy Corrigan, "The Cinematic Essay: Genre on the Margins," *Iris: A Journal of Theory on Image and Sound* 19 (Spring 1995): 90.

22. Sigmund Freud, *The Freud Reader* (New York: Norton, 1995), 126.

23. For Slayton's actual role in the manned space program, see Donald K. Slayton and Michael Cassutt, *Deke! U.S. Manned Space from Mercury to the Shuttle* (New York: Doherty, 1994); and Alan Shepard and Deke Slayton, *Moon Shot: The Inside Story of America's Race to the Moon* (Atlanta: Turner, 1994).

24. The role of race in astronaut selection in the U.S. Air Force and NASA is discussed in J. Alfred Phelps, *They Had a Dream: The Story of African-American Astronauts* (Novato, CA: Presidio Press, 1994).

25. Robert F. Reid-Pharr, "Makes Me Feel Mighty Real: The Watermelon Woman and the Critique of Black Visuality," in Juhasz and Lerner, *F Is for Phony*, 137–38.

26. Reid-Pharr, "Makes Me Feel Mighty Real," 139.

27. For discussion of portrayals of iconic black characters, see Donald Bogle, *Toms, Coons, Mulattoes, Mammies, and Bucks: An Interpretive History of Black in American Films* (New York: Continuum, 1973); James Snead, *White Screens, Black Images: Hollywood on the Dark Side* (New York: Routledge, 1994); Thomas Cripps, *Slow Fade to Black: The Negro in American Film, 1900–1942* (Oxford: Oxford University Press, 1991); Linda G. Tucker, *Lockstep and Dance: Images of Black Men in Popular Culture* (Jackson: University Press of Mississippi, 2007).

28. As documented in Michael Schmidt's 1993 film *The Truth Shall Make Us Free*, produced by Swedish Television.

3

Peter Delpeut's
The Forbidden Quest:
History and Truth in Fiction

Robert G. Weiner

Peter Delpeut's *The Forbidden Quest* (1993) is one of those rare films that is so engaging that its mockumentary stance is almost forgotten. Indeed, when I first watched the film, in the late hours of the night, I almost believed that I was watching a real documentary. Although the only indication of the film's status as a fictionalized reconstruction is found in the opening credits, there are clues embedded in the *Quest* that lead viewers to realize that all is not what it seems. This chapter examines those clues to explore the ways in which *The Forbidden Quest*, as an artistic, historical, and literary work, blurs the line between fact and fiction.

IT'S THERE IN THE PICTURES

The film, set in 1941, tells the tale of a filmmaker who, while working on a documentary about the longline fishermen of Ireland's Black Salt Bay, comes across J. C. Sullivan, who claims to be the last surviving member of the ill-fated *Hollandia* expedition to the Antarctic. Sullivan agrees to an interview and reveals that he has film canisters containing pictures that tell the tale that he is about narrate: "The Ship," he affirms, "she's still there in pictures."

Sullivan's story begins in 1905. He hears that a carpenter is needed for a boat journey in Norway, and so he becomes part of an international crew led by a Dutch captain, Van Dyke. Footage of Scott's *Terra Nova*, as it was being readied for sail, provides the context for the crew's preparations. The crew, unaware of the adventure to come, only learns of the polar journey when the sled dogs are loaded aboard. As the expedition ventures forth, the inhumanity of man and the power of nature are showcased time and again in both the film's fictional narrative and the documentary images it appropriates.

Throughout the expedition, found documentary footage gives testimony to the human assault against nature, as whales and sea lions are slaughtered. Likewise, it bears witness when nature strikes back, as storms and blinding glaciers threaten to overwhelm the crew. As images from Frank Hurley's camera illustrate Shackleton's ship *Endurance* and her crew struggling to cut through the Arctic ice, Sullivan wonders how such glacial beauty "could bring about such evil."

This battle between man and nature—the struggle to define good and evil—is, for Sullivan, the downfall of the expedition. His crewmates' inhumanity, he believes, brings the "wrath of God" upon the *Hollandia*. He refers to the "thing that started it all"—the brutal killing of a polar bear—by one of the crew members, known only as "the Italian." Sullivan acknowledges that these are "creatures that don't live there," and he sees the bear as an omen—a sign from God that the expedition should go no farther. When the interviewer expresses skepticism, Sullivan defends his story with the power of images: "It's true; it's there in the pictures." He tells how the Italian raised his gun and shot the bear over and over again, but the animal refused to die quietly, which he sees as proof that the bear was "God sent." When the Italian ate the raw bear meat, Sullivan knew that they would be punished for this sin—that the Italian had brought the "wrath of God" upon the *Hollandia*.

Wilson, the helmsman, offers a different explanation: the bear is proof that the expedition's goal exists—that there truly is a passage through the center of the earth, between the poles. The passage was purportedly found by Belgians, who then went mad from the Pandora's box of knowledge it released. A group of Eskimos—like the bear, displaced from the Arctic—appears, and we see footage of an Eskimo village and families. One is wearing a Belgian cap, reinforcing the helmsman's story.

Terror and madness, seemingly brought on by the crew's violations of a divine moral code, descend on the expedition: the Italian and others die horribly at the hands of the Eskimos, and the raw bear meat causes a fatal disease in the men who consume it. The captain dies and is laid to rest through footage of Shackleton's real-life burial. Sullivan recounts how, without a skipper, all would have been lost but for the "man of letters," Wilson, the helmsman, who took command. The ice starts to close in around them; they become "frozen fast" (as did the *Endurance*); and the crew unloads the ship (mirroring Shackleton's men) for a journey ashore. When the *Hollandia* is finally crushed, what viewers actually see is Frank Hurley's footage of the *Endurance* being torn apart by the ice.

The fantastic intrudes again, however, as Wilson directs the survivors to travel poleward in search of the entrance to the center of the earth. Their numbers steadily diminishing, they find it—at this point Sullivan almost stops the interview, fearing disbelief, but the filmmaker urges him on—and audiences see color-tinted reddish-orange documentary footage of a crew sledging and climbing near a wide gorge. When they reach the other side, the explorers find themselves in the Eskimos' land of the dead. There Sullivan sees a reddish-green light, where the "hand of God touches the earth."

Wilson went on into oblivion, leaving only Sullivan and the picture man to continue the trek. When the picture man started to slip away, he gave Sullivan the film canister, saying, "Take the pictures." Sullivan knew he had to "bring the living pictures" back because the camera saw it all. The pictures, which Sullivan believes will never lie, have the desired

The *Endurance* as the *Hollandia*.

effect. After watching the footage from the film canister, the filmmaker realizes that Sullivan's story is completely true, and he attempts to visit him again to ask many more questions. However, Sullivan had completed his mission—telling the story of the *Hollandia* and her crew's amazing journey through the wasteland of Antarctica—his final task was delivering the film canister to his interviewer to validate his story. Shortly thereafter, he died. It was now the pictures' duty to tell the tale.

FOUND-FOOTAGE FILMMAKING

Dutch filmmaker Delpeut is famous for using the found-footage technique to craft a new piece of filmmaking art. Several of his better-known works make use of variations on this technique, including *Lyrical Nitrate* (1991), Delpeut's early homage to silent films; *The Forbidden Quest*, with its tale of Arctic exploration; and *Diva Dolorosa* (1999), on early Italian divas. These films suggest that Delpeut, as a filmmaker, has more in common with found-footage directors such as Ken Jacobs (*Tom Tom the Piper's Son*, 1969), Craig Baldwin (*Tribulation 99*, 1992), Jay Rosenblatt (*King of the Jews*, 2000), and even Kenneth Anger (*Don't Smoke That Cigarette*, 2000) than with mockumentary filmmakers such as Christopher Guest (*Best in Show*, 2000; *This Is Spinal Tap*, 1984). Yet *The Forbidden Quest* also differs from many other found-footage films in that it actually attempts to build a narrative through that footage, rather than to convey a social message, as did Rosenblatt and Anger.

This technique of creating new works of filmic art by using found footage is not a new practice in the motion picture industry. Feature films have been using "stock footage" as a technique to enhance visual narratives for much of the history of commercial cinema. For example, a movie might use an airplane takeoff or a missile launch to add realism or augment available effects—closely associating use of stock footage with low-budget filmmaking. Nonfiction productions, for their part, often employ inserts of historic film to illustrate or highlight events and lives of individuals. Unlike either of these, found-footage filmmakers combine various bits and pieces of film to create something new and vibrant: not a hybrid film but an imaginative product of appropriation and reconfiguration that can stand on its own, offering glimpses of the familiar, yet unique unto itself. In recent years, various found-footage festivals have sprung up all over the world, testifying to the interest and creative use of this unique mode of filmic art.

Delpeut spent countless hours mining the archives of the Film Museum of the Netherlands to find the footage used in *The Forbidden Quest*, ultimately crafting an entire narrative around existing documentary

Arctic film footage. In so doing, he not only created a new tale but also introduced contemporary audiences to the archival footage embedded in his film: Frank Hurley's *In the Grip of the Polar Ice* (1919),[1] featuring Ernest Shackleton; Herbert Ponting's *90 Degrees South with Scott to the Antarctic* (1933),[2] featuring Robert Falcon Scott; and Odd Dahl's *Med Maud over Polhavet* (1926), featuring Roald Amundsen. These three major Antarctic explorers defined the heroic age of Antarctic exploration (circa 1895–1923), and their footage provides an iconic realism to Delpeut's film.[3] One reviewer commented, "Perhaps the greatest wonder is that these fragile images have lived to tell their own tales."[4]

This use of archival footage in *The Forbidden Quest* certainly has led to confusion among audiences and catalogers alike. The Online Computer Library Center's First Search World Catalog, a bibliographic utility used by professional librarians, has the following listing for *The Forbidden Quest* VHS: "*The Forbidden Quest* is the unknown story of the *Hollandia* South Pole expedition 1905–1906, as told by ship's carpenter J. C. Sullivan." The description heading is "Documentary Films–Netherlands," and the entry lists the interview with J. C. Sullivan as though he was a real historical figure. The catalogers also gave the film a legitimate nonfiction number/letter heading. Other records for the VHS and DVD simply list *The Forbidden Quest* as either an Antarctic drama or a silent film produced in the Netherlands.

VOICES FROM THE PAST

In addition to employing found documentary footage to tell the story of *The Forbidden Quest*, the filmmaker draws on journals and memoirs, such as the travel journals of Shackleton, Scott, and others, to spin a true-to-life tale.[5] The *Hollandia* sailed in the times and places of those great expeditions—her 1905–1906 journey situated in the years between those of Scott and Shackleton—with her crew making similar stops along the way.

And in that crew, many bore resemblance to the real-life explorers whose lives gave rise to Delpeut's story. The captain was no doubt inspired by Shackleton's skipper, Frank Worsely, and the character's name, Van Dyke, was most likely chosen to honor director W. S. Van Dyke, who directed the Arctic feature film *Eskimo* (1933). That film, which was considered a documentary at the time of its release, also blends reality with fiction, combining documentary footage of life among the Inuit with a fictional narrative about treacherous white traders. Van Dyke also directed *White Shadows in the South Seas* (1928), which may have provided additional inspiration for Delpeut's work.

The ship's carpenter, and narrator of the *Hollandia*'s journey, J. C. Sullivan, was also likely based on an actual member of an expedition crew: C. J. Sullivan, the literate blacksmith of the HMS *Erebus* of the British Antarctic expedition (1839–1843), under the command of James Clark Ross. The real-life Sullivan, whose thoughts were preserved in a journal, encountered the Antarctic with a wonder and awe that is mirrored by his cinematic counterpart. His notes relate that the polar sights were "wonderful works of nature," "[sometimes] too grand for [even] Stout hearted Sailors."[6]

Other characters in the film drew from the lives of the early explorers. Wilson, helmsman of the *Hollandia* and a "man of letters," bears more than a casual resemblance to Dr. Edward Wilson, a physician, naturalist, and painter who had been one of Robert Scott's most trusted friends and colleagues, accompanying him on both the *Discovery* and *Terra Nova* expeditions. Even Osmond, J. C. Sullivan's favorite dog in *The Forbidden Quest* narrative, bears the name of the favorite dog on Scott's *Terra Nova* expedition.

The influences of the early expedition filmmakers are also apparent in Delpeut's narrative, well beyond any appropriated bits of celluloid. In his film *90 Degrees South with Scott to the Antarctic*, Herbert Ponting, Scott's official photographer and filmmaker on the *Terra Nova* expedition (1910–1913),[7] reminisced about coming across a Christian cross that had been erected in memory of a comrade who had been on Scott's previous expedition, with the *Discovery* (1901–1904). He observed that this symbol of "Christian faith on earth seemed like a guardian angel at the gates of a *forbidden land* reminding those who would venture farther that in the midst of life we are in death."[8] It would be no surprise if this statement was the inspiration behind the story of *The Forbidden Quest*.

Delpeut's film is dedicated to Australian photographer and filmmaker Frank Hurley, who documented Shackleton's *Endurance* expedition.[9] No stranger to polar travel, Hurley had also accompanied Douglas Mawson's *Australian Antarctic* expedition (1911) and recorded those travels in the film *Dr. Mawson in the Antarctic* (1913),[10] and his addition to the crew of the *Endurance* was due in large part to the belief that some of the cost of the expedition would be offset by revenue from the film and photographs.[11] Shackleton's *Endurance* journey was a failure, but it does provide what is perhaps the greatest survival story in the history of exploration and adventure.[12] When the film *In the Grip of the Polar Ice* was finally released (1919), it was a great success, and both Hurley and Shackleton often lectured at various screenings.

There is no doubt that the picture man "who saw it all" in Sullivan's narrative was based on Hurley. In one incident in the narrative, Sullivan recounts how the picture man had been out in the Arctic weather too long and had to be massaged and rubbed for hours to bring life back into

Filmmaker Herbert Ponting. *Library of Congress.*

him. A similar incident happened on the *Endurance*: When the trapped ship was being slowly crushed by pack ice, Hurley, already evacuated, returned to the splintering vessel to retrieve film and photographs left behind and nearly froze to death. The *Endurance* crew massaged the filmmaker for many hours to save his life. In the fictional narrative, the picture man plays the most significant role, next to J. C. Sullivan. He is the one whose work ultimately testifies to the reality of the amazing supernatural journey, since "pictures don't lie." The pictures become a metaphor for the truth of the journey in the fictional narrative, and since the images used by Delpeut actually did "see it all" in real-life expeditions, there is a duality of truth here.

THE INTERPLAY OF TEXTS

Delpeut's story of the *Hollandia*'s expedition draws life from a complex intertextual relationship among literary works of exploration as well—not merely those of London, Melville, and the other great books of the sea but fictional works, as well, including such notable writings as T. S. Eliot's *The Waste Land* (1922), Edgar Allen Poe's only full-length novel, *Narrative of Arthur Gordon Pym of Nantucket* (1838), and Jules Verne's *An Antarctic Mystery* (1897).[13] The relationships among these works, Delpeut's film, and real-life polar explorations illustrate complex links that blur the boundaries among reality, fiction, and the fantastic.

Reaching as far back as the seventeenth century, to Anthanasius Kircher's *Mundus Subterraneus* (1665), we find fantastic notions about the poles of the planet—a "hollow earth," with a passage between the poles where mystical beings dwell—and these images and ideas are carried forward in tales such as Ludvig Holberg's novel *Nicolai Klimii iter subterraneum* (Niels Klim's subterranean travels; 1741), Captain Adam Seaborn's *Symzonia* (1820), Jules Verne's *Journey to the Center of the Earth* (1864), and Edgar Rice Burroughs's *Pellucidar* series, among others.

Poe's *Arthur Gordon Pym*, the tale of an ill-fated seafaring expedition, is among these early novels speculating about the Antarctic waters and polar regions. Initially dismissed as a literary hoax, the novel toys with its readers, presenting fiction as fact—an early literary parallel to Delpeut's mockumentary. The narrative is presented as a firsthand account of Arthur Gordon Pym, a stowaway on the *Grampus*, a ship bound for the South Sea Islands.[14] Pym's preface reinforces the story's status as reality, noting "Mr. Poe" has already adapted portions of his journal into a fictional story, and it is "Mr. Poe" who must finish the tale, when Pym's notes stop abruptly at his death.[15]

Numerous plot elements and character references suggest the influence of Poe's tale on *The Forbidden Quest*. The stowaway and the carpenter each experience their demons in human form—the cook, for Pym; the Italian, for Sullivan—characters whose evil influence brings about the downfall of their respective journeys and the demise of their crewmates. Murder and cannibalism taint both expeditions, and ships bound for Antarctic glory deliver both sets of survivors. And the mystical lore of "hollow earth" philosophies—beliefs and symbolism that link the supernatural and natural worlds with the fates of men—move effortlessly from Poe's pages to Delpeut's images. Mist and ash enshroud the crews; giant white Arctic bears appear, as if from another place and time, refusing to die and bringing ill fortune to those who eventually kill and eat them; and the terrible screams of the gigantic snow-white birds that haunt Pym's Antarctic struggles, "Tekel-li Tekeli-li," echo forward in time, through Sullivan's trials as well.[16]

Nearly sixty years later, Poe's narrative is carried forward, adapted, and its literary "mockumentary" status reinforced in Jules Verne's *Antarctic Mystery*. Verne, however, with his focus on the scientific, explains away all of the supernatural elements found in Poe's original tale. Verne's mystery is framed as a diary, penned by a Mr. Jeorling, in the same style as Pym's early account. Jeorling becomes involved in adventure on board the *Halbrane*, as her captain embarks on a quest to find his brother, thought lost at sea. That brother, Jeorling learns, was the captain of the vessel that rescued Pym, the *Jane*. The captain is obsessed with Poe's novel and believes that his brother may still be alive. Jeorling, who is familiar with Poe's rendition of Pym's adventure, is stunned by the realization that the tale is not fiction but fact.

Verne's novel summarizes "Poe's Romance of Pym" for the sake of those readers who are not familiar with Poe's work. The captain of the *Halbrane* believes that the Pym narrative may give him clues to finding the lost crew of the *Jane*, including his brother, and so, he retraces the former's path. Like so many vessels, real and imagined—including Shackleton's *Endurance* and Delpeut's *Hollandia*—the *Halbrane* becomes frozen fast in an iceberg, giving testimony to the perils of Antarctic exploration. However, unlike so many other expeditions, the *Halbrane*'s meets with success: The two brothers are reunited; Pym's body is found; and the remaining crew is rescued. Jeorling recants his earlier belief that Poe's descriptions of the Antarctic waters were "hallucinations of Arthur Pym" attesting "No! These were physical facts which we had just witnessed, and not imaginary phenomena!"[17]

And in the decades that followed, the chronicles of real-life expeditions—"physical facts" and the emotions and imaginings that those "facts" inspired—would find voice in countless fictional treatments.

The arduous trek in *Forbidden Quest.*

Echoes of the following passage from Shackleton's journals, telling of an eerie, otherworldly presence sensed during his twenty-two-mile journey across South Georgia, can be found in both Eliot's *Waste Land* and Delpeut's *Forbidden Quest*:

> When I look back at those days, I have no doubt that Providence guided us, not only across those snow fields, but across the storm-white sea that separated Elephant Island from our landing place on South Georgia. I know that during that long and racking march of thirty-six hours over the unnamed mountains and glaciers of South Georgia, it seemed to me often that we were four, not three. I said nothing to my companions on the point, but afterwards Worsley said to me, "Boss, I had a curious feeling on the march that there was another person with us." Crean confessed to the same idea.[18]

For the poet, Shackleton's legacy is found in these stanzas from his epic poem:

> Who is the third who walks always beside you?
> When I count there are only you and I together
> But when I look ahead up the white road
> There is always another one beside you . . .
> I do not know whether a man or a woman
> —But who is that on the other side of you?[19]

The filmmaker injects this intuition in a similar scene: The helmsman, heading the crew's desperate trek for survival after the captain's death, leads them through the Antarctic snow toward the passage between the poles. On the journey, the survivors begin to imagine that there existed one more among them—although they were only four, Sullivan relates, there was always the sense of a fifth.

The play between the real and the fictional in these examples illustrates the fragile and complex nature of our notions of "the truth," as it is conveyed through literature and film. In Delpeut's faux chronicle of Sullivan and the *Hollandia*, there are glimpses of "the real," as well as of the mysteries of the polar regions captured by Poe and Verne—and those fictional mysteries were in turn pursued by real ship captains and sailors for generations.

THE UNEASY STATUS OF FAUX HISTORY

The Forbidden Quest does not fit neatly into many of the existing frameworks for considering mockumentaries and found-footage films. The very nature of the mockumentary implies the parody, or "mocking," of the cultural status of documentary's generic codes and conventions.[20] Such parody, along with elements of critique and deconstruction, composes for mockumentary scholars such as Jane Roscoe and Craig Hight key characteristics of the genre. Roscoe argues that mock documentaries not only appropriate documentary aesthetics to create a fictional world but also construct a parody of both the documentary format and the subject at hand. In so doing, mockumentary filmmakers attempt to develop an intimate relationship with the audience, as coconspirators in the humorous content as well as in the inherent critical reflexivity of the form.[21]

Similarly, when discussing found-footage films, film scholar William Wees argues that, as with mockumentaries, the purpose of such films is often to deconstruct or recontextualize "images produced and disseminated by the corporate media" to create social or cultural commentary. Found-footage filmmaking is frequently used as political activism by filmmakers such as Marxist theorist Guy Debord who employ strategies of "detournment"—appropriating familiar images to create new works that are antithetical to the originals—using collage and montage to expose and critique ideological agendas.[22] Critic Keith Beattie explains that "found footage filmmaking may combine non-fictional images, selected from sources as commercial stock footage, newsreels, and home movies, and (even) fiction footage to construct an argument about the social historical world," making the films a kind of argument.[23]

Cultural critique of his subject, however, seems far from Delpeut's intention in filming *The Forbidden Quest*. On the contrary, the film functions more as homage to the heroic age of Antarctic exploration than as any sort of parody or commentary. Like mockumentarians and found-footage filmmakers, Delpeut *does* appropriate documentary footage from Arctic expeditions, which is paired with the interview narrative, to tell the story of the film. However, his intentions are not to use these repurposed images to create parody or advance an ideological agenda. Rather, he uses the footage to construct faux history in which, like Poe's *Narrative of Arthur Gordon Pym of Nantucket* and Verne's *Antarctic Mystery*, the commentary is focused on the audience's/reader's notions of what constitutes "truth"—pointing to its fragility and the permeable boundaries between the "real" and the "false"—creating fiction from fact and potentially creating "fact" from fiction. Anthropologist Allen Feldman observes,

> Yet despite this homage to actual film history, we are propelled into the unified fiction of the film and thus indirectly into the fictions and fantasy that organized 19th- and 20th-century Antarctic and other explorations. The diverse footage becomes a narrative continuum through expert montage and judicious use of the carpenter's voice-over. We are looking at footage culled from many historical polar expeditions, yet this film is both telling and not telling their story . . . for what we have seen is documentary reassembled as fictive events.[24]

The filmmaker thus challenges—and chides—his audiences as he entertains them, sending them away to interrogate their own received knowledge and sense of history. He combines history with literature and fantasy to craft a fantastic tale around "found" expedition footage, asking audiences, "What if?" in a way similar to that of many of the faux histories that have gone before. Sullivan's fictional tale of Antarctic survival was granted truth status by images—the picture man's pictures in the world of the narrative and the archival footage in the world of the audience. These are images of "what was" giving testimony to "what could have been, but wasn't." Like Jayne Loader's *Atomic Café* (1982), *The Forbidden Quest* provides a "cultural expression or memory of a particular time and place"[25] yet clothes it in fiction and offers it as reality. The intrinsic historical value of the images is left untouched and unblemished; they have not been ripped out of historical context, yet they receive new life in the service of a history that wasn't.

While the film has received acclaim as a work of fantasy, winning the International Fantasy Film Special Jury Award at the Festival Internacional de Cinema do Porto, in Porto Portugal, and the Special Jury Prize at the Netherlands Film Festival (1993), its blurring of statuses—truth and fiction—has created fissures in reception. Some viewers marvel at the film as a vehicle for historical artifacts embedded in fictional narrative, citing the "poetry and wonder" of Delpeut's use of found footage[26] and the value of "the silent images; ephemeral moments of life on the ice, the weird beauty of the polar landscape."[27] Others, however, such as *New York Times* critic Janet Maslin, lament that the fictional narrative "detracts needlessly, from the honest power of the film's archival scenes, which have been arranged and manipulated to suit the fictitious story." It is precisely the acceptance and valorization of that "honest power" of archival footage that Delpeut's construction of faux history calls into question. Through his use of found footage, the filmmaker reminds audiences that recontextualized images are never "innocent" or "honest" but must be probed and explored. *The Forbidden Quest* requires an interrogation of viewers' assumptions about received historical knowledge and implicitly urges its audiences to embark on their own "forbidden quest" to reconsider the nature of historical truth.

NOTES

1. Alternate titles include *Shackleton's Expedition to the Antarctic*, *Southward on the Queste*, and *South*.

2. Previously released as *With Captain Scott, RN, to the South Pole* (1911), *With Captain Scott in the Antarctic* (1912), *The Undying Story of Captain Scott* (1913), and *The Great White Silence* (1924).

3. Other films used but whose directors remain anonymous include *Storm of Zee*, *In het Land van de Yukon*, *Kerstmisheringerigen*, *Shackleton's Burial*, and *Den Store Gronlandsfilm*.

4. Juliet Clark, "Dutch Voices: Jo De Putter and Peter Delpeult," October 16, 2005, http://www.bampfa.berkeley.edu/film/FN15692.

5. Most likely from the following sources: C. J. Sullivan, *MS/Dairy*, SPRI MS 367/22, Turnbill Library, Wellington, New Zealand; C. J. Sullivan, "Narrative of Sir James Clark Ross's expedition, Excerpted in 'Two Unpublished Accounts of the British Antarctic Expedition, 1839–43'" in *Polar Record* 10, no. 69 (1961): 597–604; Fridtjof Nansen, *Farthest North; Being the Record of a Voyage of Exploration of the Ship* Fram *1893–96 and of a Fifteen Month's Sleigh Journoy by Dr. Nansen and Lieut. Johansen* (1897; repr., New York: Modern Library, 1999); Robert Falcon Scott, *Scott's Last Expedition; Being the Journals of Captain R. F. Scott*, vol. 1 (1913; repr., New York: Carroll & Graf, 1996); Roald Amundsen, *The South Pole: An Account of the Norwegian Antarctic Expedition in the* Fram, *1910–1912* (1913; repr., New York: Cooper Square Press, 2001); Ernest Shackleton, *South: The Story of Shackleton's Last Expedition, 1914–1917* (1920; repr., New York: Carroll & Graf, 1998); and Herbert Ponting, *The Great White South; or, with Scott in the Antarctic, Being an Account of Experiences with Captain Scott's South Pole Expedition and of the Nature Life of the Antarctic* (1922; repr., New York: Cooper Square Press, 2001).

6. C. J. Sullivan quoted by Francis Spufford, *I May Be Some Time: Ice and the English Imagination* (New York: St. Martin's Press, 1997), 39–40. For more on early British exploration, see L. B. Quartermain, *South to the Pole: The Early History of the Ross Sea Sector, Antarctica* (London: Oxford University Press, 1967); M. J. Ross, *Ross in the Antarctic: The Voyages of James Clark Ross in Her Majesty's Ships* Erebus and Terror *1839–1843* (Yorkshire, UK: Caedmon of Whitby, 1982); for a recent study on what actually happened to *Erebus* and *Terror*, see Martin W. Sandler, *Resolute: The Epic Search for the Northwest Passage and John Franklin and the Discovery of the Queen's Ghost Ship* (New York: Sterling, 2006).

7. For a general history of the Scott expedition, see Ranulph Fiennes, *Race to the Pole: Tragedy, Heroism, and Scott's Antarctic Quest* (New York: Hyperion, 2004); Apsley Cherry-Garrard, *The Worst Journey in the World* (1922; repr., Washington, DC: National Geographic, 2002); Michael De-La-Noy, *Scott of the Antarctic: A Concise Biography* (Gloucestershire: Sutton, 1987). For a look at Ponting's photographs, see Herbert Ponting, *With Scott to the Pole: The* Terra Nova *Expedition, 1910–1913; the Photographs of Herbert Ponting,* ed. H. J. P. Arnold (Crows Nest, New South Wales: Allen & Unwin, 2004). For a contemporary look at Antarctica and life on the continent see Nicholas Johnson, *Big Dead Place: Inside the Strange and Menacing World of Antarctica* (Los Angeles: Feral House, 2005).

8. Herbert Ponting, quoted in *90 Degrees South: With Scott to the Antarctic,* DVD, directed by Herbert Ponting (1933; Harrington Park, NJ: Milestone Film and Video/Image Entertainment, 1991–1992).

9. Also known as the Imperial Trans-Antarctic Expedition (1914–1916).

10. Also known as *Home of the Blizzard.*

11. See Frank Hurley, *South with Endurance: Shackleton's Antarctic Expedition 1914–1917; the Photographs of Frank Hurley* (New York: Simon & Schuster, 2001). Hurley wrote his own account of Antarctic adventures in *Argonauts of the South: Being a Narrative of the Voyagings and Polar Seas and Adventures in the Antarctic with Sir Douglas Mawson and Sir Ernest Shackleton* (New York: Putnam's, 1925). Also see Herbert Ponting and Frank Hurley, *1910–1916 Antarctic Photographs: Scott, Mawson, and Shackleton Expeditions* (New York: St. Martin's Press, 1980).

12. See Shackleton, *South*; Alfred Lansing, *Endurance: Shackleton's Incredible Voyage* (1959; repr., Carroll & Graf, 1999); F. A. Worsley, *Endurance: An Epic of Polar Adventure* (1933; repr., New York: Norton, 1999); Caroline Alexander, *The Endurance: Shackleton's Legendary Antarctic Expedition* (New York: Knopf, 1998).

13. Also known as *The Sphinx of the Ice Fields* and *The Mystery of Arthur Gordon Pym.* Certainly, one can also find the influence of Verne's *Journey to the Center of the Earth, 20,000 Leagues under the Sea,* and *The Mysterious Island* as well.

14. An interesting coincidental piece of history was that, like Pym, Pierce Blackborow was a stowaway on Shackleton's ill-fated *Endurance* expedition. Also like Pym, Blackborow became a valued member of the crew, but there was no murder or mutiny on the *Endurance* as on the *Grampus.*

15. Edgar Allan Poe, *Narrative of Arthur Gordon Pym of Nantucket*, in *Tell Tale Heart and Other Writings* (New York: Bantam Classics, 2004), 215.

16. These same cries are also found in H. P. Lovecraft's "The Whisperer in Darkness" (1931) and *At the Mountains of Madness* (1936).

17. Poe, *Narrative*, 318–19.

18. Ernest Shackleton, *South: The Endurance Expedition* (New York: Signet, 1999), 230.

19. T. S. Eliot, *Selected Poems* (New York: Harcourt, Brace & World, 1964), 65.

20. Jane Roscoe and Craig Hight, *Faking It: Mock-Documentary and the Subversion of Factuality* (New York: Manchester University Press, 2001), 42, 73.

21. Steven Lipkin, Derek Paget, and Jane Roscoe, "Docudrama and the Mock-Documentary: Defining Terms, Proposing Canons," in *Docufictions: Essays on the Intersection of Documentary and Fictional Filmmaking*, ed. Gary Rhodes and John Parris Springer (Jefferson, NC: McFarland, 2006), 14.

22. William Wees, "The Ambiguous Aura of Hollywood Stars in Avant Garde Found-Footage Films," *Cinema Journal* 41, no. 2 (2002): 4.

23. Keith Beattie, "The Cinema of Coming Attractions," *Metro* 151 (Winter 2007): 154.

24. Allen Feldman, "Faux Documentary and the Memory of Realism," *American Anthropologist*, n.s., 100, no. 2 (1998): 498, 500.

25. Adrian Danks, "The Global Art of Found Footage Cinema," in *Traditions in World Cinema*, ed. Linda Badley, R. Barton Palmer, and Steven Jay Schneider (New Brunswick, NJ: Rutgers University Press, 2006), 246.

26. Gary Handman, "Quick Vids," *American Libraries* 37, no. 2 (February 2006): 48.

27. Clark, "Dutch Voices," n. 1.

II

POPULAR CULTURE AS COMMENTARY

4

Polka Settles the Score in *The Schmenges: The Last Polka*

Linda Kornasky

The 1984 HBO mockumentary *The Schmenges: The Last Polka*, written by and starring Eugene Levy and John Candy as locally famous Midwestern polka-playing brothers Stan and Yosh Schmenge, is currently unavailable on DVD,[1] despite the popularity of Levy's many other mockumentaries, such as *Best in Show* (2000) and *A Mighty Wind* (2003).[2] Ironically, the target of Levy and Candy's mockumentary's parody, Martin Scorsese's 1978 classic rockumentary *The Last Waltz*, has remained both commercially successful and critically acclaimed, thanks to excellent performances by the legendary Muddy Waters, Bob Dylan, Joni Mitchell, and many other folk, blues, and rock-and-roll stars.[3] The steep rise in Scorsese's renown as a director since 1978, along with *The Last Waltz*'s unusual aesthetic sophistication for a documentary concert film, also explains the film's continuing interest for rock-and-roll audiences and critics, who routinely judge it to be the best (or among the best) and most definitive rockumentaries. The fanfare surrounding *The Last Waltz*'s release on DVD in 2002 in a twenty-fifth-anniversary restored edition has only reinforced the critical view of the film's significance to American popular culture.

Conversely, *The Schmenges: The Last Polka* has been overlooked as a mock rockumentary for two reasons—both of which should be reconsidered as two of the film's major strengths. First, as I demonstrate, its unique mockumentary approach to cultural critique entails a formal shift from a

53

respected genre to a discredited one—rock to polka—rather than the more typical and clear-cut generic parody via a ludicrous example of the type that *This Is Spinal Tap* (1984) directs at heavy metal or *A Mighty Wind* (2003) directs at folk music. In this way, among music-oriented mockumentaries, *The Schmenges: The Last Polka* most closely resembles the innovative *Bob Roberts* (1992), which features a content shift within the musical form of folk, from liberal to conservative political themes. As film scholars Jane Roscoe and Craig Hight have argued about *Bob Roberts*—and their point, I contend, applies as well to *The Schmenges: The Last Polka*—films of this type "develop reflexivity through their engagement with issues related to wider political processes, as much as from the complexity of their use of the mock-documentary form."[4] While this variation on mock rockumentary form in *The Schmenges: The Last Polka* has made it difficult to classify the film in a mockumentary field where the classic *This Is Spinal Tap* sets the standard, this variation should actually be considered a complex approach to the form that opens up potential ideological critique.

Second, one can assume that at least in part *The Schmenges: The Last Polka* has faded out of American popular culture because of its use of ethnic stereotypes. To be sure, the film dabbles in several conventional anti–Eastern European stock jokes, generally known in North America as "Polish jokes," featuring stupidly inappropriate behavior in everyday situations. While not given a real ethnic identity, the Schmenge brothers are depicted as immigrants from a fictionalized composite Eastern European country called Leutonia, a place-name that perhaps blends *Lietuva*, the Lithuanian word for Lithuania (a term known to Candy, whose mother was of Lithuanian descent), with *Polonia*, the Latin name for Poland used today to refer to the entire Polish diaspora.

The film stereotypically characterizes these generic Slavic Americans as unhip to American slang and trends; the women are depicted as disproportionately wide from the waist down, and they are unaware that they are in the midst of the second wave of the feminist movement. Similarly, the men are depicted as effeminate in gait and voice, unfashionable in their clothing, and oblivious to the fact that their large facial moles are stigmatized in America (and that other Americans would have them surgically removed).[5]

Nevertheless, one can interpret this excessive ethnic humor as a vehicle through which Candy and Levy initiate a cultural critique that examines the ethnic exclusionism inherent to rock-and-roll ideology; the film's "Polish joke" style of comedy is often undercut in telling ways that reveal the film's objective in this regard. For instance, Levy's musicianship on the accordion during the film's polka performances belies the initial images of bungling Eastern Europeans. Even as Levy and Candy suggest that many polka performers' offstage goofiness has contributed to

The Schmenge brothers perform.

polka's demise, both drop their bungling personas to reveal themselves as talented musicians while playing their instruments. Candy's Lithuanian heritage and his impressive musicianship on the clarinet also lend a sympathetically pro-polka/pro-Slavic tone to the film.[6]

Moreover, through their hilarious parodying of Scorsese's *The Last Waltz*, Levy and Candy transcend the Slavic American stereotypes they occasionally evoke, since their film's carnivalesque stance critiques the implicit ideology of rock and roll and posits in its stead polka ideology, a countercultural ethos that ethnomusicologists Charles Keil, Angeliki V. Keil, and Dick Blau have called "polka happiness," defined simply as "a ritual sense of present time in which individual freedom of expression and maximum sociability reinforce each other."[7] Candy and Levy's viewers are thereby drawn to the film to laugh at predictable "Polish jokes," but they find that their laughter is soon redirected toward the pretensions of rock and roll.

The film's critique of rock and roll's ideology, as represented compellingly by the Band, concentrates in four areas:

1. its inauthentic claims to full ethnic inclusiveness and to represent the democratic American essence, in the southern U.S. Mississippi River Delta,

2. its conception of promiscuous sex as a reward for individualistic macho celebrity status,
3. its glamorizing of drug and alcohol abuse, and
4. its generally sorrowful ethos.

ROCK AND ROLL'S FALSE CLAIMS OF INCLUSIVENESS AND REPRESENTATION

Recasting trademark scenes in *The Last Waltz*, Candy and Levy in *The Schmenges: The Last Polka* document the exclusion of the Slavic American musical ethos from the folk, blues, and rock-and-roll music of the 1960s and 1970s. Drawing on African American blues, Celtic and English folk music, and the predominantly Jewish American popular songwriting tradition of New York City's "Tin Pan Alley," rock-and-roll musicians have thereby staked a claim on behalf of their genre to a unique democratic inclusiveness in terms of representing North America's multiethnic identity. Countering this claim with their film parody, Candy and Levy suggest that North American polka has ironically been rendered virtually invisible to the rock-and-roll audience of *The Last Waltz*, even as this same audience has been encouraged to treasure its music's supposedly inclusive, multiethnic perspective on American identity.

Since the slump in the popularity of rock and roll over the past decade or so, polka has ventured successfully to market itself as stylistically cutting-edge—in the form of the urban, world music, "polka punk" style of Brave Combo (Dallas, TX), Gogol Bordello (New York City), and the Dreadnoughts (Vancouver, British Columbia), as well as in the Tejano polka style of Flaco Jiménez and others. Unfortunately, however, these developments in North American polka music have occurred without notice from those who perform and represent popular American rock-and-roll music, who have simply continued the customary 1970s self-satisfied definition of this genre as authentically diverse in representing the full ethnic heritage of North America, even though it has disregarded Eastern and Central European American polka that it might have blended into its musical fusion. Indeed, this inclusion of polka could very likely have occurred in the formative years of rock and roll given that polka was more prominent in North American popular music then than it has been in recent years. Not surprising, a few performers, such as Willie Nelson and a few other country-and-western musicians from central Texas (where Czech and German polka bands flourished in the mid-twentieth century), did draw on polka for their own sound. Sadly, though, their inclusion of polka tunes and beats was atypical in popular North American music from the 1950s to the 1970s.

Nonetheless, during these three decades, the North American polka industry was active and economically healthy throughout the u-shaped polka belt that stretches from Ontario, Canada, to the upper Midwest U.S. states (especially Wisconsin and Ohio), down south into Texas and sweeping across the northeastern United States (especially Pennsylvania and New York). Canada's biggest polka sensation was the Walter Ostanek Band, the likely local inspiration for the Schmenge brothers' parody, its bandleader being dubbed "Canada's Polka King." During the same period, in the United States, the Frankie Yankovic Band and the Lawrence Welk Orchestra enjoyed the same popularity and estimable album sales, with Yankovic having received the title of "America's Polka King" and with Welk bringing polka, along with other big band styles, to national attention in his one-hour musical variety show broadcast by the ABC network from 1955 to 1971. All three of these popularizers of polka music integrated polka rhythms with North American pop melodies and lyrics while retaining traditional Eastern European folk songs in their repertoires.

Polka's blending of pop and traditional ethnic music has often been a target of humor inside and outside the world of polka, and Candy and Levy's mockumentary makes the most of this comic trope. For instance, in what I consider to be the funniest musical performance in *The Schmenges: The Last Polka*, Rick Moranis, in his role as singer Linsk Minek, parodies middle-aged polka musicians' heavy-handed, indiscriminate attempts in the 1970s and early 1980s to integrate too many disparate genres of American popular music into polka. With the Schmenge brothers playing polka tunes to accompany his singing, he belts out a hilarious medley of pop songs, narrating them as he goes along to make connections between them. He starts with a few lines of Willie Nelson's "On the Road Again" and moves through short bits of the rhythm-and-blues standard "Kansas City," Frank Sinatra's "Chicago," Glen Campbell's "Galveston," the commercial jingle "I Love New York," and the Doors' "Touch Me," wrapping up with "On the Road Again." This medley mocks polka's understandable concern over its inevitable generational decline in the 1970s music market and the futility of the transparently commercial strategy of tacking commercially successful pop tunes onto polka. Later in the film, Stan's and Yosh's ridiculous attempt to perform a Michael Jackson tribute concert, wearing Jackson's signature red-sequined military jackets, continues this critique.

Additionally, Moranis's medley points to the problematic ideological issue of geographical origins and ethnic identity by mocking the ideologically problematic juxtapositions of interview segments and musical performances in *The Last Waltz*. The medley highlights the degree to which, via these juxtapositions, the Band's members misrepresent their geographical and ethnic origins and the unresolved ideological conflicts

Rick Moranis as Lynsk Minek.

in their original music's blend of Confederate southern alliances and civil rights activism against southern racial segregation.

Levy, Candy, director John Blanchard, and the rest of the SCTV comedy team behind *The Last Polka* are—like four of the five members of the Band—Canadians. Furthermore, like Candy, Rick Danko was of Slavic Canadian descent. His musical family immigrated to Canada from the Ukraine at the turn of the twentieth century like so many other Slavic immigrants to North America. One of the instruments that Danko played well was the accordion, the main component of polka music. Robertson is of Native American descent on his mother's side and Jewish Canadian on his father's. Yet nowhere in *The Last Waltz* are these facts mentioned.

Instead, all the Band members—especially the two front men, Robertson and Danko—present themselves as having U.S. Anglo-Celtic heritage and speak about their recruitment in the early 1960s as the backup band for Arkansas rhythm-and-blues singer Ronnie Hawkins as if it had occurred in the United States and as if he and they had primarily toured the southern United States during this period. In fact, in the late 1950s, Hawkins had relocated to Canada, on the advice of country music star Conway Twitty, who correctly believed that the region would be receptive to southern rock and roll. The Band's initiation to touring had not occurred in the South, and only drummer/singer Levon Helm, an Arkansas native like Hawkins, had even lived in the southern United States while growing up.

Moreover, Moranis's hilarious medley specifically spoofs a disparate five-part juxtaposition of scenes from the middle of *The Last Waltz*. This parodied sequence begins as Richard Manuel answers a question that Scorsese, acting as interviewer, poses about why the Band chose its generic name. Manuel says that when he and the four other Band members left Ronnie Hawkins, they first decided to call themselves the Honkies and afterward had tried the Crackers. He says that people "backed away" from these names because they were too "straight" (i.e., racially blatant), so instead, after becoming Bob Dylan's electric backup band, working with him in Woodstock, and helping to establish the famous politically liberal counterculture there, they resorted to the name everyone had come to call them: the Band.

Immediately following Scorsese's interview segment with Manuel, there is a performance of the Band's original song "The Weight," accompanied by the vocals of The Staple Singers, the legendary African American gospel-and-soul group that gained its fame as a voice of the U.S. civil rights movement. The famously cryptic lyrics of "The Weight" vaguely suggest southern working-class displacements (although the "Nazareth" in the song is actually the city in Pennsylvania where the Martin Guitar factory is located), racial or class-based discrimination (the song's first-person speaker asks a local man for help finding a room, but "he just grinned, shook his head, and 'No' was all he said"), and biblical references to Moses and to "the judgment day" that are similar to those in gospel songs. The Staples' perfect harmonies and gospel-style clapping percussion at the end of the song give the arrangement a powerful gospel effect. Next, the third segment in this sequence, Danko and Robertson's short, quirky singing of the old country song "Old Time Religion"—which is a gesture, Robertson says, meant "for the folks"—clearly establishes this gospel feel. Yet as the song continues, their singing and playing become somewhat farcical, and the scene ends with Robertson observing, with seemingly pretended regret, "Oh, it's not like it used to be."

In the fourth incongruous scene in this sequence, the Band plays "The Night They Drove Old Dixie Down," a nostalgic pro-Confederate song set in late-1860s Tennessee that casts white Confederate soldiers, who fought to retain African American slavery and the agricultural economy based on it, as heroic victims. Robertson (who, as mentioned above, is not a southern Anglo-Celtic American but a Canadian of Native American and Jewish background) wrote the song in support of the "Lost Cause" mythological motto: "The South will rise again." This racist pro-Confederate message is reinforced during a later interview segment that has a large Confederate flag hanging prominently in the background.

Without any comment on the controversially pro-Confederate theme of this song,[8] the next scene—the fifth and last of the sequence—features a New York City skyline picture behind Helm and Robertson as they are interviewed about their first trip to New York City, where they had met Carole King, Neil Diamond, and other Tin Pan Alley songwriters in the mid-1960s. Robertson and Helm describe their debauched visits to New York City to record albums there almost like going into battle or into a boxing ring. Helm refers to these experiences in the city as "an adult portion" and elaborates, "You just go in the first time, and you get your ass kicked, and you take off. As soon as it heals up, you come back. You try it again."

With this final shift to the urban U.S. Northeast, these scenes have moved through geographical space from the countercultural peace movement's most beloved place, Woodstock, to "Nazareth," an apparently segregationist southern small town unwelcoming to stigmatized outsiders, to a rural Tennessee countryside nostalgically devoted to the Confederate Lost Cause, to New York City's cosmopolitan and ethnically diverse Tin Pan Alley. Scorsese creates tenuous cinematic connections for these jumps in space, time, and politics to suggest that the Band embodies an authentically American identity, and he highlights the fact that its retirement show occurs on the quintessential American holiday, Thanksgiving. However, the ideological contradictions represented in these segments' jumps remain unresolved, and one can thus plausibly speculate that Moranis's parallel medley in *The Schmenges: The Last Polka* works on two levels—it critiques the ideal of a unified vision of America identity that can smooth over the regional and racial conflicts of U.S. history by constructing a fictional journey around the nation, as well as ribbing the polka world for its doomed attempt to redefine itself as "hip" by taking the same sort of symbolic American journey in song, emblematic of its self-conscious awareness of its culturally inferior status.

As Helm points out in a later interview segment in *The Last Waltz*, rock and roll was indeed created from several American musical forms that came into contact in the Mississippi River Delta region: African American blues, work songs, and call-and-response gospel music from the Lowland South; Anglo-Celtic American folk ballads; instrumental blue grass and other dance tunes; and country gospel music from the Upland South in the Appalachian Mountains. The Anglo-Celtic American traditions of the Upland South would eventually be commercialized through mass-marketed recordings in the 1920s and dubbed American "old-time" music. These streams of American popular culture and music are, of course, very significant, and Helm is correct to name them as the basis of North American rock and roll.

Nevertheless, the problem that emerges in Helm's and the Band's definition of rock and roll is that they represent it as a musical genre that is more authentically American than any other genre, including what cultural historian Victor Greene termed "old-time ethnic music": Polish American, Scandinavian American, Czech American, and Slovenian American polka; Jewish American klezmer music (like polka, played on accordion and clarinet); and Italian American folk accordion music.[9] While rock and roll is, of course, a distinctively American musical genre and can boast of being racially inclusive of both African American and European American rural musical influences, it does not have any more claim to representative authenticity for comprehensive American identity than urban, multiethnic music from the upper Midwest and Northeast. *The Schmenges: The Last Polka* reveals the regional and ethnic exclusions built into this concept of authentic, "melting pot" American music.

PROMISCUOUS SEX AS A REWARD FOR MACHO CELEBRITY STATUS

The centerpiece of macho sexual power in *The Last Waltz* is, without a doubt, Muddy Waters's magnificent performance of his blues manifesto "Mannish Boy," with its erotic assurances: "I'm a natural born lovers' man," "I'm a hoochie coochie man," and "The line I shoot will never miss. When I make love to a woman, she can't resist." Then again, the last lines of Waters's song, "Don't hurt me, don't hurt, don't hurt me child," are poignantly vulnerable in regard to the demands of macho sexuality and are perhaps the most erotic part of the song for female listeners, suggesting that the persona's pose of sexual supremacy is more theatrical than real and yet that believing is being.

Furthermore, in an interview segment that follows the segment about New York City and Tin Pan Alley and its logical follow-up segment—the guest performance by Neil Diamond—all of the members of the Band talk about the subject that Scorsese introduces with the following title: "women on the road." In this scene, the Confederate flag is displayed prominently behind the men being interviewed, evoking the racism, sexism, and sexual exploitation of Confederate patriarchal ideology. In response to Scorsese's invitation to discuss "women on the road," Manuel first spontaneously says, "I love 'em!" and then he and the others speak more deliberately about the sexual rewards of rock-and-roll celebrity for male stars. Manuel muses that the group's numerous and seemingly anonymous heterosexual experiences were "probably why we've been on the road," to which Robertson, who is standing just behind Manuel, slaps Manuel's shoulder dramatically and agrees: "That's it!" Manuel continues, "not that I don't like the *music*," adding a lascivious wink and a "uhmmm" sound.

Helm then jokes awkwardly, "I thought you weren't supposed to talk about *it* too much," and looking directly at Scorsese, who is off camera, meaningfully adds, "I thought we were supposedly to pan away from that sort of stuff," as he leans back in his seat to emphasize his implied point. Manuel laughs lustily in response while Scorsese jokes, "Well, I guess we're not [supposed to talk about it], and we better go on," appreciatively echoing Manuel's laugh. Danko then evaluates the Band's musical and interpersonal development by paralleling it to the numbers of female groupies who have been their sex partners and suggesting group sexual activity: "Just as we have all grown just a little bit, so have the *women*, and it's amazing." Meanwhile, the Band members laugh knowingly, and Manual jokes cryptically, "I just want to break even."

Scorsese, now vicariously satisfied, does then pan away for the next segment—to the attractively thin and blonde Joni Mitchell, one of only two female musical solo artists in the film (the pretty brunette Emmylou Harris is the other; the attractive Mavis Staples and her two sisters were onstage earlier in backup roles). Mitchell appears on the screen, shown from behind, the camera's angle emphasizing her swaying hips and narrow waist, as she walks from offstage to the microphone at center stage to begin a performance of her song "Coyote." (Her other earlier shadowy appearance in the film occurred during Neil Young's performance of his classic "Helpless," when she did not come onto the stage at all but, rather, sang beautiful background harmony from offstage.)

"Coyote" cryptically narrates a first-person female persona's experience of a sexual relationship, begun when she is picked up hitchhiking by a philandering southwestern rancher, associated in Mitchell's poetic lyrics with the sexually potent coyote trickster figure in Native American mythology. The macho Coyote man is sexually forceful: "He pins me in a corner, and he won't take 'No.'" And he openly and vigorously practices polygamy—he has a wife and another lover, as well as the song's narrator. She does not seem disappointed but instead giddily wonders that "he seems to want me anyway." Taking a male role, she returns to the road, assuring Coyote that the situation should occasion "no regrets" and "I just get off up a ways," yet she describes herself as only a vulnerable "hitcher" who is "a prisoner of the white lines of the freeway." Though Mitchell, like a male rock star, represents herself as sexually liberated and powerful, she evokes conventional male sexual mastery in the character of the Coyote rancher—the same type of male sexual mastery of which Manuel and the other members of the Band had just boasted. And Danko's appreciative gaze toward Mitchell as he plays bass to her lead guitar seems to place him in the Coyote role, especially because he had just finished discussing the polygamous rewards for stardom that he and his fellow Band members have enjoyed.[10]

However, their idealized bachelor-style sex lives were more complicated in reality than *The Last Waltz* suggests, especially for the two charismatic and handsome front men, Robertson and Danko, and for the keyboardist, Manuel. By 1967, nine years before *The Last Waltz* retirement concert, Robertson was married and, during the years of the Band's late 1960s and early 1970s fame, was a father with young children; Danko had married and was a father by 1969. Manuel was married to his first wife in 1968, and his two children were born in the early 1970s, before his divorce in 1975, just a year before *The Last Waltz* concert. Not surprising, then, to many, the Band's members' ostensibly pleased recounting of their sexual exploits seems forced and unconvincing, as reviewer Roger Ebert observes (evaluating the 2002 twenty-fifth-anniversary DVD edition), "Even references to groupies inspire creases of pain on the faces of the rememberers: The sex must have been as bad as anything else."

The Schmenges: The Last Polka responds insightfully to this aspect of the Band's macho sexual representation by Scorsese. The Schmenge brothers are both married to "Leutonian" American women, but unlike rock stars, whose marriages/parenthood are carefully deemphasized by publicists, their traditional marriages and families are part of their wholesome polka band image, which an early interview scene emphasizes, as shot in the backyard of one of their houses during a family barbecue. Thus, their sexual infidelities are not to be readily idealized. In a hilarious series of musical and interview segments in the middle of the film, their scandalous affair with a *three*-sister singing group (played brilliantly by Catherine O'Hara; her actual sister, Mary Margaret O'Hara; and Robin Duke) that illogically calls itself "The Lemon Twins" (Sylvie, Gerta, and Max [a male name that suggests the stereotype of Slavic women's lack of idealized femininity]) is recounted at length, focusing on the boost that this sex scandal had given to their album sales.

In several mock interview segments, knowledgeable insiders talk at length about the brothers' sex scandal. The commentary by Val Babbyit, the author of *Polka Today*, a polka newspaper with a front page that copies the *USA Today* design, is particularly funny because he expresses so well the virtuous, family-oriented polka world's distaste for Yosh and Stan's sexual affair with the three sisters in his very proper, accented, and soft voice:

> It was a *scandal*! That's what it was. Those two happily married men were constantly being seen with these women. And they didn't exactly go out of their way to avoid public places. It was this more than anything that distressed those of us who knew them well. And not only that—there were three of them, three women and two men. That was also distressing! And it was a terrible time for their poor wives, who suspected an affair was going on but never ever raised the question of infidelity because Leutonian wives believed that it was not their place to do so.

The Lemon Twins.

As he narrates the public's response to this affair, a montage of tabloid images flashes by on the screen showing Yosh and Stan, with Beatles-style haircuts and dark sunglasses, sporting more stylish clothing than what they usually wear, as they walk along a city street and on a lakefront with the three female singers, all clearly aware that they have been followed by paparazzi. These images are followed by images of each of their humiliated wives, photographed looking out the front window of her middle-class house, one of whom is so short (and fat) that she is barely visible. The comical incongruity of these images—for polka fans used to the wholesome media images of Walter Ostanek, Frankie Yankovic, and the other polka kings of the 1950s to the 1970s—demonstrates that the lack of sexual scandal in polka culture and polka's image as wholesome family music make it bland to consumers in a mass market where such scandal has become the norm. This contrast implicitly questions whether such sordid scandals should be considered fodder for entertainment in any context.

GLAMORIZING DRUG AND ALCOHOL ABUSE

Except for a bottle of beer visible onstage during the first song, *The Last Waltz* does not directly depict drug and alcohol use or abuse. The film's interview segments do, however, emphasize that when touring, the Band had played many gigs at seedy bars where patrons drink heavily, and at times, Manuel and Danko appear intoxicated when they are interviewed. Moreover, Danko implies that when he and the others lived in Woodstock while recording with Bob Dylan, they avoided "having too much fun" because they had limited "company" and were therefore very musically productive during this time. Danko remarks to Scorsese, "You know what happens when you have *too* much fun," and he pauses meaningfully to allow the film audience to imagine his meaning.

Additionally, a few of the original songs performed by the Band in the film refer briefly to drugs or alcohol. Their classic "Up on Cripple Creek," for instance, refers to smoking marijuana with a bong or taking a generous swig on a liquor bottle: "I swore as I took another pull" that "my Bessie can't be beat." This good-natured Bessie, a "girl that I once knew," whom the speaker in the song visits in lieu of returning home to his regular girlfriend or wife (identified as "my big mama"), is described as a "drunkard's dream if I ever did see one." Later, a short portion of Danko's recorded solo song "Sip the Wine" is also played.

More telling on the subject of drug and alcohol abuse is Robertson's later explanation about the Band's decision to retire after sixteen years together. He offers superstition as a reason, wondering whether he and the other members of the Band would be pressing their luck if they were to continue touring. And he cites Hank Williams, Elvis, Jimi Hendrix, and Janis Joplin as past victims of the road: "The road has taken a lot of the great ones." These pop music stars all died from drug overdoses, so Robertson's use as them as cautionary examples in this context highlights that drug and alcohol abuse was a long-standing issue for members of the Band as well.

Conversely, in *The Schmenges: The Last Polka*, the topic of drug addiction and alcoholism is handled with sharply comedic effect in an interview with singer Linsk Minek, the Schmenges' longtime friend and client (they became his agent when they offered to represent him for only a 50 percent cut of his earning, a much better deal than the 75 percent cut demanded by his and the Schmenges' previous agents, the elderly "Colonel Tom Cohen" and, after his "mysterious death," his fifteen-year-old widow).[11]

On the subject of life on the road, Minek complains comically: "Oh, it's a crazy business! Come on! There's a syndrome in this business. It's so easy to get hooked on women, or the pills, or booze, or drugs, or dope. In my case, it's . . . food." Since Moranis, playing Minek, is not particularly overweight but has only a few extra pounds around his middle, this switch from the more serious issue of drug and alcohol addiction to his refreshing overconcern about eating habits is very humorous. There is a clearly implied contrast meant here between the ultrathin

Robertson, Danko, Manuel, and Helm, who have perhaps become so thin due to cocaine abuse, and the more or less pudgy polka musicians who happily (and guiltily) eat while on the road and at home rather than using drugs or alcohol.

The delightfully inane refrain from the Schmenge brothers' most famous original song—"Cabbage rolls and coffee, mmm, mmm, good!"—resonates in this regard as well, especially because the audience is enthusiastically invited to sing the refrain with Yosh and Stan. And this passion for food surfaces again in the funny gag about sweet rolls, or "raisin surprise balls." (The joke is that they are called this because only an occasional roll has a single raisin in it, so if a customer finds one, it is a surprise). In his first interview segment, polka expert Val Babbyit recounts at length that, at the local bakery hangout in their neighborhood, he, Yosh, and Stan, as usual, had these rolls over coffee one day, and it was then that he first finds out that the Schmenge brothers are planning something related to their polka career, which he soon finds out is their imminent retirement. In his story, the rolls seem to have almost as much significance as the mock tragic news for the polka world. Later, in a similar depiction of food and the pleasure of eating, Catherine O'Hara's Lemon Twins character continues to gobble fluffy white frosting from a cake, in messy fingerfuls, as she is interviewed about her past work and relationship with the Schmenge brothers. In the scene, her hips are amply padded to appear exaggeratedly large and out of proportion to her upper body.

This focus on eating and on the corpulent bodies of polka fans and performers is decidedly carnivalesque—especially Candy's exaggerated stoutness as Yosh, which the faux-historical black-and-white footage from the brothers' Leutonian childhood in a pre–World War II era extends to his plump boyhood. These bodies come to represent a "festive and utopian" feature of both the food-centered polka party and the Schmenge family's pastoral cabbage-farming past and its parental devotion to beloved, well-fed children. (In these scenes, Candy plays the boys' father, and Levy, in drag, their mother, so the plumpness of the family is repeated in the two generations.)

In fact, Candy's stout body seems to represent the human condition of both bodily imperfection and gustatory enjoyment that, as Mikhail Bakhtin theorizes about the carnivalesque body, "makes no pretense to the renunciation of the earthy." The materiality of Candy's excessive body and appetites thereby exhibit "a cosmic and at the same time an all-people's character." For "the material bodily principle" realized by such representations "is contained not in the biological individual, not in the bourgeois ego, but in the people, a people who are continually growing and renewed."[12] As Bakhtin observes about social laughter directed at such excessive bodies, "certain essential aspects of the world are accessible only to laughter."[13]

Thus, the laughter directed toward these representative bodies, negatively inflected though it may be on one level, is festively positive and insightful on the issue of the regenerative pleasures of the flesh and the mistake of rejecting an ample body in favor of a bony one that is pushed to the limit of its performative endurance.[14]

ROCK AND ROLL'S GENERALLY SORROWFUL ETHOS

The rock-and-roll ideology illustrated in *The Last Waltz* generally posits that truth is more accessible through seriousness than through laughter, although there are a few exceptions to this generalization as applied to the film, such as Doctor John's "Such a Night,"[15] Van Morrison's irrepressibly joyful "Caravan," and Lawrence Ferlinghetti's reading of his comic poem "Loud Prayer," a fitting parody of the Lord's Prayer given the notice on screen at the beginning of the film: "This film should be played loud." Other than these few joyful, laughter-producing moments, the rest of the film is somber. Even the game of pool that the Band members are playing in the first scene of the film is oddly serious. Scorsese asks, "Okay, Rick, what's the game?" and Danko replies, "Cut throat," the object of which, he elaborates, is "to keep your balls on the table, and knock everybody else's off."

Reviewing the 2002 restored edition, film critic Roger Ebert observes about the Band's somber tone, "the performers, seen on screen, seem curiously morose, exhausted, played out." He elaborates:

> The overall tenor of the documentary suggests survivors at the ends of their ropes. They dress in dark, cheerless clothes, hide behind beards, hats and shades, pound out rote performances of old hits, don't seem to smile much at their music or each other. There is the whole pointless road warrior mystique, of hard-living men whose daily duty it is to play music and get wasted. They look tired of it.

Thus, the Band's ominous-sounding arrangement of the song "The Last Waltz"—played while the camera pans over blighted San Francisco city streets, moving toward the formerly elegant Winterland Ballroom—emphasizes not what Robertson rather unconvincingly claims will be a "celebration" but rather that this concert is a terminus for the heyday of rock and roll as it was played in the 1960s and early 1970s.

In the end, when introducing the encore song, Robertson remarks, understating the event's significance, "You're still there, huh? We're going to do one more song, and that's it," as he drags hard on a cigarette. The song is "Don't Do It," which is a pessimistic yet stirring rhythm-and-blues song about a man loving a cruel woman "too much," revealing his love to her and finding out afterward that this knowledge has given her a weapon to use against him, to cause him "heartache and misery." After this encore, the Band members walk off the stage, saying only "goodnight" and "good-bye" with little emotion. This encore has been repositioned by Scorsese in the chronology of the film, however, so that it both introduces the narrative and closes it but only in the audience's memory. The actual ending of the film is more footage of the Band playing the ghostly theme song "The Last Waltz" on a deserted sound stage.

In contrast, the ending of *The Schmenges: The Last Polka* paradoxically portrays the optimistic attempts by Yosh and Stan to blend the polka sound with 1980s dance music, specifically Michael Jackson's "Beat It," demonstrating all the while that polka's tongue-in-cheek hilarity, its disruptive satire of the pomposity of a popular culture that takes itself too seriously, is not lost even in that implausible imitation. Indeed, as I have argued, such sampling of popular music is a common element of polka music, and the real problem with Yosh and Stan's imitation of Michael Jackson is that they take the act too far, wearing Jackson's signature stage costume and attempting unsuccessfully to dance as well as he can. But their attempt at stardom ultimately fails not so much because their music and dancing are so bad but because the young audience fails *them*. There are not enough tickets sold to even hold the concert.

Right after this concert, which is referred to as "the Plattsburg disaster," the Schmenge brothers retire but only after a final concert that highlights their excellent musicianship in their own musical genre. This concert ends not with the solemnity of a hauntingly arranged last waltz but with the defiantly joyful last polka of the film's title. This upbeat final polka highlights the core values of polka ideology, as explained by cultural critic Ann Hetzel Gunkel: "the participatory, communal" aesthetic that counters the aesthetic of mass-marketed celebrity and the idolizing of pop stars and a "relentless emphasis on joy and ecstatic celebration."[16] Unlike the emotional control of the members of the Band, the Schmenge brothers respond emotionally to their final number. Candy, the otherwise perpetually happy brother, chokes up and sheds a few tears, yet he and Levy launch into a rousing polka to close the show that gets the elderly audience to their feet cheering.

CONCLUSION: THE COUNTERCULTURAL POSSIBILITIES OF POLKA'S "RITUAL HAPPINESS"

In the end, *The Schmenges: The Last Polka* questions the patently commercial objectives of any band's retirement concert—its potential as a market-

The marquee for the "last polka."

ing tool for future concerts and album sales. As the final credits roll, Stan and Yosh are heard speculating about their possible reunion concerts or recordings. They remark that they are the only two people who know why they retired, and then they continue hilariously:

STAN: If in fact we really are retiring,

YOSH: which we are.

STAN: Oh we are, yes.

YOSH: But what does retirement really mean? You know, think about it. It doesn't mean that *everything* has to stop.

STAN: Oh no, not in that sense, but people might think that this was all a hoax if we didn't retire.

YOSH: Oh they would if not for the fact that we are retired, and have been for the last two weeks.

STAN: Two weeks.

YOSH: And I just got to say, it's been the best two weeks of my life.

STAN: Oh, a good two weeks. We've had lots of fun. But how long can you sit around and do nothing, you know. You get itchy to work.

YOSH: And make the money.

The funny point here is that the Band had vigorously played out this plan to "make the money" while the sun shines by 1985, the year *The Schmenges: The Last Polka* was released. During most of 1983, 1984, and 1985, the Band (sans Robbie Robertson) launched three ambitious reunion concert tours. Not surprising, these tours began to stumble as they went on; the shows near the end of this period became less lucrative, as audiences apparently had begun to wonder about the veracity of *The Last Waltz* as a retirement concert and had become disenchanted with the legendary status that the Band had represented themselves to have.

The other amusing point is that such a tactic for an aging polka band such as the Schmenge brothers would obviously have no such limited lucrative effect. Indeed, since the heyday of the polka genre fifty years ago, the marginalization of this brand of polka in the music industry has caused financial drawbacks for polka musicians, and *The Schmenges: The Last Polka* stands as a comical testament to this unfortunate situation.[17] But the poor and isolated polka genre has also thereby been pushed to develop a uniquely critical perspective on mainstream American popular culture, through its carnivalesque attitude and lyrics, as *The Schmenges: The Last Polka* presages as well. Ultimately, thus, this often-overlooked mockumentary highlights that, as limiting as the genre's financial prospects and recent history may be, polka might again thrive if it were to employ its greatest strength—its authentic status as nonmainstream, *alternative* music. It may be, as music critic Jim Bessman has noted, that polka is "America's last great undiscovered genre—or, as others say, 'the real alternative.'"[18] It also provides, as Gunkel points out, "a space for the creative expression and negotiation of hyphenated and often conflicted ethnic identities."[19] Promisingly, in the case of the handful of new "polka punk" bands—especially Gogol Bordello—polka has thrived because of the genre's potential to deliver a transgressively carnivalesque critique of mainstream culture and music and a new vision of creativity in redefining ethnic fusion in more inclusive terms. Candy and Levy as the Schmenge brothers showed us that this breakthrough was only a matter of time.

NOTES

1. *The Schmenges: The Last Polka*, dir. John Blanchard, perf. Eugene Levy, John Candy, Catherine O'Hara, and Rick Moranis (HBO, 1985).

2. Cowritten with Christopher Guest.

3. *The Last Waltz*, dir. Martin Scorsese, featuring Robbie Robertson, Rick Danko, Levon Helm, Richard Manuel, and Garth Hudson (1978; MGM, 2002).

4. Jane Roscoe and Craig Hight, *Faking It: Mock-documentary and the Subversion of Factuality* (Manchester: Manchester University Press, 2001), 140.

5. Such Henny Youngman–style of "borscht belt," anti-Polish/Slavic humor is regrettable, particularly because many of these scenes feature Jewish Canadian actors Eugene Levy and Rick Moranis, the latter playing a singer named Linsk Minek, who often teams up with the Schmenge brothers for joint concerts and serves as a featured guest performer at the brother's last concert. Thus, their parodic depictions of these polka performers recall ethnic tensions between Eastern European Jewish and non-Jewish immigrants, whose largest waves of immigration to the United States and Canada coincided at the turn of the nineteenth century. It should be pointed out here, though, that polka music is popular among both Jewish and gentile fans and musicians from many Eastern, Central, and Northern European ethnic groups. Moreover, the accordion and the clarinet are used frequently in polka music and in Jewish klezmer music.

6. For these reasons, *The Schmenges: The Last Polka* was cited positively on Anna and Chris Saccheri's "Let's Polka" daily weblog, on February 2, 2007, by guest blogger David Golia. Similarly, Candy's polka band-leading character Gus Polinski (aka "the Polka King of the Midwest") in the first *Home Alone* film (1990) is another sympathetic treatment of a polka musician created by Candy.

7. Charles Keil, Angeliki V. Keil, and Dick Blau, *Polka Happiness* (Philadelphia: Temple University Press, 1992), 3.

8. Later in the film, of course, the presence of African American blues legend Muddy Waters, one of the most revered among the cadre of guest performers for the concert, provides some further contradictory counterbalancing to this problematic pro-Confederate theme. Additionally, in an interview discussion, the Band's members show their respect and admiration for the late African American blues harmonica player Sonny Boy Williamson, whom they met and jammed with at his home just a few month before his death.

9. Victor Greene, *A Passion for Polka: Old-time Ethnic Music in America* (Berkeley: University of California Press, 1992).

10. In her feminist critique of Bob Dylan's 1967 rockumentary *Don't Look Back*, Susan Knobloch contends that a shift from transgressive female sexual agency to traditional patriarchal sexual authority is common in this film genre, and she cites *The Last Waltz* in this category: "Several films follow *Don't Look Back* in a distinct strain of rockumentaries (including Dylan's own *Renaldo and Clara*, *No Nukes*, *The Last Waltz*, and *Hail! Hail! Rock 'n' Roll*), which despite their countercultural rhetoric, assert the primacy of male star subjects as all-knowing Lacanian father figures" (134). Susan Knobloch, "(Pass through) The Mirror Moment and *Don't Look Back*: Music and Gender in a Rockumentary," in *Feminism and Documentary*, ed. Diane Waldman and Janet Walker (Minneapolis: University of Minnesota Press, 1999), 121–36.

11. Colonel Cohen is shown in faux-historical film footage wearing a large Texan cowboy hat, though his Jewish surname suggests that his folksy Texan identity is an opportunistic masquerade. He is the agent who "discovered" the young brothers when they performed on his weekly radio show *Foreigners on Parade*. They remain grateful to him for helping them begin their musical career even though he exploited them economically. His character is, of course, a spoof of Elvis Presley's and Gene Autry's Dutch-born, cowboy-hat-wearing promoter

Colonel Tom Parker (aka Andreas Cornelis van Kuijk). Parker outrageously charged 50 percent commission from his star clients.

12. Mikhail Bakhtin, *Rabelais and His World*, trans. Helene Iswolsky (Boston: MIT Press, 1968), 19.

13. Bakhtin, *Rabelais and His World*, 66.

14. This emphasis on enjoyment of abundant food and this laughter at the corpulent body are common features of "polka happiness." Popular polka standards include "Who Stole the Kishka [Sausage]," "Who Likes Pierogi," and "Too Fat Polka."

15. However, Doctor John's song "Such a Night" focuses on a situation that will result in heartache for someone: the persona's friend, whose girlfriend the persona plans to seduce because, as the refrain laughingly insists, "If I don't do it, someone else will."

16. Ann Hetzel Gunkel, *The Polka Alternative: Polish American Polka as Resistant Ethnic Practice* (New Britain, CT: Central Connecticut State University Press, 2005), 419.

17. To invigorate the genre, in 1986 polka enthusiasts successfully lobbied for a Grammy Award to be established in the polka category. While it lasted, the award was especially helpful to the fortunes of the current holder of the title, "America's Polka King," Jimmy Sturr, a musical collaborator of Willie Nelson and an eighteen-time Grammy winner. This support has not, though, been enough to make polka competitive in the national music market, and in 2009, the polka Grammy Award was discontinued because of the dwindling number of album entries and their very limited distribution. See the Grammy Awards website: http://www.grammy.org/recording-academy/news/academy-spring-trustees-meeting-results-announced.

18. Jim Bessman, "Monarchs of the U.S. Polka Mainstream," *Billboard*, August 3, 1996, 108.

19. Jim Bessman, "The Polka Alternative: Polka as Counterhegemonic Ethnic Practice," *Popular Music & Society* 27, no. 4 (2004): 421.

5

Experiments in Parody and Satire: Short-Form Mockumentary Series

Craig Hight

Mockumentary has become part of the mainstream of television programming; it has become another style to be employed for both banal and artistic ends. While not a staple of all television networks, mockumentary series have nonetheless become a regular feature of television schedules throughout the world. Adapting Bill Nichols's definition of the documentary genre, mockumentary can be defined as a *discourse*, one that can be identified through reference to three levels of media practice: production agenda, aesthetics, and modes of reading.[1]

1. Mockumentary arises from a variety of agendas on the part of fictional media producers. It draws in particular from parodic and satiric traditions but is not reducible to these.
2. At the textual level, mockumentary appropriates styles not only from the codes and conventions of documentary proper but from the full spectrum of nonfiction media, including fact-fiction hybrid forms. And mockumentary discourse operates within a range of generic traditions (including, surprisingly, nonfiction itself) and intersects with a variety of forms of the media.
3. And mockumentary is capable of providing for a complexity of forms of audience engagement, often (but not necessarily) involving

different senses of reflexivity toward the nonfiction and hybrid forms that it appropriates.

It is at the interaction of these three levels of practice that mockumentary is located.[2] The more complex and effective examples of television mockumentary rely on an audience's familiarity with the array of factual-based television forms, develop a commentary on these forms and the factual discourse that they rely on, make intertextual reference to wider popular culture, and encourage identification with characters in the manner of more conventional fictional programming.

In one sense, television as a medium serves as the natural space for mockumentary. The breadth and variety of nonfiction and fact-fiction forms within television provide for extraordinarily rich sources of intertextual appropriation and commentary. From documentary proper to texts that blur the lines between argument and narrative, recording and performance, character and social actor, television offers texts that challenge the continued salience of documentary's core functions, centered on recording, argument, analysis, and expression.[3] Key documentary hybrid formats, such as reality game shows (*Big Brother* and *Survivor*), docusoaps, situation documentaries, lifestyle programs, and talk shows, have all variously integrated elements of documentary aesthetics while typically neglecting documentary's social-political agenda.

The mainstreaming of television mockumentary, with the emergence of a number of mockumentary series within a variety of national contexts, suggests a wider naturalization of reflexivity toward such forms, as television producers employ the discourse to engage in commentary on emerging television genres, the nature of television itself, and its appeal to wider cultural discourses. Within the overwhelmingly commercial ethos of television, mockumentary has often been used for pure novelty value, particularly in stunts such as April Fool's Day mock news reports, and one-off episodes of dramatic series, such as the live premiere of the 1997 series of hospital drama *ER*. Perhaps the most frequent use of the discourse is within the continual stream of television advertising, which often relies on parody and shorthand references to other aspects of popular culture. Advertising functions as an interlocutor and interpreter of aesthetic styles, appropriating at will and forming a backdrop of stylistic instability and trivial and easily discarded appropriation that characterizes commercial television as a whole.

Mockumentary has also been integral to more sustained experiments in television programming. The most high profile and celebrated of these is perhaps *The Office*, which has been replicated in other national variations and still serves as the exemplar of the new form of sitcom production, which Mills has termed *comedy verité*.[4] This series is an example of mockumentary discourse being employed to revitalize an existing television genre (much as *The Blair Witch Project* was innovatory for cinematic horror). A more limited use of mockumentary discourse informs the production of other innovative sitcoms, such as *Curb Your Enthusiasm* and *Arrested Development*, although these are not mockumentary proper.

This chapter considers four short-form mockumentary television series: *Marion and Geoff* (2000–2003), *Double Take* (2001–2003), *Look around You* (2002–2005), and *Posh Nosh* (2003). Short-form series often represent the more experimental end of television mockumentary production, although it is debatable whether this constitutes a stable avenue for the gestation of new formats. Here ideas are sketched out, trialed in off-peak time slots or one-off broadcasts, and occasionally extended to longer-series form.[5] Each of these series references a specific nonfictional television form: video diaries, tabloid journalism, 1970s educational and popular science programs, and cooking shows. Each engages with specific modes of nonfiction representation and, through these, to the wider discourses surrounding the production of factual-based television genres. Each was produced within the United Kingdom, a reflection of the prominence of mockumentary discourse within television programming within this national context. More mockumentary series have appeared here than within any other broadcasting context, a growth that is symptomatic especially of the popularity and profile of the docusoap format, with many mockumentary series drawing direct inspiration from this hybrid form.[6]

MARION AND GEOFF

The finest of this group of short-form mockumentary series, *Marion and Geoff* centers on Keith (Rob Brydon), a London minicab driver who offers monologues to a camcorder mounted on his dashboard, in the form of an ongoing video dairy. Video diaries have become a staple within television hybrid programming, typically involving participants who are given camcorders and encouraged to present an emotional confession to the lens. This is a practice and production technique derived from earlier experiments with camcorder-based formats. The key United Kingdom reference points here are *Video Nation*[7] and the related *Video Nation Shorts*, which popularized the video diary as a short-form format within British television broadcasting. These series adhere to the original promise of (digital) camcorder technology, which was to open the television sphere to more voices, to democratize the television mainstream.

Dovey discusses *Video Nation* in detail,[8] placing the series within a wider discussion on the development of the proliferation of "first-person media," particularly those television forms centered on various notions of confession.

> An enormous proportion of the output of factual TV is now based on an incessant performance of identity structured through first person speaking about feelings, sentiments and, most powerfully, intimate relationships.[9]

Adapting Foucauldian perspective toward first-person media, Dovey notes that across the continuum of such forms, everyday voices are positioned in a number of ways and not just sutured into conventional power relations. Distinctive among first-person television formats, *Video Nation* consists of a kind of self-surveillance by camcorders, incorporating parts of both performance and confession that link to wider social relations in often quite open and contradictory ways. As Dovey notes, the key debates for these forms center on

> how far this public participation in the discussion of everyday personal and public problems represents a democratisation of televisual space and how far they represent a reinscription of moral and political hegemonies.[10]

Unlike talk shows, where the hegemonic discourses offered quite clearly operate to both judge participants and prescribe corrective actions for their assumed deviant behavior, the video diary model has an inherent openness resulting in a collective of voices offering specific, limited, but nonetheless often relatively unvarnished perspectives on the everyday. Dovey argues that within *Video Nation*, the video diary segments work to establish a sense of *dialogue* with the viewer, rather than have the audience positioned as critical voyeur. This derives partly from the absence of a high degree of mediation in the series production, maintaining a commitment to low production values, as part of the effort to let participants tell their own stories in their own way—hence, the avoidance of postproduction practices that would impose a more conventional dramatic narrative onto these autobiographical accounts, in the manner that is so distinctive a characteristic of video diaries in docusoaps and other reality-based television formats. The low-grade aesthetic of amateur home movies reinforces the authenticity of participants' direct and intimate address to the audience. As Dovey notes, this also conveys a degree of instability to the form as a whole with unpredictable and perceptive social-political insights from participants, paired with the banal observations of everyday experience.[11]

The video diary itself is an adaptation of the "interactive" or "participatory" mode of documentary representation (as labeled by Bill Nichols), a format that relies on the key discourses associated with both this and the observational mode of documentary recording. The interactive mode essentially records an encounter between filmmaker and subject, where audience readings of film interviews are based on a wider belief in the authenticity of personal testimony. In this mode, the filmmaker typically plays a role ranging anywhere from interrogator to confidante. In contrast, the observational mode attempts to typically maintain the pretense that footage has been captured from a "fly on the wall" camera, which documents the everyday without intervention. Such footage develops a sense of authenticity from an implicit rhetorical stance that these events would have occurred without the presence of a camera crew (a stance that downplays or obscures the possibilities of participant performance). With the video diary, there is only the participant and the camcorder, and the assumption by audiences is typically that here is a form of interaction that is inherently more empowering of the participant than any encounter with an interviewer. In other words, this is a form that immediately conveys a sense of intimacy with participants and raises expectations of greater emotional openness. In fact, Renov argues that video is uniquely suited to the confessional mode that has become so central to contemporary visual culture.[12]

These wider frames of reference are central to the premise of *Marion and Geoff*. Rather than a gimmick, the video diary format is employed to open new possibilities for comedic narrative. The aesthetic of the series is consistent with video diaries but effectively extended by being played out over an entire series, increasing the potential to accumulate a complex narrative. In the first series of ten-minute programs,[13] Keith keeps the camcorder on his dashboard of his cab and regularly switches it on to record the latest events in his life. The "raw footage" captured by Keith has the appearance of having been edited to emphasize his personal narratives, with quick fades in the middle of scenes to skip irrelevant detail and some brief montage sequences set to music. However, there is a deliberate air of ambiguity about the series. Although Keith never gives any explicit indication that he is engaged in creating a television series nor explains what is his own motivation or agenda for participating, he has strict rules about when he might use his camera, politely turning it off whenever he has passengers or receives a phone call, out of respect for their privacy.

All we know of other people in Keith's life, then, is gleaned from his own perspective of events and from the occasional clue from locations that can be seen through the driver's-side window onto the street. Through various tales told by Keith, we identify with his character and the details of his life. His personal life is in ruins after his wife, Marion, leaves him for her business partner, Geoff, who is gradually taking over the role of father to Keith's two young boys (his "little smashers"). All his attempts to reconnect with his family or establish any form of human relationship end in disaster despite the earnestness and innocence of his intentions.

Rob Brydon, as "Keith Barrett," switches on his dashboard-mounted camcorder in series 1, episode 1, of *Marion and Geoff.*

The second series[14] extends the premise to half-hour episodes, featuring Keith acting now as chauffeur to a family that is itself disintegrating. In this series, Keith develops a series of dysfunctional relationships with each member of the family and even with Marion and Geoff, unwittingly playing a key role in each of their personal transformations, while his own life appears to be more and more out of his control.

The drama, comedy, and tragedy within these monologues derive from the tension between his relentlessly optimistic interpretation of events and the actual narrative that we can glean through the details he provides. Keith has always been a "loser" but is relentlessly optimistic in the face of crushing disappointment. It is a measure of the quality of the writing that this simple narrative form here suggests any number of wider themes that resonate with contemporary capitalist society: the sadness and emptiness of individual lives in large cities, the tragedy of those left behind in the rush for wealth and upwardly mobile ambitions, and the desperation of those outside the apparently happy norm of the nuclear family. The series could also be seen to draw on postfeminist discourses on the instability of contemporary masculinity (Keith is very much the sensitive New Age man, while Marion is an upwardly mobile alpha female).

In fact, it is the everyday nature of Keith's disappointments that encourages us to identify with him and wish that he could overcome obstacles in his path. The series becomes increasingly bleak, however, as the remnants of his former life slowly erode and the series becomes more of a black comedy. Even a brief flash of hope at the end of series 1 is bittersweet. He crashes on the way to see his newfound girlfriend, and the last shot of this series is of Keith in the passenger seat of his girlfriend's car, with her kids in the backseat. As she tells him to turn off the camera (our only glimpse of another human being through Keith's lens), he turns it toward himself, and we briefly see his body swathed in bandages. He has finally become "whole" again and no longer needs the camera as his companion and confidante.

A key aspect of the comedic tension that the series generates derives from the sense of ambiguity over Keith's confessional relationship with his camera. In part, Keith suggests the wider preoccupation of "everyday" people to place their trust in television to provide a forum for their personal failings, and he replicates the video diary's objective (as noted earlier) of establishing a dialogue with a wider audience. However, at times, Keith does not appear to have enough self-awareness to realize how he is appearing to his audience (an early episode features him playing innocently with his father's sniper rifle while looking at his wife's lover through the scope, a shot rich with suppressed violence and Freudian significance). Central to Keith's persona is a degree of naiveté, and crucially, this is where the series differs from now conventional reality television programs. His commentary and narrative are simply offered into the wide-open public space, with no expectations of a reply. Keith retains the original authenticity and clear sense of autobiography that have tended to become subsumed into more commercialist production agendas within which the video diary format typically now appears. Brydon's character indirectly suggests a more innocent period of camcorder history, before the acknowledgment of performance was such an integral part of our expectations as viewers.[15] We are unused to users of camcorders displaying such openness and lack of awareness of how they might be perceived. Keith's fictional monologues consequently retain an apparent pathos and authenticity ironically absent from most constructions of television reality, even those within *Video Nation*.

On another level, however, Keith's entire appearance is a performance of sorts, as he is at pains to not acknowledge to the camera the quiet desperation of his life that lurks just beneath the surface. We expect him to explode, to break down in tears (he does, very briefly in one episode), but we are denied the complete dropping of his beatific façade. It is the tension between the contradictory expectations that the series establishes

"Keith" innocently views his wife's lover through the sights of his father's rifle, in series 1, episode 2, of *Marion and Geoff.*

that explains much of its effectiveness: Keith is immediately familiar in his performance yet refreshingly virgin as a camcorder participant.

A later special titled *A Small Summer Party*[16] returned to the key moment when Keith finally is forced to acknowledge the relationship between his wife and Geoff, when he finds them together in his marriage bed. This extended (one-hour) special maintains the mockumentary nature of the series as a whole but abandons the dashboard video diary for another innovative approach. This special takes its cue from the ubiquitous everyday presence of amateur camcorders. Constructed as virtually a real-time account of the barbeque organized by Keith to celebrate Marion and Geoff's business relationship, the episode seamlessly cuts among four apparent continuous records of the afternoon: one from an unnamed friend whom he has invited to record the event, another by a camcorder operated by his two boys playing in and around the house in astronaut suits, and a third arriving by car with dysfunctional family guests. The fourth camcorder is carried into the house by neighbors who are trying to document evidence of Keith's family's disruption of the neighborhood but who get caught up in his personal tragedy.

All the filming uses natural lighting, and the movement and sound effects associated with each camera suggest something of the "personality" of its apparent operator. For example, we hear the sound of the boys' breaths on the soundtrack (amplified by their astronaut suits) whenever the screen cuts to their child's eye level, very shaky handheld footage, which consists of much lurking on internal stairs to spy on their parents and guests. The pathos of the events is captured in a manner reminiscent of the style of Robert Altman, that is, largely through indirect means, with Marion's and Geoff's faces appearing only toward the end, each camera accidentally overhearing conversations or framing the reactions of participants to events rather than capturing the events themselves. The special is consistent with Keith's version of this most traumatic of events in his life (outlined in episode 6 of series 1 of *Marion and Geoff*) but is less successful than the regular series because Keith's character is more peripheral to the action, and we are given a much more dispersed set of perspectives through the multiple-camcorder approach while never gaining the emotional resonance of any characters' direct confession to camera. Instead of an autobiographical portrayal of the incident, these perspectives position Keith more as the unwilling object of surveillance, as the various cameras relentlessly capture every detail of his humiliation.

DOUBLE TAKE

Produced by photographer Alison Jackson, *Double Take* is a series of programs consisting of short vignettes constructed as a pastiche of paparazzi and surveillance footage catching celebrity figures in banal and everyday activities.[17] The program is constructed of a mixture of apparent closed-circuit television tape, miniature camera footage, and especially amateur or semiprofessional video footage; pictures are grainy, sometimes blurred (or quickly coming into focus), and shot from behind obstacles and through windows, which the camera continually attempts to traverse to gain a better perspective on its subject. Jackson uses a series of look-alikes to role-play figures familiar to the British public, such as David Beckham and his then national coach, Sven-Göran Eriksson; singers Robbie Williams, Elton John, Mick Jagger, Kylie Minogue, and Michael Jackson; political figures such as Prime Minister Tony Blair, his wife, George Bush, and various members of the British royal family. At base, these are performances by carefully prepared impressionists, but viewers' awareness of the comedic impressions is given an edge by their presentation through the form of accidentally captured actuality footage.

The characters that this footage features are identifiable partly through their close resemblance to the people they are based on and partly through the accompanying audio that appears to overhear private conversations (including people apparently talking to themselves). The comedic effect of the program comes from taking existing public knowledge about a public figure and extending it into speculation about private behavior. Jackson has explained that her technique involves combining the iconic with the intimate and personal.[18] The British royal family is "seen" in everyday pursuits that are normally out of bounds of any camera, such as the queen getting her legs waxed, playing with her maid, giving driving lessons to her grandson, Prince William, simply struggling to figure out how to answer a cell phone, or playing charades with husband, Prince Philip, and the Blairs.

The overall effect is to provide a charge of authenticity, literally encouraging viewers to do a "double take" to make sure that the characters are not really who they appear to be, together with the shock and pleasure inherent to unexpected voyeurism (public figures are viewed in their underwear or in otherwise unwittingly revealing movements). Although at one level a simple exercise in titillation, in fact the series works best at those times when it encourages a layered sense of appreciation—both for the skill and quality of the impression and for the ways that those impressions play with viewers' expectations of the public persona of its targets.

The visual references made by the series range across key parts of the continuum of ways in which photographic images have become implicated within wider cultures of surveillance within contemporary society (and, crucially, these are all in contrast to the autobiographical control demonstrated by Keith in *Marion and Geoff*). Here the object of the camera's gaze is always unaware of the camera's presence and at the mercy of a dubious social and political agenda. The closed-circuit television footage

The combination of the iconic and intimate that defines Alison Jackson's faux celebrity constructions for *Double Take*.

suggests the wider regimes of law enforcement and security surveillance, aimed at identifying and recording deviant and transgressive behavior. Such footage is often implicitly and inherently accusatory; these cameras are invariably positioned in private spaces precisely to capture expected criminal or suspect behavior. Similarly, miniature camera footage has become a staple tool within investigative television reporting, extending the news and documentary camera into ever more-unlikely areas of social encounters in the service of a self-appointed public watchdog role. The erosion of public service principles at the core of commercial television news production means that such footage is often initiated as much for reasons of fulfilling a need for dramatic and/or shocking program content as for purely informational reasons. There is a clear overlap here with the other key visual reference within *Double Take*, to the small army of paparazzi photographers and camera people who provide content for the more explicitly tabloid end of popular visual culture.

The often unacknowledged aspect of tabloid culture is how deeply implicated the audience is in its maintenance and relative ferocity, through the often banal act of consumption. Viewers and readers are typically ambivalent in their acceptance of their own role within such explicitly voyeuristic and exploitative media practices. We invariably condemn the more extreme examples of tabloid tendencies and express sympathy for the objects of paparazzi surveillance (or pure harassment), yet we will continue to participate in acts of consumption and its associated gossip cultures. *Double Take* deliberately plays with this ambivalence, creating both the logical conclusion of the surveillance of public figures (the queen revealed in her most intimate and embarrassingly trivial moments) and the shock of recognition of our own complicity in such an agenda. The range of viewer readings can consequently move between appreciation of the skill of the impersonations and the success of specific instances of parody, through to a confrontation with our own guilty pleasures as voyeurs. The ultimate effect might be to encourage viewers' reflexivity toward their own fascination with tabloid culture. Certainly, Jackson, in the face of criticism of the series and the art that she has created using the same practice,[19] justifies the program ultimately as an effort to interrogate the wider public belief in the integrity of any photographic image, regardless of our understanding of the increasing sophistication of methods of selective perspective, manipulative construction, and outright fakery.[20]

LOOK AROUND YOU

The next example of short-form mockumentary series references earlier, more "innocent" forms of television nonfiction. The two series of *Look around You* respectively parody 1970s television learning modules and 1980s popular science programs,[21] offering an irreverent parody of now-dated television formats and satirizing the underlying scientific discourse upon which they drew. A key aspect of parody is a degree of ambivalence toward its target, including nostalgia toward the very aspects that are being ridiculed. Both series of *Look around You* follow this pattern, offering an affectionate re-creation of more public service–oriented and less sophisticated forms of television production.

The first series references Open University and Television for Schools and Colleges programming, where students would watch programs at home with open textbooks—each episode begins with a shot of an expectant student ready with textbook open and the instruction on which chapter viewers should turn to. Its presentation relies on voice-over, with demonstrations set in a bright white or blue studio and with various props, such as beakers and microscopes, intended to simplistically replicate the authority of a scientific laboratory. The second series parodies popular science programs from the 1980s and is fronted by four presenters (including cowriters and coproducers Peter Serafinowicz and Robert Popper). Each episode focuses on a particular subject—such as "maths," "water," "germs," "health," "sport," or "music"—which is then presented through a series of everyday textbook examples. Everything about the series is carefully re-created. The fashion of presenters and guests is staid and referenced to the specific television gender stereotypes of the 1970s and 1980s, complete with appropriate hairstyles and makeup. The production style combines a slow, measured editing pace and relies on the use of a small selection of static shots: a standard set of long, medium, and close-up compositions, all eye-level, brightly lit, carefully framed frontal shots. These are overlaid with simplistic two-dimensional graphics and cheesy synthesizer theme music.

The tone used in voiceover narration in series 1 and from the second series' on-screen presenters is measured and authoritative. The original series is directed toward a 1970s school-age audience, and the same cheerful tone is employed to address a more general audience in the second series. There are frequent pauses for effect (as if the presenters expect viewers to nod in agreement while watching at home), with comforting smiles and a friendly conversational tone of voice.[22]

The effectiveness of both series, however, relies very much on an audience's familiarity with the original forms of programming that are their targets. Without this frame of reference, the first series of ten-minute programs has the feel of extended sketches, and the content quickly becomes tedious. With the second series, the producers introduced a linking device for each episode, with an "Invention of the Week" segment featuring an award given to a budding inventor, building toward the series finale

"This is a brain": the simplistic form of science presentation demonstrated in the first series of *Look around You*.

The team of presenters in mock-1980s costume, with the "latest model of a personal computer" as a prop, in the second series of *Look around You*.

where the winning invention is judged by Prince Charles (who appears using a seamlessly integrated archival sequence of the prince from the 1970s). The in-studio presenters for this second series also serve as a stable set of characters, enthusiastically offering themselves as guinea pigs for increasingly bizarre experiments.

At another level, the series is a detailed satire of key aspects of scientific discourse. The programs' discourse could be called "television science," a reduced, popularized version of science that focuses on the everyday applicability of new technologies. These series offer the more simplistic form of mockumentary parody, creating humor through the colliding of the rational (a nonfiction address closely aligned with the sober discourse of science) with the absurd.[23] The first series insists that germs "originated in Germany," and many such nonsensical facts are accompanied with a command from the narrator for viewers to "write that down" in their copybooks.

There are frequent caricatures of the simplistic stereotype of the scientist as a white-coat and glasses-wearing male with poor social skills but also the need for science to be couched within continual references to the "latest" technology and to draw on a naive and limited sense of the future. The second series, for example, disparages previous predictions of the future (showing old science fiction portrayals of a brightly lit, antiseptic world and then returning to the bright, white television studio without any acknowledgment of the irony) and then asks viewers to participate by sending in their own predictions for what the future will be like "in the year 2000." The effect is to suggest the contextual basis of any scientific rhetoric, including how emerging technologies are popularized and made meaningful through references to implicitly historicized notions of progress.

POSH NOSH

The final example of short-term mockumentary series, *Posh Nosh*, is a mock cooking show[24] that draws on both the long tradition of instructional cooking programs, an established staple of television schedules, and the more recent popularity of celebrity chefs. The husband-and-wife team of Minty (Arabella Weir) and Simon (Richard E. Grant) Marchmont hosts the show. They are upper class to the core, with their elitist pretensions toward themselves and their food saturating every aspect of their program. Billing their program as offering "extraordinary food for ordinary people," Simon and Minty construct meals of only the finest ingredients, positioning food in crafted designs on the correct combination of plate and table setting (one episode features "architectural fish and chips," Simon's answer to the disappointment of what he terms "builder's fish and chips"). Presenting recipes from the kitchen of their country

Arabella Weir and Richard E. Grant as upper-class dysfunctional television chefs "Minty and Simon Marchmont."

mansion, the hosts reveal themselves through their chosen recipes, language, and gestures, including their idiosyncratic descriptors for cooking procedures ("disappoint the vege," "annoy the sturgeon," "disable the partridge," "thrill the mussels," and so on).[25]

As with the other examples discussed here, there are obvious satiric subtexts that can be read into *Posh Nosh*. In a wider sense, the series targets the manner in which any cooking show comes loaded with class, gender, and ethnic assumptions about the value and role of food within households. Specifically, its more blatant appeal to an elite market niche suggests the deliberate ignorance of a restaurant culture to the deeper implications of maintaining its arbitrary definition of culinary standards. At the end of each program, there is a mock ad for a top-of-the-range food item (sample product: "Costa Rican coffee-flavored chocolate coffee beans"), accompanied by choral music and a velvet-toned voiceover by Joanna Lumley extolling its virtues. Some of the products advertised are made from endangered animals or are blatantly exploitative of Third World producers.

Distanced from an awareness of the more basic and functional place of food in most people's lives, the couple are also in deep denial about their own dysfunctional relationship. The underlying tensions in their marriage, revealed through the slippage in their façade of a happy couple, forms the real narrative of the series. As with *Marion and Geoff*, key narrative details are presented inadvertently through their address to camera narration. Simon is transparently gay and snidely hostile toward Minty and her more modest class background, but she pretends not to notice and rather sublimates her unhappiness through cooking and eating. Their oblique references to unhappy past events and their true feelings are aided by both Minty's and Simon's partaking of frequent drinks through each program (Simon has a tendency to save his most eloquent pronouncements for identifying and assessing the flavors of his wine). Unlike *Marion and Geoff*, however, the series features somewhat abbreviated character development. The limited space for action and the necessary focus on actually presenting a complete (though fake) recipe mean that the series tends to operate on one-liners rather than accumulating the narrative complexity that characterizes the more effective examples of television mockumentary.

Collectively, these series suggest some of the range of mockumentary discourse, the potential complexity of its engagement with the media and cultural practices associated with nonfiction television forms, one key to the consequently layered senses of engagement that mockumentaries can provide for audiences. The expansion of factual-based television programs, together with the emergence of mockumentary television series, suggests that producers are becoming more sophisticated in understanding and exploring the potential of mockumentary for parodic and satiric commentary. Taken together, the short-form series discussed here also demonstrate the challenges that producers face in employing mockumentary discourse. The finest examples of mockumentary occur not in pursuit of a one-off stunt but where filmmakers and producers commit to using the appropriation of nonfiction codes and conventions as the central premise of a text and aim to develop audience identification with characters to service the demands of conventional narrative construction.

NOTES

1. Nichols defined documentary in relation to the professional and institutional practice of filmmakers, the specific modes of documentary representation that characterize documentary texts, and the assumptions and expectations of the genre's audiences. B. Nichols, *Representing Reality: Issues and Concepts in Documentary* (Bloomington: Indiana University Press, 1991), 12–31.

2. This is a definition discussed in more detail in Craig Hight, *Television Mockumentary: Documentary and Satire in the Televisual Space* (Manchester, UK: Manchester University Press, forthcoming).

3. M. Renov, ed., *Theorizing Documentary* (New York: Routledge, 1993), 22–35.

4. B. Mills, "Comedy Verité: Contemporary Sitcom Form," *Screen* 45, no. 1 (2004): 63–78.

5. There is not space here to outline other pathways into television production, including the importance that radio has had in the gestation of new comedic formats.

6. Again, *The Office* is a key example here. For an excellent detailed discussion of this series, see B. Walters, *"The Office"* (London: British Film Institute, 2005).

7. See http://www.bbc.co.uk/videonation/, which provides information on the series, a brief history, and its progression into an online series of shorts in which amateurs negotiate the production of their footage to the final edit.

8. J. Dovey, *Freakshow: First Person Media and Factual Television* (London: Pluto Press. 2000), 103–32.

9. Dovey, *Freakshow*, 104.

10. Dovey, *Freakshow*, 116.

11. This is a pattern that is replicated on a far-greater scale through user-produced short videos uploaded to sites such as YouTube.

12. Like Dovey, Renov employs a Foucauldian perspective on the cultural significance of confessions within the contemporary moment. M. Renov, *The Subject of Documentary* (Minneapolis: University of Minnesota Press, 2004), 191–206.

13. Series 1 of *Marion and Geoff* first screened on BBC2 from September to November 2000. All screening dates listed in this chapter are taken from M. Lewisohn, *Radio Times Guide to TV Comedy* (London: BBC Worldwide, 2003).

14. Series 2 screened from January to March 2003.

15. Again, this tendency has become even more dominant outside the television medium, as demonstrated by the plethora of autobiographical performance videos that feature on YouTube and other Web 2.0 sites.

16. The special was screened by BBC2 in September 2001.

17. Although not short form in length, with episodes of thirty minutes, the structure of the series is for each episode to be very fragmented with segments lasting only a few minutes each. A fifty-minute pilot screened on BBC2 in December 2001, with the series following in March to April 2003.

18. Alison Jackson in an interview included on the DVD for the series.

19. See http://www.alisonjackson.com.

20. Jackson, DVD interview.

21. The first series of ten-minute programs screened on BBC2 in December 2002. A second series was extended to thirty-minute episodes, screening from January to February 2005.

22. Both series are supported by online sites that replicate their educational tone of address, graphic style, and absurdist content. See http://www.bbc.co.uk/comedy/lookaroundyou/.

23. Taken to more extremes, the series would closely resemble a key strand within the style of *Monty Python's Flying Circus*, where an adherence to a rational mode of presentation is married with increasingly absurdist content.

24. The series of ten-minute episodes screened February 2003 on BBC2.

25. As with *Look around You*, an accompanying website maintains and extends the fiction, in this case offering recipes and further details on the food philosophy of Simon and Minty. See http://www.bbc.co.uk/comedy/poshnosh/.

6

Commando Raids
on the Nature of Reality

Gary D. Rhodes

Films exist in many places: a film is in a reel stored inside of a can; a motion picture is encoded onto a shiny DVD that sparkles like a rainbow when held up to the light. But at the same time, those are just objects that contain films. We experience films not by staring at a reel or at a disc but by gazing elsewhere, at a screen. But even the theater or television screen is not a film's permanent home, certainly not in the same way that a frame provides to a painting. No, at best it's a fragile, temporal relationship, with the film bounded by opening credits and fades to black. The film exists for a short while, until it reaches THE END and the screen goes dark.

That's not to say that we don't try to provide frames for our cinematic paintings. We attempt to fix them in our memories, honing in, for example, on particular scenes that we like to recall, over and over again—lines of dialogue as well, even when the memory that we create constitutes something different from our original experience with the film. Humphrey Bogart's Rick never actually said, "Play it again, Sam" in *Casablanca* (1943), but he certainly did—and continues to do—in our cultural memory.

But perhaps our favorite way to combat the temporal is to hinge particular adjectives onto films, as if a single word or two can encapsulate what they are. Movie X is "heart-warming"; it is "uplifting"; it is—like so many other films before it, of course—"inspirational." By contrast, Movie Y is "bold" and "daring" and "original." And then, of course, there is the darker underbelly of cinema, as exemplified by Movie Z, which is "shocking" and "graphic" and—egad—"titillating." Running time runs, but we can screech the experience to a halt with such adjectives, equally suitable for use in our own conversations as they are for the text on movie posters and videotape boxes.

If most films exist (at least when they are not being viewed) as adjectives, I'd argue that a small number are verbs. They just *are*. In some cases, such as Bob Quinn's *Poitín* (1979) and the Coen brothers' *No Country for Old Men* (2007), perhaps it is because they are so unadorned, so unvarnished, so raw, they require no flowery adjectives. In other cases, ranging from *The Great Train Robbery* (1903) and *The Cabinet of Dr. Caligari* (1919) to *Citizen Kane* (1941) and *Á Bout de soufflé* (1960), they exist as if they have always existed. And they exert a gravitational pull, causing so many other films to orbit around them, tied irrevocably to the gravity of their influence, which is so strong as to just *be*.

And then, well, then there is Norman Mailer's 1970 film *Maidstone*. He directed the film and starred in it, both as the fictional character Norman T. Kingsley, a movie director who runs for president of the United States, and as Norman Mailer, playing himself as the director of *Maidstone*. After limited engagements in 1971, the film essentially disappeared from sight until a DVD was released in France in 2006, which was followed by a number of public screenings, including that at the Lincoln Center's Walter Reade Theater in 2007.[1] For over three decades, then, *Maidstone* had no screen on which to appear; its running time had stopped; and words were all that it had.

Norman Mailer as film director and possible presidential candidate Norman T. Kingsley. *Photograph © Daniel Kramer.*

Though Mailer would insist that the medium of film was "once re-moved from words," the words through which *Maidstone* existed dur-ing its hiatus were largely his own.[2] Mailer's essay "A Course in Film-Making," published in the *New American Review* in 1971, described his theory behind shooting *Maidstone*. A slightly different version of the essay appeared that same year in his book *Maidstone: A Mystery*, which also printed the film's dialogue and stage directions, transcribed after the fact since *Maidstone* did not have a shooting script.[3] Many words, to be sure, but one in particular surfaces repeatedly. Not an adjective or even a verb but a noun: for Norman Mailer, *Maidstone* was a "raid."

Specifically, it was "analogous to a military operation, to a commando raid on the nature of reality—[the persons involved in making the film] would discover where reality was located by the attack itself, just as a company of Rangers might learn that the enemy was located not in the first town they invaded, but another."[4] Or as Mailer (while playing him-self as film director) would say in a scene in *Maidstone*,

> we made a movie by a brand new process. . . . Now what we did is we made a movie as a military operation. When you have a military operation, what happens is you set out to take a given town and your objective is to take that town, and as you go forward all sorts of unforeseen contingencies arrive, and as they do you go around them, or you go through them or you go under them.

Around the unforeseen contingencies, through them, under them. For Mailer, *Maidstone* was something far more than a single film. It was an important opportunity to put his theory of filmmaking into practice.

OPERATION LEVIATHAN

Maidstone tells the story of film director Norman T. Kingsley, who mounts his new movie while simultaneously considering a run for the presidency of the United States. Though Kingsley promises that his new film will not be "sexploitation," it is set in a bordello and features nudity and copula-tion. While working on it, Kingsley meets with a number of supporters and detractors for his emerging political career, ranging from the presi-dent of a women's college to a group of young African Americans.

Fearful that Kingsley might actually get elected, a group of "High Of-ficials" contemplates an assassination attempt. But we soon learn that many others might be plotting against Kingsley as well. Rumors suggest that television reporter Jeanne Cardigan (Jean Campbell) could be a mem-ber of an organization that inadvertently encourages assassinations. And then there is the Cashbox, a kind of Rat Pack that hangs around Kingsley, headed by his half brother Raoul Rey O'Houlihan (Rip Torn). Kingsley purports to have them under control, but they are clearly a dangerous group. The film director's life is clearly at risk.

Mailer chose to film *Maidstone* with no script, using a combination of professional actors (such as Ultra Violet, fresh from her work with Andy Warhol, and Hervé Villechaize, later famous as Tattoo on television's *Fantasy Island*) and amateurs (including two of his ex-wives, his current wife, and the owner of the Maidstone estate, where the film would be shot and from which it would take its title). During the filming, rumor had it that at least one cast member was armed, and there was no doubt that numerous others engaged in all sorts of debauchery. Sex, drugs, and booze: according to one anecdote, Villechaize nearly drowned in a swimming pool.[5]

Five groups of cinematographers followed the actions of the large cast for one week of shooting, each group operating independent of the others. They included D. A. Pennebaker (who directed *Monterey Pop* in 1968, a film that Mailer much admired, as well as *Don't Look Back* in 1967) and Richard Leacock (who had helped shoot *Monterey Pop*). Both men had played key roles in the cinema verité documentary movement.

As much as anything else, that movement inspired Mailer. Handheld cameras and handheld sound recorders allowed for small, mobile crews, offering what at least *seemed* to be unfettered access to reality. With natural lighting, shooting could occur easily, including that in confined spaces. It could occur hour after hour. And it could even occur surreptitiously, as one young woman performing oral sex would learn during *Maidstone*'s production. That was all part of the process, of course, for a crew that filmed forty-five hours of footage, some of it residing in the land of Plot, some of it residing in the land of Behind the Scenes, and some of it occupying territory on the borderland between the two.

We get, for example, footage of Mailer playing Mailer the film director. We also get footage of Mailer playing Kingsley (which was in fact Mailer's own middle name), using an affected accent. Two Normans. But then there's also footage of Kingsley in which Mailer largely drops the accent, blurring the division between the two. As Mailer the director explains during an on-screen discussion with the cast, "You can't say that this is real now, what we're doing, you can't say what we were doing last night [while filming a Kingsley scene] was real."

And so, this commando raid represented for Mailer a "Leviathan of the thesis."[6] It was "pure cinema," a "prime example of the logic of film."[7] His strategy of attacking the nature of reality was rooted in what he claimed was a "brand new process" of making movies. He would cling to that view in large measure, later suggesting that it was a "conception which was more or less his own, and he did not feel the desire to argue about

Norman Mailer directing the cast on the set of *Maidstone*, 1968. *Photograph ©
Daniel Kramer.*

it," even while admitting that precursors abounded, ranging from Cassavetes's *Shadows* (1959) to silent two-reelers that were shot without scripts.[8]

As for important precursors, *Maidstone*'s narrative engages in an interesting conversation with *Citizen Kane* (1941), a film that Mailer much admired. Both Charles Foster Kane and Norman T. Kingsley are well-known men but are simultaneously unknown. They are mysteries. We learn the "salient facts" about Kingsley in the opening minutes of *Maidstone*, though some of them are oxymoronically "unconfirmed facts." We hear rumors, such as the possibility that he might be homosexual, but such rumors are nothing more than loose ends, false leads. Kinglsey's opinions on major political debates are also unknown. A Kingsley associate tells the High Officials, "You haven't begun to get to know what he really is," but then has to admit that she doesn't "really know what he is any more than anybody else knows." As a result, journalists attempt to unravel the mystery of Kingsley, just as they do Kane. Still puzzled by Kingsley in one of her final scenes, Jeanne Cardigan asks, "What is he?" confronting a problem none too different than the reporters at Xanadu face at the conclusion of *Citizen Kane*.

Of course, the marvels of *Kane* are cinematic as much or more as they are narrative. Rather than being imperfect eyesores, scratches on certain shots in its *News on the March* newsreel beg to be believed because they appear old and are thus historic and trustworthy. And in those images that seem to grow in majesty and prescience with every viewing, we see handheld footage of Kane in a wheelchair, "stolen" footage as it were, shot through an opening in a privacy fence. We return then to the issue of the handheld camera, which of course predated the cinema verité movement, and we must reckon with its importance not just in the acquisition of images on location but also for its unique aesthetic and thematic potential.

Because if its handheld, whether as early as in *Kane*, a later film like *Shadows*, or in, for example, Vietnam footage on the nightly television news of the 1960s and 1970s, the image possesses a particular urgency that at least seems to evoke reality. The unsteadiness of the camera and the resulting shake of the image become pivotal in *Maidstone*. During the Assassination Ball, for example, a failed attempt on Kingsley's life evokes all too clearly the chaotic footage of Bobby Kennedy's death, which was still horrifyingly fresh in the minds of *Maidstone*'s cast and crew when they shot the film.

Rather than the medium being the message, Mailer's message was to disrupt the medium, to disrupt the complacency of the film audience with what it sees and hears. His Leviathan thesis was a strategy, using tactics that ranged from a preexisting shooting style and an improvised storyline to the combined use of amateur and professional actors who would appear on screen as characters and—in some instances and to some degree—as themselves. It was every bit a commando raid of a shoot.

DEEP IN MY DUNGEON

According to Mailer, improvisation during a film shoot "obviously gave more freedom to the cutter."⁹ *Maidstone*, despite its brief production schedule, would become what Mailer described as "a work of months [to edit], and then finally of a year (and a second year to follow) of mistakes and losses, blunders and mislaid gems of film strip, but when done, it would be his conception, he would by then have *written* a movie using strips of film rather than words."¹⁰ Mailer's conception of editing was to control the battlefield and the airspace by using the booty he had seized during the commando raid.

The completed film clocked in at 110 minutes. Mailer broke it into twelve sections, or—to continue his writing metaphor—chapters, each featuring a number and title. With the exception of "12: Silences of an Afternoon," the titles are immediately straightforward and obvious within the context of the plot and its dialogue: "1: A Meeting of High Officials," "2: The Director," "3: PAX, C" (the acronym of an organization name designed to prevent assassinations but which might in fact encourage them), "4: Instructions to the Cast," and so forth.

He controls and manipulates the images in each section. Along with all the visual signs of "reality"—from handheld camera to light leaks on the image and the occasional appearance of a microphone in the shot—*Maidstone* features various techniques that show an editor's intervention, including slow motion, echo effects, and audio played backward, as well as images of a shoreline intentionally edited upside down. During "5: Politicking in the Grass," the film offers a few very abrupt edits, an indicator of an editor cutting unwanted words or visuals. It features jump cuts without apparent need in "6: A Commencement of Filming," as well as dissolves connoting the passage of time. It even illustrates a curious control over the optically printed section titles: all of them feature numerals, except for "EIGHT: Return of an Old Love," which curiously spells out the number.

And then there is what at first seems to be duplicated footage. In "7: Portents," when the "European Agent" asks if someone should "forcefully" remove Kingsley, the "Worried Fellow" responds that he "couldn't make that decision." Mailer then offers another take of the same characters having the same conversation in the same location. But their words have changed ever so slightly, placing pressure on us to consider whether or not this is in fact a repetition or whether it constitutes something else, the second of the two takes representing perhaps an alternate reality or a kind of memory of the first take. In moments like these, the editing choices simultaneously remind us of the improvised raid and Mailer's subsequent control over the spoils of war.

On a larger scale, Mailer transforms the improvised images and dialogue into various themes, such as a sustained meditation on the connection between sex and death. He tells a story in which a director is making a film about a brothel while an assassination plot against him is apparently underway. Possible assailants cavort with unabashed hedonism in and out of character. The first visual in the film (after a television broadcast by Jeanne Cardigan) is of an architectural structure that looks like a gallows; later, we hear that hangings from it involve orgasms. And—in what is certainly the most experimental section—"9: The Death of a Director" offers orgasmic moans and images of nudity and sex intercut with shots of animal bones and Kingsley lying on the ground as if he were dead. Elsewhere in the same section, Jeanne Cardigan, with breasts partially exposed, licks the microphone before she smears a baby doll and then herself with what appears to be blood while shouting that she hates "NTK," Kingsley's initials.

And despite some critical and audience complaints to the contrary, Mailer offers a largely clear, understandable narrative structure that overtly projects a destination point in Kingsley's assassination, with characters as early in the film as "2: The Director" discussing "whether or not we're going to allow this man to live." Such an event is foreshadowed elsewhere as well. While boxing, Kingsley says that he "can't take too many shots to the head"; he later suggests that "being president is equivalent to being a monkey in a shooting gallery." More obliquely—and more ominously as result—Lazarus warns him, "There's a storm coming."

Perhaps, given his comparison of editing to writing, Mailer would have desired, indeed expected, such narrative and thematic coherence to be shaped in postproduction. After all, during "11: A Course in Orientation," he expresses his hope that all of the different footage taken from the commando raid will not prove "incompatible." And he also defends "10: The Grand Assassination Ball" from on-screen criticism voiced by the cast, who were unhappy that no character assassinates Kingsley, a narrative conclusion that Mailer had planned rather than improvised.

The film, as he would later write, "kept promising developments of plots which never quite took place, even as we travel through our lives forever anticipating the formation of plots around us which do not quite form."[11] It was as if he preferred the sound of the fist punching through the air to its landing on a head that "cannot take too many shots."

So he had "staged," as he said, the Grand Assassination Ball with no assassination, crafting a story structure leading to an event that seems not to occur. During the editing process, he chose to begin his film with audio of a singer proclaiming,

> Deep in my dungeon, I welcome you here.
> Deep in my dungeon, I worship your fear.
>
> Deep in my dungeon, I dwell
> I do not know if I wish you well.

Mailer directing a scene on the *Maidstone* set. *Photograph © Daniel Kramer.*

Mailer knew that the unexpected can and does occur during commando raids. That a regiment can raid the wrong town, for example. And also that the captor can so easily become the captive.

The words written about *Maidstone* while it remained hidden from view all those many years often focused on "12: The Silences of an Afternoon." By the time that it was captured on film, Mailer had "come to the erroneous conclusion his movie was done"; the shoot had wrapped.[12] Then a small number of cast and crew traveled to Lonetree Hill, where—as Robert Griswold suggests on screen—"those wonderful birds are." Rip Torn was in that group, percolating with unease and anger over Mailer's decision to avoid the violence, to avoid the narrative conclusion the story promised, to avoid the assassination of Norman T. Kingsley.

With cameras still filming, the group disperses, walking around Lonetree Hill as we hear a wordless vocal from the singer of "Deep in My Dungeon." Rip Torn slowly retrieves a hammer from his satchel and throws off his sunglasses. His face appears strained, then a dissolve transports us to his apparently unexpected attack on "Not Mailer" but on "Kingsley," who "must die." Even if (at first, at least) it is Rey the film character attempting to assassinate Kingsley the film character, it is also (apparently) Mailer the man (no longer the director?) who will struggle with Torn (the actor run amok?). Of course, that description is possibly too simplistic, as their roles could have reconstituted themselves repeatedly during the attack, which becomes the most captivating in *Maidstone*.

After announcing that he "must die," Rey/Torn twice hits Mailer/Kingsley with a hammer over the head. The two struggle with each other until falling onto the ground. Mailer then bites Torn's ear, drawing blood. Their hands grab at each other's necks, with Torn gaining an upper hand just as Mailer's wife and children appear. His wife begins screaming and the children begin to cry.

"I'm taking that scene out of the movie," Mailer yells at Torn shortly after the fight ends. They continue to talk, trading barbs and insults in between Torn's attempts to explain that he did what he *had to do*. Writing about the event later, Mailer admitted, "Torn had . . . been right to make his attack. The hole in the film had called for that. Without it, there was not enough."[13] On screen, the attack and struggle last roughly two minutes, with another six minutes covering Torn and Mailer's ensuing and quite heated conversation.

The Torn sequence causes us to reconsider the whole of Mailer's military campaign, just as he did while editing. The fight gave "him a whole new conception of his movie." He believed that his commando raid created a "presence" that outlived the conclusion of his original storyline, that outlived what had only *seemed* to be the end of shooting; it was that

Norman Mailer and Rip Torn's famous fight scene. *Photograph ©
Daniel Kramer.*

presence which triggered Torn's attack. It was an event that took *Maidstone* closer to the "possible real nature of film."[14]

Perhaps that was the case. But it's just as possible that including the
scene moved Mailer closer to the kind of filmmaking that he dismisses on
screen in "11: A Course in Orientation." Once he was in postproduction,
Mailer crafted a film that featured—on a larger scale—a clear narrative
that used dialogue and visuals in a manner not entirely dissimilar to some
Hollywood norms, to—on a smaller scale—standard editing devices such
as the sound bridge that connects "10: The Grand Assassination Ball" to
"11: A Course in Orientation" and the dissolve that transports us from
Torn's scheming face to his attack on Mailer.

Complaints from the cast over the lack of an assassination in "11: A Course in Orientation" anticipated similar unhappiness in the future film audience. Torn's attack aimed to rectify that perceived problem. The result means that, in its basic form, the structure of *Maidstone's* conclusion can be read as not so different from that of many Hollywood films in which we the audience think the film reaches an apparent climax ("10: The Grand Assassination Ball") only to be tricked thanks to a brief delay ("11: A Course in Orientation") before the villain returns a final battle (Torn in "12: Silences of an Afternoon"). It is possible that the dungeon of Hollywood storytelling has welcomed Mailer, who was trapped into including the very kind of conclusion that he had originally sought to avoid.

MINING FOR THE INELUCTABLE ORE

It would be wrong of course to focus too much attention on the word *dungeon*. It would be wrong because doing so would force *Maidstone* into a place in which it does not belong. Whatever allowances the Rip Torn attack makes for an audience, whatever minor similarities the film shows to Hollywood storytelling, *Maidstone* is not a studio film or really a commercial film of any kind. After all, we could just as easily invoke the relationship between "9: The Death of a Director" and the experimental film movement of the sixties and seventies. But in neither case can *Maidstone* be imprisoned by a word like, say, *repetition* or *recapitulation*. No, Mailer's film is something far more than a set of narrative structures or visual styles chained to the cinematic past.

Though intended to be a commando raid on the nature of reality, *Maidstone* raided a different, though equally fascinating, place. It became a unique raid on the way in which the cinema *depicts* reality. It places a degree of faith in a certain kind of depiction, meaning cinema verité, but remains skeptical of it all the same. Let's not forget that, in his essay "A Course in Film-Making," Mailer refers to the "director" in the third person. He knows that Norman T. Kingsley was a fictional character, but he also knows that Norman Mailer on screen—the "director"—was also, in varying degrees that may shift from moment to moment, a fictional character. "Behind the Scenes," at least as captured on film, is very much a plural location.

And that takes us back once again to Rip Torn's attack. Though *Maidstone* has still not garnered a large audience, the attack scene has become a part of the YouTube world, watched online as a clip and viewed outside of the context of the film. And yet it evokes an array of user comments that would no doubt excite Mailer, providing some verification of his

Leviathan thesis. Some viewers believe it's real; some don't. Others argue for it being somewhere in between. As Mailer himself wrote,

> *Maidstone* had been filmed not only as an imaginary event but as a real event, and so was both a fiction and a documentary at once and then become impossible to locate so precisely, for what came nearest to the hard hide of the real. Was it [the attack] Norman T. Kingsley, the self-satisfied director, instructing his cast for the last time, or was it suddenly the real head of Norman T. Kingsley that Torn as suddenly attacked. (Yet his hammer had been held carefully on the flat to reduce the damage.) For if the attack were real, the actor upon whom it was wreaked should not be, and would not be unless the attack became fiercer still, fierce enough to kill him indeed. Then Kingsley would have become undeniably more real than Mailer.[15]

But whatever happened at Lonetree Hill during the attack, *Maidstone* reveals to us only a depiction of it, a cinematic depiction. After all, those eight tense minutes between Mailer/Kingsley and Torn/Rey include six edits. Something is there for us to see, whatever it is and whatever it depicts, but something has been left out as well, removed from our view. The cutting-room floor also occupies an important place in the nature of (cinematic) reality.

With *Maidstone*, Mailer was acutely aware of what he had achieved, as well as of its limitations. The film is not an end but a means to an end. He quite rightly predicted that "with the advent of electronic editing from videotapes, the notion of *writing* one's movie out of the film at one's disposal" was inevitable. Such editing—in the form of computer, nonlinear editing—has indeed changed the ways in which films are compiled, crafted, *written*. And he hoped that his discovery of a new way to make films would prove influential.

Though its direct influence was largely stifled due to limited screenings in 1971, *Maidstone* was certainly at the vanguard of what became mockumentary filmmaking in the 1970s and beyond, a less complex and certainly less interesting kind of commando raid than Mailer had staged. Indeed, perhaps *Maidstone*'s most important heir came in the form of Orson Welles's *F for Fake* (1974), in which Welles, not unlike Mailer, also believed that he had created a new kind of film. But in *F for Fake*, Welles searched for and celebrated the frauds and the phonies, whereas Mailer had pursued something quite different.

Mailer concluded his essay "A Course in Film-Making" by suggesting that he was "mining for the ineluctable ore of the authentic."[16] Adjectives, nouns, and verbs might try to freeze-frame a film with words, but Mailer's goal was a continuous and ongoing project. The reemergence of *Maidstone* means that we no longer have to depend on a word or even a group of words to replace it, whether Mailer's or someone else's. Words can shed light on a film but only the kind of light that causes the shiny DVD to sparkle like a rainbow. They cannot act the part of a stand-in for the film. Experiencing *Maidstone* flickering on a screen reveals Mailer valiantly, sometimes indescribably, in pursuit of *something*, whether it is the authentic or merely a cinematic simulacrum of it. *Maidstone* is a commando raid forever searching perhaps for the ineffable, even the impossible, rather than ineluctable, but so much the better. That way, the running time keeps running.

NOTES

1. *Norman Mailer: Wild 90/Au-dessus de lois/Maidstone*, DVD (Cinémalta: Paris, 2006).

2. Norman Mailer, "A Course in Film-Making," in *New American Review 12*, ed. Theodore Solotaroff (New York: Simon & Schuster, 1971), 232.

3. Norman Mailer, *Maidstone: A Mystery* (New York: New American Library, 1971).

4. Mailer, "A Course in Film-Making," 201.

5. Mailer, *Maidstone: A Mystery*, 16.

6. Mailer, "A Course in Film-Making," 202.

7. Mailer, "A Course in Film-Making," 232.

8. Mailer, "A Course in Film-Making," 217.

9. Mailer, "A Course in Film-Making," 231.

10. Mailer, "A Course in Film-Making," 226.

11. Mailer, "A Course in Film-Making," 239.

12. Mailer, "A Course in Film-Making," 201.

13. Mailer, "A Course in Film-Making," 238.

14. Mailer, "A Course in Film-Making," 201.

15. Mailer, "A Course in Film-Making," 239.

16. Mailer, *Maidstone: A Mystery*, 180.

III

DARING TO BELIEVE

7

Aching to Believe:
The Heresy of *Forgotten Silver*

Scott Wilson

The "point" of the exercise was not to con viewers, but to give delight, and offer a tongue-in-cheek tribute to Kiwi ingenuity.[1]

As a result of this programme I am now going to pay my broadcasting fee in Monopoly money.[2]

On the 29th of October 1995, New Zealand's state-owned broadcaster TV One offered its public the documentary *Forgotten Silver* as part of its "television of quality" series *Montana Sunday Theatre*.[3] As the broadcast that closed the 1995 season, this was a documentary nestled among a number of admittedly higher-brow dramas that seemed to pass without question among the program's estimated 40,000 viewers. The reason for this lay at least in part in the amount of publicity leading into this broadcast of a documentary that offered a unique revelation: hidden in New Zealand's cultural past, it seemed, was a long-lost cinematic pioneer who, having been revealed by the work of Peter Jackson and fellow cineaste Costa Botes, now "deserves a place among the luminaries of early cinema, like Edison, Méliès and the Lumière brothers."[4] As a fundamental part of the lead-in to the broadcast, the New Zealand weekly television listings magazine *The New Zealand Listener* ran an article—"Heavenly Features"—that primed viewers to anticipate these remarkable findings while leaving some of the more impressive details for the documentary itself to reveal.[5]

Peter Jackson leads viewers up the garden path.

Further to this and as part of its own celebrations of the centenary of cinema, the New Zealand public had been made aware of a drive by the New
Zealand Film Commission to discover and restore lost and forgotten film
footage, so discoveries and restoration were very much in the air when
the time came to reveal *Forgotten Silver* to a public primed to accept such
discoveries as entirely possible.[6] Thus, the pieces of the *Forgotten Silver*
story were in place, and the broadcast itself has subsequently entered
both New Zealand broadcasting and mockumentary mythology.

The purpose of this chapter is not to reflect on the techniques of the documentary text itself but to instead consider the aftermath of the screening
and the ways that public reaction to *Forgotten Silver* is as intimately tied
to the considerations of such things as national identity and cultural history as the documentary that works to critique them.[7] Furthermore, I am
keen to link the material of *Forgotten Silver* to the ways in which particular
kinds of critically directed texts—and mockumentaries are perfect examples of this—seem to generate responses that, in hindsight, are far more
revealing of the broader conditions of their production and reception
than might otherwise be considered, for, exactly as Conrich and Smith
note, "the negative response that the filmmakers experienced, once the
hoax was revealed, highlights the extent to which many New Zealanders
wanted the story to be true."[8]

To that end, I think that it is important to consider the kinds of work
that this text is engaged in, because that will reveal the source texts so
skillfully lampooned by the artifice that Jackson and Botes are able to
wield. Thus, it is important to recognize—particularly for viewers of

Forgotten Silver, without the cultural references essential to understand some of the more arcane humor of the piece—that much of the criticism that *Forgotten Silver* attempts has its origins in the foundation myths of this country's settlement: foundation myths that are necessarily tied to colonization and that must therefore implicate ethnicity as much as they do the development of some kind of putative national identity.

Central to the story of Colin McKenzie, the long-forgotten cinematic pioneer, is the function of the pioneer in the mythology of this postsettlement society. As Peter Limbrick notes, the colonization and settling of New Zealand by Europeans,

> which began in a scrappy, ad hoc fashion and which, even when eventually organized and systematic in its usurping of Maori land and its imposition of foreign language and culture, left the country with unpredictably diverse and messy cultural practices and transactions.[9]

Therefore, because the colonization and settlement of New Zealand proceeded with fragmented and diverse objectives and drives (as, one suspects, occurred with many nations formed through settlement), the possibility for a singular national identity for the colonizing settlers is rendered difficult, if not impossible. Indeed, as Mark Williams observes, the problems inherent in the desire to create or inhabit any mythology of New Zealand national identity reflect

> the fundamental weakness of nationalism in New Zealand, a weakness going back to the late-colonial period when its early Pakeha [white European] manifestation emerged not as a break with imperial affiliation but as a confirmation of New Zealand's special place within empire.[10]

Williams's point is that New Zealand, as a land of settlement, exists as an ambivalence, caught between the desire to become a land with its own identity and the wish to both extend and represent English dominion.

Of course, what Slavoj Žižek refers to as the "obscene underside" of ideology is captured exactly by this tension, demonstrated neatly in the critical responses to *Forgotten Silver*'s commentary: a national identity is a made thing, expressed materially in the lived rituals of nationhood and embodied, not necessarily in actual individuals, but in creatures of the media who are themselves textual fabrications: sportspeople, cultural figures, politicians, celebrities who come to function as and embody what Lee Tamahori referred to as the "defining documents of our nation."[11] None of this is "real," *Forgotten Silver* is offering, and yet it is invested in nevertheless. What is more, this construction *works* for those who invest in it but only for so long as the construction is not revealed to emerge *as a made thing.* Prior to *Forgotten Silver,* the myths of nationalism so neatly parodied were never so sacred as to not be made light of, but the making light of stood in relation to the original thing in such as way as to preserve its veracity.

FORGOTTEN SILVER AND THE MYTHS OF SETTLEMENT

Central to the work of *Forgotten Silver* are two important factors, both of which lie within the criticisms that the broadcast itself received. The first of these, and most often commented on in local considerations of the text, is the manner with which it draws attention to and then parodies symbols and performances that all, in their part, contribute to a particular version of New Zealand's national identity. As Hight and Roscoe argue,

> a crucial part of the effectiveness of the program for New Zealand audiences was based on the subtlety and variety of ways in which its filmmakers exploited cultural stereotypes and accepted notions concerning the nature of New Zealand history and society.[12]

The fact that we must consider the version of identity represented in *Forgotten Silver* as just that—a version—itself draws attention to the fragility of national identity and the manner with which any nation, particularly those with settler or colonial experiences, must negotiate the ambivalences of settlement and colonization.

The second factor that we must examine is broader than the specific target of *Forgotten Silver* but is necessarily implicated in the success of the hoax and forms a central thread of the negative responses: the manner with which the documentary text relies on a particular set of filmic or televisual techniques to anchor its access to truth and reality. This second factor is explored later in more detail. For now it is enough to note that both these factors worked to make *Forgotten Silver* the particular text that is was and is, and both are present in the tone and content of the responses the broadcast received.

To deal with the local and particular aspects of national identity that find their way into the content of the text, we must detour first and briefly to New Zealand literature. It is there that we first find the figure of the "Man Alone," a singular presence explicitly named in the 1939 eponymous novel by John Mulgan but whose presence can be seen through the development of postsettlement art and cultural (read: European) representation. The Man Alone embodies an entire series of ambivalences regarding the act of settlement and the ability of the settler to actually settle and make a home in this "newfound land." Thus, for Mulgan's novel (and subsequently throughout New Zealand literature and into cinema), the Man Alone figure, often functioning as a kind of "everyman," must negotiate a variety of binary positions as these occur in the narrative; here we see ambivalences around isolation and friendship, male companionship and heterosexual relationships, the barren or empty landscape and the overfull urban environment played out across the figure of the Man Alone, who is, most often, damaged, destroyed, or cast out by these forces that, conversely, seem not to trouble those indigenous inhabitants who might feature in these texts.

As a result of these ambivalences, the Man Alone figure develops a kind of laconic self-sufficiency as a form of protection against the misunderstandings of the society that both needs and refuses them. The Man Alone may very well be temporarily accompanied by companions, friends, or lovers, but his path—these narratives offer us—is one of isolation, doomed not to be recognized by his peers but instead to be retrospectively respected and mourned if he is remembered at all. It is exactly from this kind of cloth that the figure of Colin McKenzie is cut, and we can see that the narrative of *Forgotten Silver* is careful, with its "air of portentous reticency,"[13] to provide him with temporary companions only to have them forcefully removed at significant moments in the McKenzie mythology. His brother Brooke dies as part of the ANZAC assault on Gallipoli during World War I, and Colin's bride, Maybelle (now the widow of recently deceased Brooke), miscarries and dies during the filming of McKenzie's lost epic, *Salome*. Even Hannah McKenzie, Colin's widow, who eventually donates his stored footage to "young" Peter Jackson, is present only for enough of Colin's story to provide some degree of veracity to her position as witness to much of Colin's later suffering.

McKenzie's self-sufficiency that, the documentary makes clear, occurs partly as a kind of "native" intelligence and partly in response to a dour and dominating colonial father, functions also to link him to another beloved settler mythology: the backyard inventor-genius who, as Hight and Roscoe accurately comment, "perseveres despite a wealth of natural, personal, financial, and political hardships."[14] Thus, the figure of Colin McKenzie is a clever and complex conflation of a number of mythological elements essential to a particular variant of national identity. He is both the lone genius, isolated by his achievements and driven from a society ill-equipped to contain his excessive abilities, and the self-sufficient man whose brilliance is played out in invention after invention, each innovation drawing him closer to the monumental vision that will make his fortune despite the obstacles faced, thereby demonstrating "the sense that New Zealand technological innovation could triumph over size, power and capital."[15] There is therefore a degree of narrative inevitability that McKenzie fails in his own lifetime, and it is similarly appropriate that he be rediscovered after his time so that he be both mourned appropriately and seen as contributor to and proof of the veracity of the settler mythology itself.

An example of Colin McKenzie's pioneer spirit.

Lest we forget, the narrative of McKenzie, like the narrative of this version of national identity itself, is a story of whiteness. There are no Maori in *Forgotten Silver*, a fact that is not mentioned in any of the responses I have seen. Of course, there is no reason to expect such a fact to figure at all, except that the story of McKenzie's exceptional innovation does include other ethnicities beyond European settler identities. There are two moments in *Forgotten Silver* where nonwhite ethnicity intrudes into the story, which reveals the fact that Jackson and Botes have deliberately chosen to ignore Maori representation as a way of highlighting the perceived activities of the settlers themselves.[16] McKenzie's first, pre-*Salome* feature film, *The Warrior Season*, is noted because it marks the first use of a synchronous sound technology. However, the film itself fails beyond its novelty because McKenzie has chosen to make a film about Chinese immigrant gold miners, and, without subtitles, the Mandarin dialogue is impenetrable to the New Zealand audience.

Another moment reveals how the McKenzie brothers, in an attempt to revive their flagging fortunes, travel to Tahiti to perfect an early color cinema technology, using native berries to provide the chromatically sensitive chemicals required. However, after some months of preparation, the thirty seconds of test footage is ruined because bare-breasted Tahitian maidens intrude on the shot, leading to a conviction for exhibiting a lewd document upon their return to New Zealand.

What these examples reveal is a complex set of responses to ethnicity and multiple acts of settlement, discourses still in problematic and irresolvable circulation today. The representation of the "dusky maiden," a later feature of such kitsch media as velvet paintings and lounge-music

Colin McKenzie's tests with color footage.

album covers,[17] has clear antecedents in the work of artists as diverse as Robert Louis Stevenson and Paul Gauguin and represents a particular Eurocentric viewpoint similarly critiqued by *Forgotten Silver*'s diegetic audience's inability to recognize the technological triumphs inherent in McKenzie's color footage and synchronous sound experiments.

THE HERESY OF PETER JACKSON

Forgotten Silver is engaged in a clear critique of these myths—of both settler and national identity but also of the very mechanisms of documentary itself. Yet what is clear is that the parody occurs by highlighting and then extending to the breaking point the content of the original myth to reveal its constructedness via this visibility. The offense of *Forgotten Silver*, for the numerous viewers outraged by the hoax, is that it shows up the usually invisible apparatus of ideological construction by its overextended appeal to exactly these mechanisms. Again, it is Žižek whose work provides a way to understand and use this kind of complicated ideological criticism as well as the nature of the response generated to the text itself.

For Žižek, *all* ideological demands are arbitrary in nature, a fact usually hidden by the imperative to comply that typifies these stipulations. However, there can occur moments where the arbitrary imperative is revealed to be exactly that, and this is in those moments where the demand is not just obeyed but, in effect, overobeyed. These moments of overdelivery or overattendance function as a form of heresy because they render visible the ways in which ideological demands are necessarily compromised to function across populations. Thus, as Žižek comments, any ideological imperative *"has* to compromise its founding radical message—and the ultimate 'heretics' are simply those who reject this compromise, sticking to the original message."[18]

Within Žižek's formulation, one becomes a heretic by refusing to compromise on the, at literal face value, demands that are made in ways that would render the original demands possible within a normal social situation. These compromises, Žižek suggests, are usually vital to the functioning of society; they render the original demand possible to fulfill, and they hide the fact that the imperative is constructed and not a natural consequence of one's lived experience. In opposition to this, the heretic refuses to compromise and reveals all. We can therefore consider *Forgotten Silver* to both detail a kind of heresy (that of McKenzie's excessive genius, which is, for those offended by the hoax, a heresy that is easily recuperated into the mythology it is seeking to comment upon) and function as a form of heresy in that it extends the characteristics of national identity myths to and beyond the breaking point. For, as Žižek explains in an earlier text, much more subversive than actually breaking the law is to *"simply* . . . do what is allowed, that is, what the existing order explicitly allows, although it prohibits it at the level of implicit unwritten prohibitions."[19]

In essence, what *Forgotten Silver* does is provide a single figure who confirms all the various mythological requirements ordinarily associated with a variety of postsettlement figures (both fictional and historical). Colin McKenzie—the individual forgotten by history—confirms the relationship between the contemporary society and its antecedents, while Colin McKenzie—the fictional character—overextends the possibilities of national mythmaking by embodying more of these characteristics than could ever be humanly possible.

The question then becomes, how do we know that *Forgotten Silver* had this effect on its audience? It must be mentioned that not all responses to the broadcast were negative, but it is to the negative responses that we turn first. In relation to the points made so far, the criticisms themselves can be gathered along particular themes. A number of these orient their anger along the lines of the mockumentary itself, insofar as they are offended by the relationship between documentary form and fictional content. As one irate viewer noted,[20]

> The credibility of TVNZ and its documentary makers has gone out the window, and that is a pity, for they have produced and screened some fine films. But more than that, TVNZ has created a hoax, and, in effect, has used public funds . . . fraudulently. For that reason it should be called to account.[21]

Another expressed "disappointment that so much talent, technical resources and public funds should have been used with the sole purpose of a hoax,"[22] while a third noted that "if this film was, in fact, made with the support of the New Zealand Film Commission . . . as was claimed in the credits, then I think it was an outrageous waste of my money."[23]

The perceived misuse of public monies, with funding for *Forgotten Silver* coming in part from a national television-licensing fee, is a common thread to these complaints. When this is coupled with the fact that *Forgotten Silver* played out on *Montana Sunday Theatre*—a prestigious Sunday-evening prime-time series ordinarily dedicated to showcasing high-end drama—and was further supported by expert testimonial from such experts as Leonard Maltin, Sam Neill, and Harvey Weinstein, we can see that the documentary uses both interior diegetic techniques and extrafilmic associations to locate and stabilize its claims to truth. In contrast, what these specific complaints reveal is the clear sense of loyalty that these members of the viewing public feel toward the Reithian impulses that drove the development of local television content in this country from its earliest days. Here television can serve multiple purposes (for example, as Lord Reith would have it, to "educate, inform, entertain") but never to deceive: fiction is fiction, and documentary must necessarily always and only reflect the "truth."

However, aside from these outraged responses, another set of concerns emerges; these respond to the content of the text itself and the manner

McKenzie's "Lost City."

with which *Forgotten Silver*'s "tongue-in-cheek tribute to Kiwi ingenuity"
is experienced as a wholesale attack on those ideas that go to make up this
particular form of national identity. One viewer wrote,

> As one of the "gullible" who viewed *Forgotten Silver*, I feel I was not deceived
> or cheated at having been victim of such an elaborate ruse. But I am sad-
> dened that Colin McKenzie is not part of my heritage as a New Zealander,
> and that the display of determination and spirit was not more than a figment
> of imagination in the guise of a documentary.[24]

Another lamented,

> Afterwards the radio was crammed with people wanting to express their
> delight at the extraordinary story that in a brief 70 minutes gave us a hero,
> gave us an extraordinary past and also shows "proof" that we were the first
> nation to fly. [Signed] I'm Not Laughing[25]

Finally, another noted,

> I admit to being completely taken in, and found the phenomenon of McKen-
> zie truly inspirational—worthy to stand alongside Rutherford and others in
> New Zealand's legend. I can't express my disappointment at having lost a
> genius and gained another "clever" film-maker.[26]

For these authors, among a number of others, the overwhelming sense
of disappointment comes with the fact that Colin McKenzie turned out
not to be true when, because he conformed to the expectations set up by
the presence of these mythological structures, he so readily appeared to
be a viable candidate for mythologizing. But, perhaps more than this, we
see reflected in these complaints the idea that because *Forgotten Silver*
used these myths in its fiction, the myths themselves have been revealed
as fictions. While not explicitly claimed, it is hard not to conclude otherwise when one letter writer laments,

> If this sort of thing is allowed to develop where will it end? From now on
> anything that the media produce, whether it be by word or film will be
> regarded with disbelief. This is a sad state of affairs when we can't believe
> what we read, see or hear.[27]

CONCLUSION

As noted, not all the responses to *Forgotten Silver* were negative. TVNZ,
the state broadcaster involved, received a large number of positive comments and enquiries immediately after the screening, and New Zealand's

national newspapers featured many letters to the editor that were much more positive (including a number from believers who were pleased to have their suspicions of such a figure confirmed or who offered extra information regarding the family McKenzie). However, in responding to the negative criticism from public and media professionals, both Botes and Jackson offer interesting comments that, in the light of the discussion presented here, reveal exactly the ways in which the heretical text can upset or interrupt ideological processes. In a postbroadcast article, published again in the television listings weekly *The New Zealand Listener*, Jackson offers no apology, believing that "the people who dumped on them [Botes and Jackson] are the same people who would have dumped on McKenzie had he been real."[28] Instead, he explains,

> There's a lot of Colin McKenzie's out there, and a lot of backyard people are nobbled in New Zealand. They're nobbled by the "go out and get a proper job" brigade. And the negative reaction to our programme seems a very good example of that."[29]

With these comments, as Conrich and Smith make clear, Jackson and Botes

> identify with the subject of their film not only by way of their shared professions but also in the way in which they experience an under-valuation of their originality, innovations and skills.[30]

Thus, the parody of these settler mythologies becomes, in its way, a quiet celebration of and identification with them when embodied by the perpetrators of the hoax. Therefore, it may very well be the case that "all national identity formation is to some extent a scam,"[31] but the scam works only for as long as it remains hidden or, at the very least, not commented on. *Forgotten Silver* instead reveals that the work in progress of mythologizing that constitutes any national identity is itself based entirely on conceits that are as fictional as they are ideological. Jackson's comments illustrate that, perhaps disingenuously, the filmmakers perceived the documentary's parody of settler myths to be in fact an homage to them, which may or may not be true but which certainly demonstrates the fact that even if Colin McKenzie is false, the desire to continue the possibilities of such a figure remain firmly in place, both for the text's creators and for the program's various audiences.

If there is any irony in the postreception furor surrounding the broadcast of *Forgotten Silver*, it lies in the fact that the "imagined community" disassembled by the parody of the text forms anew and effective in its response to the insult felt. In this fashion, *Forgotten Silver* calls into being a national identity for its offended viewers through the act of calling that identity into question, proof that the tropes of postsettlement (white) identity are both as effective and—for these viewers—as necessary as ever.

NOTES

1. Costa Botes, letter to the editor, *Otago Daily Times*, November 10, 1995.
2. L. McLauchlan, letter to the editor, *The New Zealand Listener*, November 25, 1995.
3. Costa Botes and Peter Jackson, *Forgotten Silver* (New Zealand: Wingnut Films, 1995).
4. Peter Jackson, quoted in D. Welch, "Heavenly Features," *The New Zealand Listener*, October 28, 1995, 32.
5. D. Welch, "Heavenly Features."
6. A perfect example of the kind of climate that surrounded *Forgotten Silver* can be seen in Steve Pennells's article "Cinema's Holy Grail" (*Sunday Star Times*, February 14, 2010, C5), which details the 2005 discovery, in New Zealand's National Film Archive, of a near-complete hand-tinted print of F. W. Murneau's *Metropolis* (1927)—a print that, due to inadequate censorship, contained eleven scenes previously thought lost.
7. Readers interested in a thorough examination of *Forgotten Silver*'s techniques are directed to Craig Hight and Jane Roscoe, "*Forgotten Silver*: A New Zealand Television Hoax and Its Audience," in *F Is for Phony: Fake Documentary and Truth's Undoing*, ed. Alexandra Juhasz and Jesse Lerner (Minneapolis: University of Minnesota Press, 2006).
8. Ian Conrich and Roy Smith, "Fools Gold: New Zealand's *Forgotten Silver*, Myth and National Identity," *Studies in New Zealand Cinema*, ed. Ian Conrich (London: Kakapo Books, 2009), 139.
9. Peter Limbrick, "The Flotsam and Jetsam of Film History: *Hei Tiki* and Postcolonial Rearticulations, *Journal of Visual Culture* 6 (2007): 247.
10. Mark Williams, "A Waka on the Wild Side: Nationalism and Its Discontents in Some Recent New Zealand Films," in *Contemporary New Zealand Cinema: From New Wave to Blockbusters*, ed. Ian Conrich and Stuart Murray (London: I. B. Taurus, 2008), 183–84.
11. Davina Thornley, "'White, Brown or 'Coffee'? Revisioning Race in Tamahori's *Once Were Warriors*," *Film Criticism* 25, no. 3 (2001–2002): 22–36.
12. Hight and Roscoe, "*Forgotten Silver*," 171–86.
13. Stanley Kauffmann, "On Films," review, *The New Republic*, November 3, 1997, 28–29.
14. Hight and Roscoe, "*Forgotten Silver*," 178.
15. Williams, "A Waka on the Wild Side," 183.
16. Although it may be the case that, with this "tongue-in-cheek" text, a lighthearted exploration of Maori identity in a text exploring white settler anxiety would have far too problematic an aspect to include. It should also be noted that the European ethnicity of the filmmakers does give them some license over the

myths they choose to parody, even as it renders other identities (particularly indigenous identities) potentially off-limits.

17. See the award-winning documentary *Velvet Dreams* (1997) by Sima Urale. Excerpts can be seen at http://www.nzonscreen.com/title/velvet-dreams-1997.

18. Slavoj Žižek, *The Fragile Absolute; or, Why Is the Christian Legacy Worth Fighting For?* (London: Verso, 2000), 8.

19. Slavoj Žižek, *On Belief: Thinking in Action* (London: Routledge, 2001), 147.

20. The University of Waikato has gathered a selection of letters to the editor of various daily newspapers, and these are divided into three categories: negative, positive, believers. The archive can be accessed at http://www.waikato.ac.nz/film/mock-doc/fs.shtml.

21. D. E. Drake, letter to the editor, *Timaru Herald*, November 1, 1995.

22. A. McCambridge, letter to the editor, *Timaru Herald*, November 1, 1995.

23. J. Hoffmann, letter to the editor, *Nelson Evening Mail*, November 3, 1995.

24. O. Rathgen, letter to the editor, *Timaru Herald*, November 6, 1995.

25. Letter to the editor, *TV Guide*, November 10, 1995. The author is referring to the story of Richard Pearse, who, local legend has it, achieved powered flight on March 31, 1903, nine months before the Wright brothers.

26. G. A. De Forest, letter to the editor, *The New Zealand Listener*, November 25, 1995.

27. Rathgen, letter to the editor.

28. G. Chapple, "Gone, but Not Forgotten," *The New Zealand Listener*, November 25, 1995, 26.

29. Jackson, quoted in Chapple, "Gone, but Not Forgotten," 26.

30. Conrich and Smith, "Fools Gold," 147.

31. Ruth Brown, *Cultural Questions: New Zealand Identity in a Transnational Age* (London: Kakapo Books, 1997), 3.

8

"That's Not Zen!" Mocking Ethnographic Film in Doris Dörrie's *Enlightenment Guaranteed*

Heather Merle Benbow

The popular German filmmaker and writer Doris Dörrie is well known for her ironic interpretations of film genres such as the romantic comedy (*Men*, 1985; *Nobody Loves Me*, 1994), the road movie (*Am I Beautiful?* 1998), and film noir (*Happy Birthday*, 1991).[1] She also has a long-standing interest in Japan and Buddhism (*Nobody Loves Me*, *Der Fischer und seine Frau*, 2005; *How to Cook Your Life*, 2007). *Enlightenment Guaranteed* (2000), a feature film set in Germany and Japan, appears both to draw on her interest in Buddhist themes and to represent an emerging concern with the documentary genre.[2] The film uses documentary elements such as digital video cameras, the casting of nonactors, a lack of nondiegetic sound and music, and ethnographic-style observation of daily rituals. Described by Dörrie as an example of cinéma vérité, the film ostensibly documents a journey undertaken by two German brothers, the feng shui consultant Gustav and Uwe, an unpretentious kitchen salesman. Gustav, a practicing Buddhist, is unexpectedly joined on a much-anticipated retreat to a Zen monastery in Japan by Uwe, who has recently been abandoned by his wife and children. The two key actors—Uwe Ochsenknecht and Gustav-Peter Wöhler—are known in the film by their own first names. The monks in the monastery, as well as the actors in most of the other Japanese locations, are amateurs, and Dörrie has said that the crew was often able to film in Japan without declaring it was making a feature film, due to the ubiquitousness of the video camera in Japan.[3] After making a documentary film on digital camera with cameraman Hans Karl Hu, Dörrie says that she became interested in making a feature film with the same equipment. She then teamed up again with Hu for *Enlightenment Guaranteed*, a film that she says was possible thanks only to the mobility of the digital camera and the small cast and crew, which enabled her to film what I suggest are ethnographically styled scenes in an actual Zen temple in Japan.[4]

According to Roscoe and Hight, mock documentaries are fictional films that "appropriate documentary codes and conventions in order to represent a fictional subject."[5] The extent to which Dörrie was inspired by factual filmmaking is apparent when she describes the filmmaking process:

> The actors had their biographies, in part they also had approximate guidelines for their dialogue. For example, we were at a Japanese train station, with seven minutes to change trains, and an old Japanese woman sat down next to Uwe Ochsenknecht and Gustav-Peter Wöhler. And I asked the two of them to speak very sensually about their memories of their mother. And this old Japanese woman became a metaphor for the mother, for transience. We worked this way all the time. We always had the opportunity to look: What comes to us courtesy of reality?[6]

Dörrie describes here a filmmaking process in which the fictional story is informed and shaped by encounters with reality, with real people. As primarily a fiction filmmaker, Dörrie uses the flexible tools of the documentary mode to gain access to a certain reality and to obtain inspiration from real events and encounters with real people.

While Roscoe and Hight insist that what they prefer to call the mock documentary is "still too underdeveloped to endure any exhaustive categorization,"[7] they outline three degrees of "mock-docness," "which are derived especially from the type of relationship which a text constructs with factual discourse."[8] These degrees range from texts in which the main intention is to "parody some aspect of popular culture," using documentary codes and conventions to do so, through to texts that above all provide a critique of the documentary mode itself.[9] Dörrie's film must sit somewhere in the middle of Roscoe and Hight's spectrum, for the film contains a good-humored critique of the fetishization of all things Oriental in German popular culture, as well as critical comment on the ethnographic mode of documentary observation. On one hand, the film critiques Gustav's Orientalist longings and New Age posturing, which is only interested in an ancient, ostensibly untouched and authentic Eastern culture.[10] On the other, the protagonists' reflexive use of a digital video camera disrupts the expected dynamic of Western observer and Oriental observed. This chapter situates *Enlightenment Guaranteed* relative to ethnographic film practices, showing that the film has a precedent particularly in critical or reflexive approaches to ethnographic film. It suggests that the film can best be regarded not just as a mockumentary but specifically as a mock ethnography, a fictional film that undertakes a critique of ethnographic film practices.

ENLIGHTENMENT GUARANTEED AND ETHNOGRAPHIC FILM

Enlightenment Guaranteed documents the encounter of its two German protagonists with Japanese culture. Asked why she sent the two brothers to Japan, Dörrie responded,

> To send them to another planet! In Spain, we can all more or less understand the menu. But in Japan you don't know anything anymore. There the rug is pulled out from under you. And that is of course another principle of Zen, around which my story is conceived: To lose everything, to give everything up, to become homeless.[11]

Although Japan is described here as "another planet," this is not simply evidence of a Eurocentric worldview, for the encounter with cultural difference is conceived of as a destabilization of *Western* identity ("the rug is pulled out from under you"). This comment is echoed in a scene immediately after Uwe and Gustav lose each other on a busy intersection. Uwe is filming people on the streets of Tokyo and comments from behind the camera, "Somehow, among all these Japanese, I feel like I'm on another planet." The comment precedes a jump cut, which reverses the subject of the camera's gaze. Uwe has turned the camera on himself and is spinning on the spot. "Everything is spinning," he says into the camera. This scene is indicative of a reflexive approach to the documentary mode and of a critical stance toward the Eurocentric values of traditional ethnography. Thus, we might begin to regard the film specifically as a mock ethnography. A brief consideration of changing conceptions of ethnographic film will help us to locate Dörrie's feature film within a tradition of critical, or reflexive, ethnographic film practices.

In his seminal critical work *Ethnographic Film*, Heider urges us to "think of *ethnographic* as a continuously variable property of many films."[12] In some ways, he suggests, all films are somewhat "ethnographic," for they are all in some sense about people. More strictly, the principles of ethnography toward which ethnographic films should aspire are enunciated by Heider as follows: ethnography is "a way of making a detailed description and analysis of human behavior based on a long-term observational study on the spot"; it "relates specific observed behavior to cultural norms" and strives for "holism"; that is, "things and events must be understood in their social and cultural context. From this principle come the

Gustav, confused.

related dicta of 'whole bodies,' 'whole people,' and 'whole acts.' They emphasize the ethnographic need to present bodies, personalities and behavior in context."[13] Dörrie's film can be assessed against these ethnographic
aims and found to be at least somewhat ethnographic in Heiderian terms.
The film involves two layers of ethnographic observation. First, there
are the scenes filmed by Hu, both in Germany before Gustav and Uwe
depart for Japan and during their Japanese journey. These include long
scenes observing cultural ritual, such as the opening sequence juxtaposing the chaos of Uwe's family life and the tranquility of Gustav's morning
meditation: the camera lingers over the breakfast table as Uwe berates his
wife, then cross-cuts from this noise and conflict to the contrived peace
and quiet of Gustav's solitude. We are privy to the banal daily routines of
the two brothers—Uwe's morning jog, followed by a fortifying cigarette;
Gustav's silent train commute with his wife, Uli—shot in relatively long
takes devoid of nondiegetic sound or a musical soundtrack. The scenes
in the Japanese monastery are even more recognizably ethnographic in
their lingering observation of the rituals of a functioning monastery and
temple.[14] Interestingly, however, the scenes shot in Japan fail to provide
the cultural context expected of ethnographic film that would enable the
viewer to understand the rituals she or he is observing. We are dealing
here with a kind of ethnography that frustrates any pretensions to really "know" the other. Moreover, in both contexts, the film transgresses
Heider's dictum of "holism" by creating empathy with certain characters
via close-ups, most noticeably in a lingering shot of Uwe's distressed but
silent wife and the countenance of a similarly frustrated wife in Uwe's

Searching for enlightenment through meditation.

kitchen display suite. These close-ups, which provide the viewer with an insight that Uwe lacks, represent a more obviously fictional approach to filmmaking. The second layer of ethnographic observation includes those scenes filmed by the brothers themselves, distinguished from the rest by appearing as though the viewer were looking through the viewfinder of the video camera (a red "record" button flashes; the elapsed time is displayed; the image is grainy). This second, "reflexive" layer of observation is discussed in detail later.

Crucially, Heider distinguishes the goals of fictional filmmaking from those of intentionally ethnographic film because of the latter's "goal of truth":

> The conventions of cinematographic honesty are quite different. Cinema has developed primarily as a medium for imaginative statements in which questions of scientific-type accuracy are often irrelevant. Much of what is taught in film schools is how to translate or distort reality for aesthetic effect. These techniques include selective composition of shots, staging acted scenes, editing for continuity effect, and utilizing sound recorded in other contexts. Some of these reality-distorting effects are inevitable in even the most scrupulously ethnographic films.[15]

Dörrie purposively uses numerous "reality-distorting effects" in her film, particularly in the way that scenes are edited suggestively—the contrast established between the two brothers, Gustav's adverse reaction to an encounter with a gay client. Rather than a strictly "scientific-type accuracy," Dörrie is supplying an imaginative narrative, but she borrows extensively from ethnographic conventions and uses "reality" as an inspiration for her story: "Usually I have to try to recreate reality. So I come into an empty room and then try to create reality. This way, though—with this little digital camera, without a huge crew—I sneak back into reality with fiction."[16] While it has been suggested that there is a certain technological determinism in some accounts of the emergence of direct cinema and cinéma vérité,[17] Dörrie emphasizes the importance of the portable digital video camera for this particular film. The camera enables her to "sneak into reality" with her fictional narrative.

CRITIQUING ETHNOGRAPHIC FILM

Enlightenment Guaranteed doesn't entirely adhere to Heider's prescriptions for ethnographic film. Instead, it is indebted to the genre's "reflexive turn,"[18] which sought to interrogate the Eurocentric values of ethnography. Beattie explains how these values influenced the practice of ethnographic filmmakers:

> The tradition of the ethnographic film, like ethnography itself, is deeply imbued with the "us" and "them"—self and Other—dichotomy and its attendant differential relations of power. Throughout most of its history from the time of Regnault, the ethnographic film has been constructed as a representational practice in which the culture of the non-Westernized "Other" has been treated as a form of scientific datum subjected to the objectifying methods of Western ethnographic science.[19]

This objectifying dynamic has been critiqued and commented on by filmmakers in various ways. Reflexive practices in ethnographic film are now as common as the postcolonial-style critique described earlier. Dörrie's film draws on these reflexive documentary practices. In particular, her film would seem to have an important precursor in ethnographic film, which it would be instructive at this point to consider in some detail. Dennis O'Rourke's critical ethnographic film *Cannibal Tours* (1987) follows a group of German, Italian, and North American tourists as they travel along the Sepik River in Papua New Guinea in the ship *Melanesian Explorer*.[20] This film shares with Dörrie's a concern to critique the tourist's gaze as an expression of the self–other dichotomy inherent in the tourism experience. The similar treatment of these themes in the two films shows that Dörrie's fiction film has a pedigree in the narratives of critical ethnographic film and that it can rightly be regarded therefore as a mock ethnography.

Dennis O'Rourke is an Australian documentary maker perhaps best known for *The Good Woman of Bangkok* (1991). He lived and worked in Papua New Guinea for five years in the postindependence period. In *Cannibal Tours*, he follows a group of tourists visiting the country for the first time, looking for an encounter with people they assume to be living in a state of nature. The film begins with the epigram, which sets the tone for this critical ethnography: "There is nothing so strange in a strange land as the stranger who comes to visit it." Although the tourists have come to look at and photograph the Papua New Guineans, it is the tourists who are actually the subject of the film's ethnographic gaze. The tourists have a romanticized attitude to the Papua New Guineans. Two Italian men on the ship discuss whether the Papua New Guineans might not have a better way of life than Europeans, who are not so close to nature. The Papua New Guineans, one of the men asserts, are happy, well provided for, with no worries. This comment is followed by a cut to a shot of the hardworking crew of the *Melanesian Explorer*, all Papua New Guineans, providing a contrast to the idealized picture painted by the Italian tourists. This juxtaposition suggests that these men are simply not acknowledged by the tourists as Papua New Guineans, for they are not living in this Edenic state of nature. Similarly, we see an American woman photographing a Papua New Guinean woman and children in traditional dress. Another Papua New Guinean woman in Western dress, who is standing nearby, is asked to move out of the shot to preserve its authenticity.

For their part, the Papua New Guineans are cynical about the tourists' need to take photographs of everything they perceive as exotic. "We sit here confused while they take pictures of everything! . . . We don't understand why these foreigners take pictures," says one old man. The spiritual dimension of Papua New Guinean culture is yet another commodity to be captured by Western visitors, first the missionaries and the colonizers, now the tourists. The locals charge $2 per person for the tourists to enter and photograph the spirit house. But the building has long since been plundered, a local man explains: "All of the sacred objects, the Germans took them, the English and Australians took them . . . everything." In an essay on the making of *Cannibal Tours*, O'Rourke writes that the film is about

> the whole notion of "the primitive" and "the other," the fascination with primitivism in Western culture and the wrong-headed nostalgia for the innocence of Eden . . . this nostalgia is inseparable from our pessimism, religious, sexual and otherwise. I believe that we all have a particular longing to be elsewhere, to be alive in a timeless past. And the film is about voyeurism and the act of photography itself.[21]

This is the message of this critical ethnography, and it is a self-consciously crafted narrative. O'Rourke makes it clear that in telling this story, he creates "characters" out of the film's subjects:

> All of these real tourists are, in part, invented characters and they should not be vilified because of what they reveal about us. This can be understood by accepting that all my films are not so much "documentary" but "fiction,"

because they don't purport to be the objective truth. In the act of first imagining a film and then photographing and editing it, all my subjects lose their authenticity as individuals and become manipulated characters in the drama that is created.[22]

Similar techniques to those of O'Rourke's fictionalized ethnography are deployed in Dörrie's ethnographic fiction; both films craft a critical narrative about Western cultural consumption by observing a Western touristic pilgrimage. Both films disrupt the expected power dynamic of the Western observer and the Oriental observed. As O'Rourke writes, "the voyeuristic experience in tourism works both ways. On the Sepik River, where tourism is a relatively new phenomenon, the natives still do experience the thrill of looking at the tourists."[23] O'Rourke's lengthy interviews with the locals show us how the locals look back at the tourists, sometimes in anger, as in a lengthy scene when a woman complains that the tourists don't buy her handicrafts. "You white people!" she shouts. "You have all the money! . . . You've got money—not us 'backward' people." Because of this economic disparity, O'Rourke is skeptical of the tourism experience. He rejects the idea of tourism as "a dialogue between cultures" as a "myth," also because the "encounters with the people who are the culture are too short—squeezed into the three-week annual holiday and the 'free days for shopping' before going home."[24] The touristic commodification of a way of life, of "the actual act of living of a group of people,"[25] can only result in a "doomed search for meaning."[26] O'Rourke's film depicts a failed spiritual pilgrimage. Moreover, as Beattie observes of *Cannibal Tours*, as the tourists' journey progresses, "the roles ascribed to 'them' and 'us' are inverted; the villagers are astute and pragmatic, and the tourists become 'savages.'"[27] This inversion is most evident for Beattie when at the end of the film, the tourists have their faces painted and pose on the ship for photos. They dance around wearing the various accoutrements they have acquired, such as jewelry and headdresses. For Beattie, this is "an embarrassing charade based on [the] notion of 'the primitive.'"[28]

ENLIGHTENMENT GUARANTEED AS MOCK ETHNOGRAPHY

Dörrie's film similarly demonstrates the failure of the touristic project and the disrupted dynamic of self and eroticized Other. *Enlightenment Guaranteed* foregrounds the brothers' use of the video camera, placing them in the role of reflexive ethnographers, for they film themselves and their reactions to Japan. From the outset, though, the Japanese refuse to be objectified. A shot of a Japanese man with a video camera on the airplane to

Modeling divine peace.

Tokyo suggests immediately that the Japanese are already looking back, that they will not be perplexed by the camera-wielding tourist. Similar to O'Rourke's naive tourists, the brothers cannot foresee to what extent their cultural consumption will be reciprocated. Gustav, the consumer of Oriental wisdom and culture, will, along with his brother, experience this dynamic of cultural consumption from the other side.

In the first part of the film, set in Germany, we see that Gustav styles himself as an expert in matters Oriental: he practices mediation; he works as a feng shui consultant; and his apartment reflects his cosmopolitan interests, with its indoor fountain, miniature Zen garden, rice-paper screen, and pictures of children from the Third World.[29] When Uwe joins Gustav on his pilgrimage to Japan, Gustav takes it upon himself to educate him in the ways of Zen Buddhism. He earnestly tells Uwe a parable about a monk in a cave, only to find that Uwe has fallen asleep before the end of the story. On the plane, as Uwe is feeling miserable about the loss of his wife and children, Gustav coolly hands his brother a book of Zen teachings. Uwe reads aloud: "To live is to suffer. Thanks, Gustav." He returns the book unimpressed, and Gustav smiles condescendingly: "That's the first precious truth from Buddha. And that's the good news! It means namely, that it's completely normal to suffer." Pointing out the airplane window, he says that Uwe is like the sky and the clouds are his worries and fears: "But you don't recognize it. It's something you just have to practice." At the hotel in Tokyo, Gustav continues to showcase his expertise, persuading Uwe to leave his money, passport, and air ticket in his hotel room because "here in Japan, nothing gets stolen."

When the brothers leave the hotel, though, Gustav's self-assurance and Oriental expertise begin to unravel. The first phase of his would-be spiritual journey turns out to be an encounter with the noisy metropolis of Tokyo, represented by shots of Japanese chatting into mobile phones, the auditory assault of talking advertisements and pachinko parlors, and the visual pollution of neon signs. Along with Uwe, Gustav quickly slips into the role of the crass tourist, getting drunk in a bar and singing loudly in German with chopsticks stuck on his nose—all recorded by the brothers themselves on their video camera. The contrast of their drunken behavior with Gustav's lofty intentions is emphasized when he shouts into the camera, "Tomorrow it's off to the monastery!"

When the brothers lose their hotel, have their credit cards swallowed by a bank machine, and spend their last money on a taxi ride to nowhere, Gustav reaches for his Zen book for inspiration. "It's about becoming homeless," he reads aloud, unconvinced. "If you feel well in your own skin, you'll feel well anywhere." When Uwe lightheartedly throws his few remaining coins into a slot machine ("I've simply let go. That's how it is."), Gustav becomes angry: "I'm tired. I'm thirsty. I want to go home. [*screaming*] I'm fed up!" Like a petulant tourist, Gustav wants to go to the German embassy and be ushered home. The Zen advice to become homeless has become a reality, and the two men crawl into cardboard boxes, like so many of Tokyo's homeless, and spend their first night in Japan there. When Uwe and Gustav lose each other the next day on a busy pedestrian crossing, they feel their foreignness all the more keenly. Uwe—filming his own reactions—observes that he feels as though he's on a different planet. Gustav seeks solace in his Zen book, but the aphorisms provide little comfort: "Only the melon knows nothing of the brisk wind in the early morning. [*looks up confused*] Was it the blossom, the fruit, that fell into the moisture from summer trees? . . . To be desperate is very bad. You lose your dignity." Gustav's putative expertise is failing him in Tokyo because the city doesn't correspond to his romanticized image of Japan.

Before he finds his way to the object of his Orientalist imagining—the monastery on a provincial hilltop—Gustav learns that, as O'Rourke writes of *Cannibal Tours*, "the voyeuristic experience in tourism works both ways."[30] At his lowest ebb (busking in the Tokyo subway), he meets Anica, a German dressed in a traditional dirndl, and after a reunion with Uwe, the two brothers go to work with Anica in the Münchener Hofbräuhaus, a chain restaurant with a Bavarian theme. The brothers, dressed in lederhosen and suspenders, are mere bit players in a Japanese performance of a commodified Germanness. On a stage at one end of the dining room, Japanese perform a parody of German identity with randomly Germanic objects, such as a Swiss horn, a steering wheel, and an accordion. This Occidentalizing performance sets the scene for the ethnographic-style sequences that follow when the brothers travel to the monastery. The audience—and the main characters—sees here that the Western gaze is reflected back at them in Japan. This commodifying, stereotypical take on German identity disrupts the observer–other dynamic prevalent in conventional ethnography. Moreover, the brothers have little direct access to the Japanese, further hindering the ethnographic project. For example, after the Hofbräuhaus stage show, Uwe shows Anica video footage of a palm reading done for him by an old Japanese woman when he was lost and wandering the streets of Tokyo. The film doesn't provide subtitles for the Japanese dialogue, and the viewer, like Uwe, is dependent on Anica for an approximate interpretation of the woman's wisdom.

Only after this sobering experience, with a little money in their pockets, can the spiritual part of the journey begin. Even here, though, Gustav's expertise is of little use. He struggles with the daily routines, the cleaning, and the long hours of meditation. Having boasted to his brother that mediation helps one find oneself and that it works for him, he initially attempts to romanticize the difficulties he experiences in the monastery: "Meditation was pure hell this morning. Really . . . really beautiful in terms of the energy in the room. But my leg, my left leg, it hurt like hell. . . . Everything hurts." The two brothers work through their experiences when alone in their room. They film each other in a kind of video diary format, practicing the skills they are learning, such as wrapping and unwrapping the bowls and utensils used for eating. In a striking parallel to O'Rourke's tourists on the *Melanesian Explorer*, Gustav performs a farcical Oriental dance in his room

Uwe, lost in the city.

for Uwe's camera. While Uwe provides a soundtrack of Beijing opera–like sounds, Gustav prances, bows, and preens pretending to speak Japanese. The would-be Zen Buddhist and cultural expert is here revealed as little better than a crass tourist of the kind in *Cannibal Tours*. He may have prepared for this spiritual journey, but it seems, as O'Rourke writes of the touristic search for meaning, doomed to failure. The difficulty of any kind of meaningful interaction at the monastery is underlined when Gustav tries to repeat to the camera a parable he has heard from the abbot about snow on the well. He makes several failed attempts to recite the parable but, like the Zen phrases from his book, cannot make it yield any meaning. When each brother has a private audience with the abbot, he is addressed in Japanese. No subtitles are provided, and a non-Japanese-speaking audience must experience, like the main characters, the frustration of not understanding. As an ethnography of the Japanese, of life in the Zen monastery, the film thwarts expectations. It fails to provide the all-important context necessary in a conventional ethnography. Neither the main characters nor the viewer gain particularly significant insights into modern Japan or the putatively traditional way of life in the monastery. The viewer is dependent on the mystified Uwe and Gustav for an explanation of the monastic rituals.

We are dealing here with a critical approach to the practices of ethnographic film. This approach is indebted to postcolonial revisions of the ethnographic project, which have regarded the discipline of ethnography as part of the broader Western colonialist enterprise. This critique has led to some self-examination by ethnographic filmmakers, as Beattie explains:

> One response to [the postcolonial critique of ethnography] has been the rise of what documentary film scholar Michael Renov refers to as "domestic ethnography" in which the practice of participant observation abandons cross-cultural representation and focuses on the observer's own culture. . . . Such works function as a form of autobiography.[31]

Dörrie's film abounds in such domestic and autobiographical sequences, including Uwe's filming of his children at the breakfast table and the scenes filmed by Gustav and Uwe on the video camera in Japan, many of which take the form of self-shot confessionals performed with an outstretched arm. Confronted by the limits of their cultural knowledge and the impossibility of a meaningful cultural exchange with those whose lifestyle they have fetishized, the protagonists reflect instead on themselves and their responses to these limitations. Gustav and Uwe are also the unwitting subjects of the metanarrative told by Hu's camera. Significantly, Gustav and Uwe are not aware of Hu's camera, unlike several young Japanese men who, in a scene shot at a train station as the brothers wait for a connection, look straight into the camera, smiling. This suggests again that Uwe and Gustav are the real subjects of this mock ethnography. The Japanese, like the viewer, are the amused observers of their existential and material travails. The inclusion of this shot is a wink to the viewer, emphasizing that this is a mock ethnography, a fictional construct placed in a documentary context. This shared insight with the viewer represents the kind of in-joke that, as Roscoe and Hight note, is prevalent in the mockumentary form, and it presumes that its viewer is a sophisticated media consumer:

> To varying degrees, the audience is expected to be conscious of the fictionality of the text; to "get the jokes" and to appreciate the intention behind the appropriation of documentary codes and conventions. To engage with the text at this level does require the viewer to watch it "as if it were a documentary," but, nevertheless, to do so in the full knowledge that it is a *fictional* text. The mock-documentary addresses a knowing and media-literate viewer.[32]

In *Enlightenment Guaranteed*, Dörrie offers her viewers two layers of critique. First, at the level of the film's narrative is the critique of the Orientalizing discourses in contemporary Germany, which express themselves as commodification of Eastern spirituality, and the touristic project. When Gustav's knowledge of Eastern culture is shown to be superficial, viewers are prompted to reflect on the fetishization of Eastern culture in contemporary Germany. Dörrie is alert to the cultural consumption that expresses itself in the "urgent project"[33] of the Western tourist, armed with his video camera. Second, Dörrie critiques ethnographic filmic modes as a process of othering. The film mocks ethnographic observation by turning the camera on the German tourists. They become ethnographers of their own way of life. Like O'Rourke's European tourists in Papua New Guinea, Gustav and Uwe are involved in "the commodification of the actual act of living of a group of people."[34] But—more so than O'Rourke's tourists, who remain ignorant—the German brothers find that those they have come to observe are actually looking back and that their own culture can be subjected to farcical appropriation.

CONCLUSION

While it co-opts some ethnographic elements, *Enlightenment Guaranteed* frustrates any desire to know the foreign culture it depicts. Instead of offering the expected excursion into Japanese culture, it can give insight only into the lives and attitudes of its German protagonists. The periods of ethnographic observation in Japan lead not to any particular revelations about the Japanese but to personal epiphanies for the two German tourists. Uwe reaches a peaceful acceptance of his wife's actions, and Gustav outs himself as a gay man to his understanding brother, revealing the significance of his earlier encounter with a gay feng shui client. Back in Tokyo, the brothers recall with a disproportionate nostalgia the rituals of the monastery, which they have become accustomed to over just five days. They remain outsiders, even back in Tokyo. Looking around bemused, Uwe asks, "Where are all these people going?" The focus here is entirely on the brothers and their personal journey.

The final scene finds them accepting the Zen exhortation to become homeless, and it illustrates their isolation from their Japanese context. It is nighttime, and they are sitting in the tent that was Uwe's response to their night in the cardboard boxes. Inside the illuminated yellow tent, they chant sutras in Japanese, an empty ritual perhaps, for neither they nor the German viewers can presumably understand the text. As the credits roll and the camera pulls out in a series of widening shots, we see that they have erected their tent on a tennis court and that the court is being used by some unperturbed Japanese tennis players. Dörrie's German tourists might feel deeply changed by their one-week visit to Japan, but they have not really emerged from their own cultural bubble. They have acquired some personal insights, but Japan remains for them another planet.

NOTES

1. *Enlightenment Guaranteed*, dir. Doris Dörrie (2000).

2. Dörrie's latest film, called *How to Cook Your Life* (2007), is a documentary about a Buddhist chef.

3. Hartwig Tegeler, "'Frei Wie Nie Zuvor.' Doris Dörrie Über Zen, Die Digitale Kamera Und Ihren Neuen Film 'Erleuchtung Garantiert,'" *Morgenwelt: Magazin für Wissenschaft und Kultur*, January 17, 2000.

4. Tegeler, "'Frei Wie Nie Zuvor.'"

5. Jane Roscoe and Craig Hight, *Faking It: Mock-Documentary and the Subversion of Factuality* (Manchester: Manchester University Press, 2001), 2.

6. Tegeler, "'Frei Wie Nie Zuvor.'" Translations of the Tegeler interview with Dörrie and of dialogue from the film are my own.

7. Roscoe and Hight, *Faking It*, 5.

8. Roscoe and Hight, *Faking It*, 64.

9. Roscoe and Hight, *Faking It*, 68.

10. Edward Said, *Orientalism* (1978; repr., London: Penguin, 2003), 52–53.

11. Tegeler, "'Frei Wie Nie Zuvor.'"

12. Karl G. Heider, *Ethnographic Film* (Austin: University of Texas Press, 1976), 3.

13. Heider, *Ethnographic Film*, 6–7.

14. The style of the film can also be understood in terms of Nichols's observational mode, described by Beattie as follows: "The observational mode . . . is closely linked to developments in camera and sound recording technologies during the late 1950s. These developments culminated in portable 16mm cameras and portable sound recording equipment synchronized to the camera. Liberated from

the restraints of the studio, the camera was free to simultaneously record image and sound in almost any location. The impression of unmediated observation achieved within the mode is informed in the editing phase in which footage is assembled with respect to temporal and spatial continuities, eschewing voice-over commentary, intertitles, non-diegetic sound effects and a complementary music track. The result of these practices is an attempt to replicate an immediate 'slice of life' which is presented in lived or real time." Keith Beattie, *Documentary Screens: Non-Fiction Film and Television* (Houndmills, UK: Palgrave Macmillan, 2004), 21. These technological developments were driven in France by the needs of ethnographers, so the observational mode and ethnographic film are intimately linked.

15. Heider, *Ethnographic Film*, 7.

16. Tegeler, "'Frei Wie Nie Zuvor.'"

17. Beattie, *Documentary Screens*.

18. Beattie, *Documentary Screens*, 45.

19. Beattie, *Documentary Screens*, 45–46.

20. *Cannibal Tours*, dir. Dennis O'Rourke (1987).

21. Dennis O'Rourke, "On the Making of *Cannibal Tours*," CameraWork, 2004, http://www.cameraworklimited.com/articles.html, 8.

22. O'Rourke, "On the Making of *Cannibal Tours*," 8.

23. O'Rourke, "On the Making of *Cannibal Tours*," 4.

24. O'Rourke, "On the Making of *Cannibal Tours*," 5–6.

25. O'Rourke, "On the Making of *Cannibal Tours*," 5.

26. O'Rourke, "On the Making of *Cannibal Tours*," 7.

27. Beattie, *Documentary Screens*, 59.

28. Beattie, *Documentary Screens*, 59.

29. Uwe, although he laughs at Gustav's interest in Zen Buddhism, invokes Eastern thought in his own way when he describes cutting vegetables to a customer as a kind of "aerobics for the soul." This shows how prevalent a kind of pop Buddhism is in contemporary Germany.

30. O'Rourke, "On the Making of *Cannibal Tours*," 4.

31. Beattie, *Documentary Screens*, 61.

32. Roscoe and Hight, *Faking It*, 52.

33. Said, *Orientalism*, 157.

34. O'Rourke, "On the Making of *Cannibal Tours*," 5.

9

The Mind behind the Mockumentary: *The Proper Care and Feeding of an American Messiah*

Chris Hansen

As a filmmaker, I come at this business of mockumentaries from a different perspective. So, while I have certainly analyzed the mockumentaries of other filmmakers, I have done so for a very practical reason—to understand the function and purpose behind their usage of the mockumentary form and, ultimately, to prepare for production of my own film and examine my own intentions in the use of the mockumentary mode in my feature film.

Some background information is probably required here, for my film has yet to achieve the reputation of a *Zelig* (1983) or a *This Is Spinal Tap* (1984). Nevertheless, I wrote and directed a feature film titled *The Proper Care and Feeding of an American Messiah*, a mock documentary about "Brian B.," a middle-class family man in his midthirties who believes that he is a messiah. Not *the* messiah, mind you, but rather a local, regional messiah for his hometown, descended from a long line of "local messiahs" who all denied their own divinity. But Brian isn't the messiah type. He has a bad temper and an annoying tendency to neglect his wife and child and heap verbal abuse upon his siblings in pursuit of his grandiose dream.

In this chapter, I take you through some of the events in the film to examine its structure and its use of the mockumentary mode to convey the practical realities that filmmakers face in making any film and how those realities affect the use of the mockumentary form.

Brian (Duston Olson) embraces his role as local messiah. *Author's collection.*

First, in general, the mockumentary form, in contrast with what I'll call the traditional narrative form, allows a filmmaker to make fun of a character's quirks without appearing to because the form implies that the character is presenting his or her own views. Thus, the character is indicted for his or her own sins or stupidity, but by virtue of the so-called objectivity of the documentary form, the filmmaker is released from any role in the judgment of the character. It allows a filmmaker to present ludicrous views and tear down a figure while appearing to stand objectively on the sideline, claiming only to have caught the ludicrousness on film. And while this isn't true, and we all know it's a *mock* documentary, the feeling of objectivity on the part of the filmmaker lingers. If the film preserves its stance as a mock documentary through its use of documentary tropes and techniques—such as the handheld camera that follows subjects and action, the use of on-camera interviews, and the acknowledged presence of a camera crew and documentarian—audiences can't help but feel the "truth" of the movie's objectivity in spite of its obviously fictional nature.

There is an obvious ethical consideration here. How a filmmaker treats his or her subject, even if it is a fictional one, matters. The power of the documentary, as established by documentary tropes, can create in the viewer a belief that the material is true simply because it occurs within the context of a documentary, in spite of the filmmaker manipulating the content and sometimes taking images out of context. In other words, film-makers can and do lie to tell the truth (or to tell what they believe to be the truth). While this ethical issue is not the focus of this chapter, it does require mentioning to recognize its significance.

INFLUENCES AND INSPIRATIONS

The technique that I used in this film—the clear establishing of a docu-mentary style at the outset, with a gradual move toward integrating traditional narrative form—was selected after studying other mockumen-taries, the best of which employed this practice. The mockumentary mode would be established up front, often for comedic purposes and as an efficient method of presenting character, and the traditional narrative style would be introduced after audiences had presumably accepted the reality of the story, with the filmmaker alternating between modes as necessary.

Specifically, I referenced three pieces more often than others. The first was the mockumentary *Bob Roberts* (1992), written and directed by Tim Robbins, which uses a handheld camera throughout but nevertheless often uses a traditional narrative shooting style too complex to have been done with a single-camera documentary crew. What surprised me about this observation was that I had always thought that this film was shot in a pure documentary style. It wasn't until I rewatched the film to study its shooting style that I realized just how many shots and angles could never have been accomplished by a small documentary production crew. It was testament to the power of a few documentary tropes that, even though I knew the film to be fiction, I was convinced that it was staged and shot as a documentary.

The second film I studied in preparation for my film was *Larry David: Curb Your Enthusiasm. Curb Your Enthusiasm* (1999) is best known as a series on HBO, but it originated as a one-hour mockumentary purporting to follow Larry David around as he planned a one-hour comedy special for HBO. This original special on HBO employed a simple mockumentary form that also integrated traditional narrative form, albeit with a hand-held, cinema verité style. It did not have interviews with the characters, though they did occasionally address the camera while engaged in the events of the story. In its current series form, *Curb Your Enthusiasm* is not a proper mockumentary. It doesn't attempt to convince the audience that what they are seeing is being filmed by a documentary crew, specifically eschewing interviews and other direct-to-the-camera references. Yet, while it doesn't make use of all the documentary tropes that mockumentaries use, it still employs the handheld cinema verité style and limited cutting to create in the viewer the sense that he or she is "right there" with the characters, seeing their actual lives unfold. This is, of course, reinforced by the fact that Larry David plays a fictional version of himself in the show, using his real name and his real life as the wealthy but neurotic cocreator of the hit series *Seinfeld*.

Also of interest in *Curb Your Enthusiasm* is the way that the show's shooting style has evolved over its six ten-episode seasons on HBO. While it started out with a clear documentary aesthetic, Larry David has indicated that they ultimately found the form too limiting in certain cases and began to move away from it by the second season. In its current form, the show still uses the handheld camera and the idea that the show is supposedly Larry David's "real life," but the shooting style is more flexible, allowing unusual shots for comedic purposes and never shying away from including shots that would not be part of a documentary.

The third piece I analyzed for my film was the BBC production *The Office*, a mockumentary television series purporting to tell the story of the daily work lives of a group of employees at a small-town paper-products company. *The Office* is presented as a documentary, using direct-camera address in the form of interviews and characters looking at the camera or speaking to an off-screen presence. Occasionally, the show highlights the limitations of the documentary form by having characters shut the crew out of their conversations, closing office doors to maintain an occasional sense of privacy, though the characters are presented as wearing wireless microphones at all times, so even when the documentary crew is shut out, it still manages to record what it needs to.

In one of the show's finest moments, the mockumentary form and the traditional narrative form merge successfully when the character of Tim decides to express his affection for his coworker Dawn. He goes into an office to speak with her and promptly takes off his microphone. The documentary camera watches in complete silence as Tim speaks with Dawn. When he walks out of the office, he turns his microphone back on and explains that she turned him down. Interestingly, this scene uses the limitations of the mockumentary form to give the characters a moment of privacy when one is needed. Tim seems to regard the camera and the microphones, in this moment at least, as an invasion of his privacy, and the filmmakers behind *The Office* must agree because the documentary camera is restrained from doing anything more than watching the door of the office that Tim has entered to speak with Dawn.

This moment is effective because it is different. The audience has grown to appreciate these characters and the access we have to them. When we are shut out, the moment feels that much more significant. But it is also effective simply because it lets some things remain unspoken (at least to us). A traditional show might choose not to let the audience hear Tim's confession of love to Dawn, but it would have to do so in a self-conscious manner, with music or general crowd noise drowning out their speech, as used in the final scene of Sofia Coppola's *Lost in Translation* (2003). In *The Office*, Tim's disregard for the documentary of which he is a part seems completely natural at this moment, and so the switching off of the microphone is highly effective as a way to create a private moment where the silence makes it all the more poignant.

What I find especially interesting about *The Office* and its influence, especially the American adaptation of it on NBC, is the way in which these documentary tropes are beginning to be used in fictional television shows, movies, and even reality shows to create a sense of "reality" in the audience where there is none or where reality is being manipulated.

The concept of manipulating reality becomes especially relevant in documentaries such as *Super Size Me* (2004) and *Fahrenheit 9/11* (2004) and television shows such as *Survivor*. In these examples, documentary form is employed, but at the same time, elements exist that cause the audience to question the truth of some events and facts that are presented as real. This issue is at least worth further study as filmmakers like me use these techniques in more and more films and television shows to signify that something is real when it might not be. In other words, how much does the documentary form itself influence the audience's perception of what is real in such works, and how ethical is it to employ this form to create such perceptions?

FOCUS ON CHARACTER

The Proper Care and Feeding of an American Messiah opens with an extended introduction to its main character, Brian, through interviews with him, his wife, and his two siblings, Aaron and Miriam, both of whom live with him and serve as his support group and his only "followers." These interviews are shot in standard documentary form, with interview subjects speaking in response to questions from an unseen, off-camera interviewer, ostensibly the documentarian within the reality of the film.

The mockumentary form allows me to introduce the character of Brian to the audience through his own words and to introduce his surroundings—his family environment—through similar interviews. This goes to the heart of my intentions with the mockumentary form in this film. It allows me to follow Brian around, as it were, to get inside his head and see what makes him tick. He is such a unique character that it became clear that we could better understand him by hearing his beliefs from his own mouth (and this idea works with Brian's character as well, because the idea that Brian would want to sit down for extended interviews to talk about himself emphasizes the role that his ego plays in his delusion).

I should be clear that what Brian says may not accurately reflect his character; the film, in fact, uses Brian's lack of self-knowledge and his denial of possible abuse issues in his childhood to help the viewer understand his character. So I am not advocating here that the mockumentary form is some kind of shortcut to understanding characters by letting them speak their own minds; that would be a poor use of the form. Rather, the form allows me to present the character's inability to understand himself because the audience can clearly see the contrast between his lofty ambitions and his current reality. This, too, is the source of much of the film's comedy, and I would contend that it is the source of much of the comedy of other mockumentaries, such as *A Mighty Wind* (2003), *Best in Show* (2000), and *Waiting for Guffman* (1996).

Brian is able to present his own bizarre worldview directly to the camera through the documentary-style interviews. If I were to ensconce the same character in a more traditional narrative, it would require the film to jump through all sorts of narrative hoops to communicate the same information that is communicated so efficiently in these scenes. For example, at one point early in the film, Brian chooses to demonstrate his miracles for the camera. One of these miracles consists of catching plums with his mouth as they are tossed from ten yards away. The presentation of this, which helps to establish the ludicrous nature of Brian's delusion, could not have been accomplished using traditional narrative form without much story-based reasoning behind his choice to do it *at that moment*.

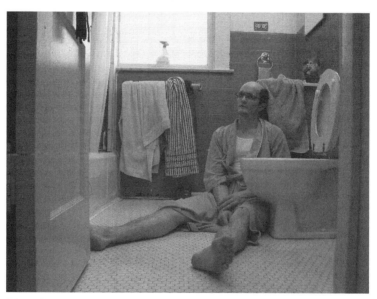

Brian discusses how his stomach ailments relate to his messianic role.

That is, it would have required a much stronger causal link between it and the scenes preceding it. In the film, Brian presents his "miracle" as a way of proving his status as a deity to the documentarian, who has wondered aloud whether someone who claims to be "a messiah" should be able to perform miraculous acts. Without this need for proof, showing the miracle would be tantamount to poor exposition, a character explaining himself to another character simply for the sake of the audience. But because Brian is a "documentary subject" who has a direct relationship with the "director," the film is able to present the scene both for the comic effect of seeing Brian trying to catch plums in his mouth and for the narrative purpose of illustrating Brian's lack of understanding about what is genuinely miraculous.

The mockumentary form, in this example at least, frees the filmmaker from the constraints of traditional narrative, allowing the film to explain aspects of the character's personality that might only be implied in a story using traditional narrative form or that would require causal narrative links to get to those points in the story, thus undercutting the comedy by taking much too long to "set up the joke." In addition to the "freeing" nature of the technique, much of the comedy in the film is achieved through the contrast between this supposedly objective documentary form and the ludicrous actions of the character.

THE DIRECTOR AS CHARACTER
AND THE POINT-OF-VIEW CHARACTER

In many documentaries and mock documentaries, such as the films of noted mockumentarian Christopher Guest (*Waiting for Guffman*, *Best in Show*, *A Mighty Wind*), the questions that prompt the character responses in on-camera interviews are only implied; the audience is never privy to the actual questions, nor is there a significant focus on the presence of a narrator or a camera crew. But other mockumentaries, including *Bob Roberts* and *This Is Spinal Tap*, have used the controlling authority, the "director" of the documentary, as a character in the film. In those cases and in many where the documentary director is a character, the director-character appears on-screen and is often seen asking the questions of the interview subjects.

The Proper Care and Feeding of an American Messiah features a director-character, but he is unseen and seldom heard. The presence of the director-character, asking questions of the other characters, underlies the documentary nature of the film; but, as a filmmaker, I didn't want that character to overwhelm the film with his physical presence. I felt that his aural presence, as a "voice only" character, would add to the film's "authentic documentary" tone without requiring that it deal with the character himself as a real person whose motives and intentions might come into question as a result of the reactions that he might give to some of the stranger things that the main characters do and say.

In a self-reflexive form like the mockumentary, the camera serves as the de facto point of view, making the director-character, in whatever form he or she appears (even if the presence of such a character is merely implied), the authority behind that point of view. A physically present director-character would logically become the audience's point-of-view character, the person whose perspective on the action most closely aligns with the audience's perspective, thus serving as the audience's "pathway" into the film. The director-character in *The Proper Care and Feeding of an American Messiah* clearly thinks that some of what he is seeing is crazy (as evidenced by the tone of his voice and condescending character of some of his questions), so if the audience is influenced too strongly by his point of view, it might have only disdain for the family, seeing it as nothing more than a source of laughs.

But *The Proper Care and Feeding of an American Messiah* is not simply about ridiculing the behavior of its characters. It is, at its core, about a family in crisis, and there is an emotional component to this that must make itself known even as the comedy remains at the forefront. I wanted Miriam, Brian's sister, to be the audience's point-of-view character in the film because she has a more sympathetic view of her family. It is through Miriam's almost-silent witness that we should experience the family and look beyond its insanity to see what might be at the root of it.

But if the self-reflexive nature of the mockumentary form grants the authority of the point of view to the camera and the director-character, how does a filmmaker alter that? In this case, I created a character who resists participating in the events of the film (even in the making of the documentary itself, as she resists answering the director-character's questions) and who acts primarily as an observer. Miriam observes and reacts, and so she begins to replace the director-character as the controlling point of view because she mimics the behavior of the camera and also the viewer. That is, she watches. But Miriam does more than simply watch. She also provides insight and understanding through simple visual reactions to things. When she does insert herself into a situation, something that occurs rarely, she does so quietly and meekly and quickly returns to being an observer when she is rebuffed or rebuked.

The director-character himself seems to understand that Miriam has some insight to offer because he seeks out Miriam's thoughts about the family's craziness. When his direct questioning of her fails because she refuses to answer, he takes a different approach, using the camera to catch her reactions to Brian and Aaron's antics. These reactions are primarily visual and only occasionally verbal. This focus on Miriam is intended to comfort the viewer, who might be disturbed to be enmeshed in a narrative filled with characters who are potentially unlikable and maybe even dangerously delusional. Miriam's reactions mirror the audience's own take on this family, from her disbelief at some of Brian's proclamations to her desire to correct him. Driven by her love for her brother and her desire to prevent him from losing whatever grip on his sanity he still retains, Miriam corrects him gently and seeks not to "pop the bubble" of his delusion too abruptly. The audience, seeing this and relating to the Miriam character as an observer of the action, gives Brian a little more latitude, as a family member might.

By making Miriam the point-of-view character, my hope as a filmmaker was that, while the audience may (and should) laugh at Brian's antics, it might also see these actions in light of their effect on Miriam and the family as a whole. She provides a more sympathetic lens through which to view the events, so when Brian gets ridiculously angry or despondent, the audience might laugh at him, but it also relates to Miriam's sisterly love and sense of familial obligation.

USE OF TRADITIONAL NARRATIVE MODE

The strict adherence to the mockumentary mode carries the story through the first significant plot "event," when Brian's desire to understand his "special purpose" for being a messiah manifests itself in a decision to rent out the local civic center for a "messiah rally" to announce his deity to his people. This move requires money, so the film is launched into the loose plot engine that will inform the rest of the action: the pursuit of money with the goal of finally reaching self-actualization.

Brian, in one scene, believes that he sees his own face miraculously appear in a stick of butter, and this vision prompts him to hold a rally. He believes the miraculous "face in the butter" is God's promise to him to "go all the way"—if Brian is himself willing to do so. Brian's version of "going all the way" is to show his trust that God will soon tell him his special purpose as a messiah by scheduling a big rally at which he plans to announce this news. Of course, as the director-character implies with his questions to Brian, one could easily interpret this decision as Brian's attempt to force God to reveal to him his purpose by setting a deadline for this to occur at the rally because, after all, how would it look to the town if Brian had a rally but didn't yet know his mission as a messiah?

At this point, though documentary tropes continue, their emphasis is lessened significantly. With the documentary style of the film having already been established by the teasing tone of the first twenty-five minutes, audiences are now "on board" for the ride with Brian as a "real" character in this supposed documentary, so the film can ease up on the mockumentary mode and begin to play out in a more straightforwardly traditional narrative style.

For example, in one scene around the middle of the film, Brian goes door-to-door to raise money for his rally. After having multiple doors slammed in his face, he encounters an unnamed homeowner who, upon hearing that Brian's "home blessing" can get rid of evil, invites Brian and his siblings into his home. After a brief negotiation over price, Brian is surprised to find out that the homeowner expects him to get rid of a set of invisible houseguests, whom the homeowner identifies with names associated with demons. In this case, however, the invisible demons like lemonade with salt instead of sugar, which infuriates the homeowner. Brian, faced with a delusion perhaps even more powerful than his own, makes an excuse and beats a hasty retreat out of the home.

This scene is more obviously a traditional narrative scene in that it employs multiple angles and shots and occurs over multiple locations. While the main action occurs in the living room, it jumps to both the hallway and the kitchen when characters are in those rooms. This is accomplished with a simple cut to the new location, as one would expect from the traditional narrative form, instead of having the camera follow the characters from room to room, as one would expect from documentary form. Obviously, this kind of technique violates the documentary style that the film employed throughout the opening act, unless the documentary crew within the film has somehow suddenly acquired multiple cameras and additional camera people to capture all the different angles in all the different rooms.

The fact that the homeowner in the scene simply doesn't acknowledge or question the presence of a documentary crew leads one to believe it's not even there. In addition, to maintain the illusion of documentary in spite of the obviously fictional nature of the material, the scene employs the use of the handheld "documentary camera," thus maintaining a surface style that allows for continuity between this and other scenes in the film.

SHOWING VS. HIDING THE "DOCUMENTARY CAMERA"

Most mockumentaries, even those that make a character of the documentary director, do not show other documentary crewmembers or camera equipment (a few, such as *The Big Tease* [1999] do). As a filmmaker, I had to ask myself what showing the "machinery of the production" would accomplish for the film. Since the documentary form is already established by other techniques, I decided that showing the camera or other equipment might reflect an attempt to be too clever for our own good, an appeal to other filmmakers and film professionals who might be viewing it rather than to general audiences.

So there are several scenes in *The Proper Care and Feeding of an American Messiah* where a documentary camera and camera operator, were they actually present, would be seen. For example, in one scene, Brian walks down a quiet neighborhood street with his siblings as they debate the merits of recruiting more "disciples" for his ministry. When Brian stops and turns to his brother and sister, the film cuts to the "reverse shot" of Brian addressing them. But if a documentary crew were filming this scene, at least one crewmember and camera would be seen in the reverse shot because of the angle.

Capturing these images would require at least two documentary cameras operating simultaneously, and each of them would be able to "see" the other in its shot.

The fact that this scene could not and would not have been shot in this manner if it were a true documentary was the subject of some debate between the director of photography and me. He was concerned with breaking the documentary "reality" that we were striving to establish in the story, and I was focused on the most efficient and visually interesting way to tell the story while maintaining an *illusion* of reality. The relationship between any film's director and its director of photography is a significant one. In the case of this film, we were constantly negotiating the approach to the visuals in the film, with the director of photography concerned at times that the mixed shooting style we were employing would not work for audiences. As is often the case in creative endeavors, the initial tensions of collaboration led us to a middle ground of sorts that worked better than either of our original preferences.

From this point in the film, with both mockumentary and traditional narrative forms established, it moves freely back and forth, employing the mode that makes the most sense at any given time. So when the film needs to convey things that might take an extensive amount of time in traditional narrative, it can use documentary tropes. And when the emotional resonance of a moment will be better conveyed in narrative form, it can use that, as in one tender scene between Brian and his sister that a true documentary might never have been able to capture but which was essential to my conception of the film as having deeper intentions than silly comedy.

In the scene, Brian goes to the bus station to find Miriam, who has left the family to start a new life in California but has found herself unable to actually get on a bus and abandon them completely. As Brian finds Miriam and tries to convince her to return home with him, the audience begins to understand the nature of their relationship, and Miriam sees, perhaps for the first time in a very long time, that Brian does have a selfless side.

The sequence begins in a documentary style, with the camera following Brian and Aaron as they rush into the bus station in search of Miriam. But as soon as Brian locates her and sits down to talk with her, the film shifts to the traditional narrative form, cutting between a wide master shot of Brian and Miriam sitting in the bus station and matching close-ups of each character.

Even if one might believe that the fictional documentary production had access to the multiple cameras and operators needed to capture this scene, the intimate nature of the conversation would prevent them from doing anything but perhaps viewing it from a distance. It would be quite an intrusion on Brian and Miriam's reconciliation for them to have cameras sitting over their shoulders as Brian comes to terms, to a degree, with his failings as a messiah. And even if they were able to capture those close-ups, the camera that is capturing the wide shot of this scene would "see" those other cameras and camera operators. In a scene like this, where the reality is created by allowing the viewer to experience people "being real" with each other, the presence of realistic documentary cameras and crew members would only destroy the emotional impact, not to mention the fact that it would be an outrageous violation of Brian and Miriam's privacy if this were a legitimate documentary.

MIXING DOCUMENTARY AND TRADITIONAL NARRATIVE MODES

The ending of the film illustrates the best use of both modes. Aaron, Brian's brother, accidentally shoots Brian at the rally. In the process of treating him, doctors discover that Aaron's bullet dislodged a serious bowel obstruction that might have killed Brian had it not been discovered. This leads to the characters questioning just whose "special purpose" was really at work here. Aaron now believes it is *he* who is the family's messiah (and he has a small following, thanks to newspaper reports of his supposed miracle). And Brian expresses some serious doubts about his own understanding of his purpose.

At this point, the director-character asks Miriam about her own special purpose. She hesitates, unsure of how to answer, and before she can decide, the action behind her draws the audience's attention. Aaron, who now believes that he is the family's resident messiah, has absconded with Brian's Jesus costume, which they use when they are playing "Bible time." Brian chases after Aaron in a wheelchair as Aaron crashes into a trashcan. Miriam, witnessing this, turns back to the camera and shrugs a little.

While the film clearly makes use of the documentary style interview in this scene, it also subtly employs the traditional narrative form as well. Miriam observes something in the background that provides the obvious answer to the question posed to her by the director. This serves as a traditional narrative response—a visual response—to the director's question, rather than as a spoken documentary interview response. What is Miriam's "special purpose"? It is to serve as caretaker and surrogate parent to the bickering, childish siblings behind her. But in the film, the moment is left unexplored, allowing the viewer to draw his or her own conclusions, rather than following up and requiring a statement or answer, as an actual documentary might do in this situation.

Ultimately, as a filmmaker, I've observed that the best mockumentaries do two things very well. First, they subtly integrate the traditional narrative storytelling style after establishing the film as a documentary form by using standard documentary tropes. Second, they create comedy through the contrast between the sometimes-bizarre actions of their characters and the supposed seriousness and objectivity of the documentary form. And in the more serious of these films, those that have something to communicate beyond the craziness of their characters or the comedy of their situations, this contrast and comedy are used to make serious points about sometimes-controversial issues, thus making the ideas more palatable. In essence, the comedy serves as a spoonful of sugar that helps the medicine of the message go down.

IV

THE WAR THAT WASN'T

10

It (Might Have) Happened Here: How Nazi Germany Won the War

John C. Tibbetts

Kevin Brownlow's *It Happened Here* (1966) begins with a series of animated maps illustrating the Nazi takeover of Britain. "The German invasion of England took place in July 1940 after the British retreat from Dunkirk," intones an off-screen voice. "Strongly resisted at first, the German army took many months to restore order. But the resistance movement, lacking outside support, was finally crushed. Then, in 1944, the resistance movement reappeared."

It Happened Here is a "rewrite" of history, an alternative time track, a paraphrase, as it were, of past historical events.[1] What would have happened . . . if Operation Sea Lion—the Nazis' plan to invade England in 1940—had succeeded and if the Nazis had defeated England in World War II? Brownlow's title is significant, of course, since it is a variant of Sinclair Lewis's novel *It Can't Happen Here*, published in 1935. Lewis's cautionary fable, which appeared at a time when fascism seemed on the rise in an America fraught with demagoguery and fanatical political groups, envisioned the nightmarish spread of an American dictatorship, from a small town in Vermont, to Washington, DC, and finally to the entire nation.[2] Nowhere in Brownlow's account of the making of *It Happened Here* (1968) does he mention the Lewis novel as a possible inspiration, but the parallels seem obvious enough.[3]

It Happened Here occupies not just a unique position among Brown-low's films, which primarily are devoted to the documentation and restoration of silent films, but in cinema history in general.[4] It is one of the first commercial feature historical films to challenge the conventions of history on film with the strategy of what has come to be referred to as the "counterfactual narrative."[5] What if . . . it conjectures. The young British historian Niall Ferguson defined this form of speculative history in 1997 in the introduction to his anthology *Virtual History: Alternatives and Counterfactuals*. "What if???" he asks rhetorically. . . . What if there had been no English Civil War, if Ireland had never been divided, and if Hitler had invaded Britain? Why concern ourselves with a history that *didn't happen*? "The business of imagining such counterfactuals," Ferguson writes, "is a vital part of the way in which we learn."[6] The approach is acceptable inasmuch as it bids the historian to deploy the methods of a scientist to test hypotheses about historical determinants. "In short," says Ferguson,

> by narrowing down the historical alternatives we consider to those which are *plausible*—and hence by replacing the enigma of "chance" with the calculation of *probabilities*—we solve the dilemma of choosing between a single deterministic past and an unmanageably infinite number of possible pasts. The counterfactuals we need to construct are not mere fantasy: they are simulations based on calculations about the relative probability of plausible outcomes in a chaotic world (hence "virtual history").[7]

Although the word *counterfactual* has only recently achieved currency in theories of historiography, the concept has always been operative in all dramatizations of historical events and peoples. More than forty years ago, historian Hayden White began proposing that there is no such thing as "objective" history, that historiography is subject to the same assumptions and narrative techniques that shape dramas, novels, and films. "What if" questions demand to be addressed the instant that a biographical or historical event is chosen and isolated. Upon the presumed *familiarity* of the past is layered a set of speculations, alternatives, and contingencies that evoke a sense of strangeness and mystery: *It did happen that way . . . didn't it???* Moreover, the historical film, writes Robert A. Rosenstone in *Revisioning History*, "must be taken on its terms as a portrait of the past that has less to do with fact than with intensity and insight, perception and feeling. . . . To express the meaning of the past, film creates proximate, appropriate characters, situations, images, and metaphor."[8]

Admittedly, traditionalist historians have tended to regard counterfactual propositions about history more as dubious exercises in whimsy than works of responsible historiography, even though examples may be seen in the work of historians reaching back to Thucydides. The "what if" approach to history nonetheless can't help but be intriguing: In his book *If It Had Happened Otherwise*, J. C. Squire declared, "There is no action or event, great or small (leaving predestination out of account) which might not have happened differently, and, happening differently, have perhaps modified the world's history for all time."[9] Recent examples of literary counterfactuals include Ward Moore's *Bring the Jubilee* (1953), which was set in 1938 in the aftermath of the South's victory in the Civil War; and William Gibson and Bruce Sterling's *The Difference Engine* (1990), which postulates how history would have changed had a steam-based computer technology been developed in 1855.[10]

In particular, speculations about the implications of a German victory over the Allies in World War II have generated many books, plays, anthologies, and at least one other film in addition to *It Happened Here*: Alberto Cavalcanti's *Went the Day Well?*[11] Books in the war years included Douglas Brown and Christopher Serpell's *If Hitler Comes* (1940), Anthony Armstrong and Bruce Graeme's *When the Bells Rang* (1943), and Martin Hawkins's *When Adolf Came* (1943). In 1948, Noel Coward's play *Peace in Our Time* created a minor stir—the first act begins with a radio broadcast from the BBC Home Service describing the reopening of Parliament by Adolf Hitler, Air Chief Marshal Goering, and Dr. Goebbels![12] Among more recent books are Philip K. Dick's classic *The Man in the High Castle* (1962), which dealt with the Axis victory in World War II, leading to the partitioning of America into zones controlled by Germany and Japan; C. S. Forester's *If Hitler Had Invaded England* (1971); Frederic Mullally's *Hitler Has Won* (1975); the Gregory Benford and Martin Greenberg anthology *Hitler Victorious: Eleven Stories of the German Victory in World War II* (1988); Robert Harris's *Fatherland* (1992); and Peter Tsouras's *Disaster at D-Day: The Germans Defeat the Allies, June 1944* (1994).

And in one of the essays in Ferguson's *Virtual History*, Andrew Roberts's "What If Germany Had Invaded Britain in May 1940?," several of Brownlow's key themes find support—for example, that before the war, there was a strong presumption in England among many citizens that there was a racial and political affinity of long standing between the Anglo-Saxons and the Germans; that Operation Sea Lion could very well have succeeded had it been better prepared; and that had the Germans arrived in May, after Dunkirk, they likely would have encountered poorly armed defenses.[13] As for the issue of British accommodation, Roberts cites the activities of the British Union of Fascists under Sir Oswald Mosley, declaring, "There was no shortage of people in 1930s Britain who would have viewed a British accommodation with Hitler positively."[14]

It Happened Here begins in 1943. The inhabitants of small English towns have been evacuated by the Nazis to a demilitarized London, where they are impressed into service in the cause of forging a "New

Europe" against the common enemies of Communists and Jewish Capitalists. This is a London where German troops ride the subways and flirt with the girls, where barbed wire separates a "Jewish Residential Quarter" from the rest of the city, and where detachments of English SS work side by side with their German counterparts (the English uniform arm patch displays the Cross of St. George placed directly beneath the traditional eagle and swastika).[15]

One of the evacuees, Pauline (Pauline Murray), is a trained nurse who arrives in London after narrowly escaping a deadly skirmish between the Nazis and English Partisans in Salisbury. In London, she decides that the best thing for her is to accept England's defeat and to cooperate with the occupation forces. After a highly regimented indoctrination, she goes to work as a nurse in the Fascist-controlled Immediate Action Organization (the IA). An old friend, Dr. Richard Fletcher (Sebastian Shaw), a physician who has refused to cooperate with the IA, is shocked by her decision. Suspected of collaborating with Fletcher, Pauline is taken into custody by the SS and dispatched to work at a country hospital. To her horror, she discovers that this stately mansion, staffed by kindly doctors and nurses, is actually an extermination center for Slavic men, women, and children. Placed under arrest by the SS for refusing to cooperate, Pauline is handcuffed and shipped out. Soon after, her train is ambushed by English Partisans, and she is ordered to a field dressing station in a forward area, where the Army of Liberation is staging a counteroffensive. While she tends to the wounded, Pauline listens numbly to radio accounts of Partisan successes as the English slaughter a captured SS unit with machine guns.

Pauline's fate is emblematic. She is neither heroine nor villain, merely a woman whose instinct to survive has turned her into a passive pawn—and, ultimately, the victim—of both oppressor and oppressed. As Nazis and English Partisans slaughter each other, their respective propaganda campaigns and acts of violence grow indistinguishable. Even the ideological lines separating them seem to have disappeared. Dr. Fletcher's words to Pauline echo in our ears: "The most appalling thing about Fascism is that it takes Fascist methods to get rid of it."

Remarkably, the newsreels and documentary-style narrative techniques throughout *It Happened Here* contain not one foot of period or stock footage. Every shot is original. For the ersatz World War I newsreel, for example, Brownlow used a 1922 hand-cranked 16 mm Kodak camera to re-create the "look" of handheld, grainy images. His codirector Andrew Mollo provided his own collection of original military uniforms and equipment. And numerous prop masters contributed a variety of trucks, taxis, private cars, and buses (according to Brownlow, wartime London buses are about the rarest vehicles on wheels). The simulated radio broadcasts heard throughout were recorded by veterans of the BBC wartime staff: Alvar Lidell, Frank Phillips, and John Snagge. It is Snagge's voice that is heard at the very beginning of the film—which is singularly appropriate, considering it was he who in real life had announced on the BBC the declaration of war. Exteriors were shot in and around London (including Parliament Square for a Nazi marching sequence and the former home of opera librettist W. S. Gilbert for the country hospital scenes). Most of the cast were nonprofessionals, including the lead actress, Pauline Murray, a doctor's wife from Wales.

Pauline (Pauline Murray) is a trained nurse who joins the Fascist-controlled Immediate Action Organization in *It Happened Here.* *Courtesy of Kevin Brownlow.*

Brownlow and Mollo were just teenagers in May 1956 when they first conceived the ideas behind *It Happened Here*. Brownlow was a trainee in the cutting rooms of World Wide Pictures, a Soho-based documentary film company, and Mollo was an art student who in his spare time pursued a passion for collecting World War II artifacts. Of the two, only Brownlow had any filmmaking experience, having just completed an amateur project, *The Capture* (1952–1955), an adaptation of a story by Guy de Maupassant.[16]

Brownlow and Mollo belonged to an emerging generation of would-be filmmakers determined to rejuvenate what they regarded as a moribund British film industry. Beginning with the so-called Free Cinema movement of the mid-1950s and fostered by publications such as *Sequence* and *Sight and Sound*, writers, directors, television producers, and critics such as Tony Richardson, Karel Reisz, Lindsay Anderson, Penelope Huston, and Gavin Lambert sounded an alarm and a prophecy.[17] Writing in 1956, at precisely the moment when Brownlow and Mollo were planning *It Happened Here*, Anderson charged that the current "irresponsible commerce" of distribution and exhibition in the commercial cinemas has caused too many filmmakers to abandon the treatment of contemporary life in their films. A year later, in a seminal essay in *Sight and Sound*, Gavin Lambert took up the cry, declaring, "Our cinema has suffered intermittently since birth from . . . [a] lack of concern with vital contemporary issues and a consequent isolation from many important factors of national life."[18] And Tony Richardson, one of Free Cinema's most vocal partisans, deplored the industry's "resistance to new ideas, new subjects, new attitudes." Richardson concluded that alternatives to the British commercial system had to be found: "If we are to have the right sort of freedom to experiment, which is the only way any art can be kept alive, we have got to be able to try to do things more cheaply. So long as there are the extremes of profit and loss, so long will there be this constant urge to play safe. . . . Only then can the economic blackmail be reduced and imagination really freed."[19] Within the next three years, with the release of Jack Clayton's *Room at the Top* (1959), Penelope Houston acknowledged that "something, however tenuously and uncertainly, seems to be stirring in the British cinema. What happens next will depend on the talent and persuasiveness of half a dozen writers and directors, on the imponderables of public response, and on whatever weight the critics are prepared to throw into the scale."[20] Indeed, in the next five years Richardson's *Look Back in Anger* (1959), Karel Reisz's *Saturday Night and Sunday Morning* (1960), and Lindsay Anderson's *This Sporting Life* (1963) spearheaded an internationally acclaimed British "New Wave" of working-class dramas and satires that took an unvarnished, street-level view of British contemporary life.

Not as well known or experienced as these filmmakers and working far more economically, Brownlow pursued in his own modest way the ideal of a direct, personalized, and economical cinema that stayed close to the realities of the British experience.[21] "I'm too eccentric a filmmaker to work within the system," he confessed in a 1980 interview as he looked back on his early experiences. "While I admire so much of Hollywood as a historian, I reject it as a filmmaker. I go out into the field with the smallest crew possible and make pictures which are extremely documentary in their style, extremely non-commercial."[22]

But frugality and commitment exact their own price. It would take Brownlow and codirector Mollo eight years to make *It Happened Here*— eight years working outside the industry, in his spare time, on a miniscule budget (ultimately just $21,000), depending on the kindness of friends and strangers (including assistance at the eleventh hour from Tony Richardson and Stanley Kubrick).[23] As the project grew and grew—from 16 mm to 35 mm, from scribbled notes to tentative scripts, from hastily wrought vignettes to carefully planned mass rallies and battle scenes—the boys themselves grew up. And the film inevitably reflected the process of their maturation. "God knows one would not wish anyone the privations of the first six years of *It Happened Here*," wrote David Robinson.

Yet the film may owe not a little of its rigorous quality to the disciplines that poverty imposed. . . . Perhaps it was the very fact that the ethical bases of the film were worked out like this, empirically, on the spot, as part of the real-life development of moral and political discernment in the film-makers, that makes their picture, if not a specially profound examination of a human predicament, at least a soundly human one.[24]

Despite (or because of) its scrupulously documentary-like surface, *It Happened Here* is a nightmarish parable suggesting that "a vast fascist potential" (Brownlow's words) exists close to the surface in all of us, in even the most democratic society. The readiness with which Pauline joins the Fascist IA, while shocking in itself, is nonetheless understandable. Ideological allegiances take second place to immediate needs for survival.

As a result of attending meetings of the British National Socialist Movement, Brownlow had become convinced that "the germ of a Nazi revival had taken root" in England: "It provided an expected and alarming topicality for our film," he later wrote.[25] Sure enough, by the end of the picture, as Nazis and English Partisans slaughter each other, the propaganda and brute force of one have become indistinguishable from the other. The ideological lines separating them have disappeared. Dr. Fletcher's words to Pauline echo in our ears: "The most appalling thing about Fascism is that it takes Fascist methods to get rid of it."

Scenes such as this, depicting Englishmen cooperating with the Immediate Action Organization, aroused indignation in viewers. *Courtesy of Kevin Brownlow.*

How close we all are to these extremes is revealed in the storm of controversy that greeted the film's release. Singled out for attack—and ultimately censored before its initial release—were, not scenes of battlefield slaughter and street riots, but an unscripted, spontaneous discussion among actual members of the British National Socialist Movement regarding topics such as euthanasia, Aryan superiority, and the "Jewish Problem." The speakers are not ranting despots and thugs but ordinary people, looking for all the world like properly tweedy Englishmen in their club recounting the daily news over brandy and cigars. "No film since the end of the war had given National Socialists *carte blanche* to express their opinions," wrote Brownlow, "with the result that few people had a clear idea of what they stood for, or of the insidious threat they represented."[26]

It Happened Here began making the rounds at distributors' screenings and festivals in August 1964. Five months later, United Artists agreed to pick it up for worldwide distribution. However, protests from Jewish organizations, angered by what the *Jewish Chronicle* considered a "credo against the Jews," resulted in United Artists' threat to withdraw the film from circulation unless Brownlow and Mollo cut the offending scene.

Critic Kenneth Tynan was among many critics and commentators who protested the excision:

> We learn with concern that [United Artists] is contemplating the deletion of a vital sequence from the film in case its anti-Semitic content causes offense. In our view the function of such a sequence emerges quite clearly: the nature of the views is a most effective form of self-indictment and one that will come as a salutary shock to people who are unaware, or do not wish to be persuaded, that views of such monstrous intensity are still rife in certain quarters in Britain.[27]

Stanley Reed, director of the British Film Institute, agreed: "The total argument of the film is so overwhelmingly anti-fascist that . . . to cut this particular sequence, which is among the most telling in the film, would not only seriously damage the film artistically, but would reduce the propagandistic effect, which in my view can only be beneficial."[28] A more balanced assessment came from David Robinson in *Sight and Sound*:

> In a way, the filmmakers themselves are seduced. They communicate their own delight in the uniforms and military show, in the spectacle of an admirably staged Nazi torchlight funeral. This sort of thing is as insidious as dry rot; history has shown that. This admirably achieved, admirably intentioned film could be hot stuff for an audience with the wrong preconditioning. It is an important factor: to an extent the success or failure of the propaganda is tied with the success of the film. It does not, however, diminish the importance of the discovery of two new film-makers of undoubted talent.[29]

Ten years later, in *Cineaste*, Lenny Rubenstein was still on the defensive, noting that the film "succeeds in revealing fascism as an evil mass movement rather than the expression of several cruelly gifted psychotics." Moreover, it "carries a degree of shock, since it is not often that one hears fascist statements uttered with English accents by people not recognizable as actors."[30]

But the damage was done. Although the censored version of *It Happened Here* played for a very successful run for six weeks at the London Pavilion, its box office take of 23,000 pounds was absorbed by distribution and advertising costs; thereafter, the film received only limited distribution before being withdrawn entirely in 1968. Brownlow's career as a director suffered a setback. "Our eight years of production netted us not one penny," he wrote at the time. "On the official returns, promotion costs swallowed up our profits." Fortunately, he continued philosophically, "we did not make *It Happened Here* for money. We made it because we had to. It gave us an apprentice course in the problems of film production. Whatever its financial and artistic shortcomings, the experience has been endlessly rewarding."[31]

Now, after more than forty years, the scene is restored, and audiences, as Brownlow had intended all along, can see and hear for themselves how the Nazis "condemn themselves out of their own mouths."[32] The film's presentist view of history that so struck viewers in 1965 is, if anything, even more disturbing today. Historian Linda Holt reports that when the film was presented in Berlin in May 1996, German audiences were purportedly alarmed because, among other reasons, it was an unwelcome reminder of the persistence of the Nazi ideology at home and abroad.[33]

Many of Brownlow's colleagues on the project went on to exemplary screen careers on their own—including cinematographer Peter Suschitzky (*The Empire Strikes Back*, 1980) and producer Andrew Mollo (production designer on *Pascali's Island* and *Dance with a Stranger*). None were more directly influenced by the experience, however, than production assistant Peter Watkins. His *The War Game*, released in 1965, is not a "what if" so much as a "what *surely must be*" speculation on the devastation of nuclear holocaust. Using the techniques employed in *It Happened Here*—maps, handheld cameras, narration, and simulated newsreels—Watkins created an entirely plausible fiction that looks and sounds *real*. "It is based on conjecture," acknowledged Watkins. "You have to be convinced that what you do, even without an historical record, rings true. . . . You constantly say to yourself—'You are in a newsreel situation. What is the sort of thing that you would have taken if you were there.'"[34] Watkins would carry this newsreel agenda to extremes, says Brownlow, ultimately abandoning entirely the "look" of a feature film in this and subsequent work.[35]

It Happened Here presents a history that might have happened—or, in some ways, actually *is* happening. It is to be expected that in our postmodernist world—fraught with theories about multiple, alternative universes and nets of infinitely diverging, converging, and parallel timelines—that we should increasingly regard the past and the present as tangles of unexplained riddles, intertwined options, subjective views, and objective data. "Time forks perpetually toward innumerable futures," said Jorge Luis Borges in his "Garden of Forking Paths."[36]

And *It Happened Here* has been—or continues to be—one of them.

NOTES

1. Earlier versions of portions of this article appeared in my "Kevin Brownlow's Historical Films: *It Happened Here* (1965) and *Winstanley* (1975)," *Historical Journal of Film, Radio and Television* 20, no. 2 (June 2000): 227–51.

2. "Where in all history has there ever been a people so ripe for dictatorship as ours?" prophetically declares Doremus Jessup, the newspaper editor protagonist in Sinclair Lewis's *It Can't Happen Here* (22). Doremus watches in bemusement,

growing alarm, and outright fear as one "Berzelius Windrip" gains the Republican presidential nomination, is elected, and quickly transforms America into a Fascist state. Although he is overthrown by the end of the novel, America is left in conflict between Fascist and democratic factions. In the end, Doremus realizes that any ideology turned fanaticism was dangerous: "He was afraid that the world struggle today was not of Communism against Fascism, but of tolerance against the bigotry that was preached equally by Communism and Fascism" (432). See Sinclair Lewis, *It Can't Happen Here* (New York: Collier, 1935). Lewis's biographer, Mark Schorer, notes that it was the story's "extraordinarily detailed kind of fantasy" and "documenting" about the transformation of America's political structure into Fascism that made it a "tour de force" of today might be called a "counterfactual"; Mark Schorer, *Sinclair Lewis: An American Life* (New York: McGraw-Hill, 1961), 610. The story was adapted to the stage a year later, but plans by MGM to produce a film version were blocked by a nervous Production Code Administration on grounds that it was too controversial.

3. "The title was inspired by the British wartime cliché," says Brownlow—"'It couldn't happen here!'" Brownlow continues: "By the way, my original title was a more emphatic 'It *Did* Happen Here'" (letter to author, November 6, 1998).

4. For overviews of Brownlow's career, see the following: John C. Tibbetts, "Life to Those Shadows: Kevin Brownlow Talks about a Career in Films," *Journal of Dramatic Theory and Criticism* 14, no. 1 (1999): 79–94; Richard Corliss, "Silents Are Still Golden," *Time*, July 1, 1996, 64; J. Hoberman, "Digging the Past," *The Village Voice*, January 12, 1999, 98; Peter W. Kaplan, "Reconstructing Video Versions of Silent Classics," *The New York Times*, September 21, 1985, 50; John C. Tibbetts, "An Interview with Kevin Brownlow," *Literature/Film Quarterly* 25, no. 1 (1997): 74–76.

5. Arguably, it could also be described as an early example of what is known today as a "mock documentary," wherein fiction is presented in a way characteristic of the codes and conventions of documented facts.

6. Niall Ferguson, ed., *Virtual History: Alternatives and Counterfactuals* (London: Macmillan, 1997), 2.

7. Ferguson, *Virtual History*, 83–85.

8. Robert Rosenstone, ed., *Revisioning History: Film and the Construction of a New Past* (Princeton, NJ: Princeton University Press, 1995), 19. See also Slavoj Žižek, "What If We Don't Act Now?" *London Review of Books*, August 18, 2005, 23; Michael Shermer, "What If? Contingencies and Counterfactuals," in *Science Friction: Where the Known Meets the Unknown* (New York: Holt, 2005), 153–72. See also, a collection of essays pertinent to this subject by writers such as Hayden White, Robert Brent Toplin, and John E. O'Connor in *The American Historical Review* 93, no. 5 (December 1988).

9. J. C. Squire, ed., *If It Had Happened Otherwise: Lapses into Imaginary History* (London: Longmans, Green, 1932), v.

10. Essays on *Bring the Jubilee, The Man in the High Castle*, and *The Difference Engine* may be found in the four-volume *Magill's Guide to Science Fiction and Fantasy Literature* (Englewood Cliffs, NJ: Salem Press, 1996).

11. In 1942, Alberto Cavalcanti's *Went the Day Well?* (U.S. title: *Forty-Eight Hours*) portrayed a contingent of German paratroopers who, disguised as members of the British army, take over the village of Bramley End, in Gloucestershire.

They are ultimately defeated by the villagers. The scenario was based on a story by Graham Greene. Writing in *The Nation*, James Agee praised its "melodramatically plausible actions" and concluded that the film has "the sinister, freezing beauty of an Auden prophecy come true." See *Agee on Film: Reviews and Comments* (Boston: Beacon Press, 1968), 104.

12. Noel Coward's play, like Brownlow's *It Happened Here*, centers on a number of English characters caught up in the Nazi invasion of Britain. They debate the issue of whether British citizens should accommodate themselves to Nazi domination. One character parades his patriotic fervor: "But don't give in—don't ever let them win you round with their careful words and their 'good-behavior' policies. They are our enemies—now and forever. If other people find it expedient to be nice to them—do remember that they don't count, those thinking, broken reeds—they're only in the minority in this country and they'll never be anything else" (49). Another character argues the opposite position: "I prefer to see life as it is rather than as it should be. Being a realist I have adapted myself to the circumstances around me. . . . The world is changing swiftly. . . and to cope with its changes you need better equipment than a confused jumble of high-school heroics" (151–52). See Noel Coward's *Peace in Our Time: A Play in Two Acts and Eight Scenes* (New York: Doubleday, 1948). According to Brownlow, the play was revived in 1997. "I was struck by its similarity in tone to our script," he writes (letter to author, April 28, 1999).

13. Andrew Roberts, "What If Germany Had Invaded Britain in May 1940?" in Ferguson, *Virtual History*, 296–302.

14. Roberts, "What If Germany," 291.

15. According to Brownlow, modern-day Fascists in England have adopted the Cross of St. George as their symbol after an unsuccessful attempt to requisition the Union Jack (letter to author, April 28, 1999).

16. Although not available today, *The Capture* was an important first step in Brownlow's filmmaking aspirations. It was shot over a three-year period, from 1952 to 1955. Brownlow updated de Maupaussant's short story from the Franco-Prussian War to wartime France in 1940. It told the story of how a German patrol was captured by a forester's daughter and taken into custody by the local national guard. Ironically, the guard, not the girl, is given credit for the capture. "After *The Capture*, I knew I was capable of making films," says Brownlow. See his *How It Happened Here* (Garden City, NY: Doubleday, 1968), 25–26.

17. Important writings contemporary to the Free Cinema movement include Lindsay Anderson, "Free Cinema," written in 1957 and anthologized in Richard Meran Barsam, ed., *Nonfiction Film Theory and Criticism* (New York: Dutton, 1976), 70–74; and Gavin Lambert, "Free Cinema," *Sight and Sound* 25 (spring 1956): 173–77. For a book-length overview, see Alexander Walker, *Hollywood UK: The British Film Industry in the 1960s* (New York: Stein and Day, 1974).

18. Gavin Lambert, "Free Cinema," 177.

19. Tony Richardson, "A Free Hand," *Sight and Sound* 28, no. 2 (spring 1959): 174.

20. Penelope Houston, "Room at the Top," *Sight and Sound* 28, no. 2 (spring 1959): 58.

21. "For what it's worth," declares Brownlow, "in the beginning Andrew Mollo and I had nothing to do with Free Cinema and *Sight and Sound*—we were light years away from all that. Amateurs in the UK have no contact whatever with even semi-professionals, as they were" (letter to author, April 28, 1999). Nonetheless, Brownlow would eventually establish many contacts with the Free Cinema filmmakers in later years, including Karel Reisz, Lindsay Anderson (for whom he edited *The White Bus*), and Tony Richardson (for whom he worked as an editor on *Charge of the Light Brigade* in 1968). For Brownlow's account of these associations, see James M. Welsh and John C. Tibbetts, eds., *The Cinema of Tony Richardson* (Albany, State University of New York Press, 1999), 31–37.

22. Quoted in "Gilbert Adair from London," *Film Comment* 16, no. 3 (May–June 1980): 6.

23. For Brownlow's account of the making of the film, see his *How It Happened Here*.

24. David Robinson, "*It Happened Here*," *Sight and Sound* 34, no. 1 (winter 1964–1965): 39.

25. Brownlow, *How It Happened Here*, 25–26.

26. Brownlow, *How It Happened Here*, 138.

27. Quoted in Brian Dean, "Film Critics Protest over Cuts in Nazi Scene," *Daily Mail*, February 26, 1966.

28. Stanley Reed, "*It Happened Here*," *The Times*, March 3, 1966.

29. Robinson, "*It Happened Here*," 39.

30. Lenny Rubenstein, "*It Happened Here*: A Second Look," *Film Comment* 6, no. 4 (1975): 36.

31. Brownlow, *How It Happened Here*, 177.

32. Brownlow, *How It Happened Here*, 138.

33. Sophie Walker, "British Nazis' Film to Be Shown Uncut after 30-Year Ban," *The Independent*, September 29, 1996, 2.

34. James Blue and Michael Gill, "Peter Watkins Discusses His Suppressed Nuclear Film," *Film Comment* 3, no. 4 (1965): 16–17.

35. Letter to author, April 28, 1999.

36. Borges's short story describes this mysterious garden: "The Garden of Forking Paths is an enormous riddle, or parable, whose theme is time. . . . [It constitutes] an infinite series of times, in a growing, dizzying net of divergent, convergent and parallel times. This network of times which approached one another, forked, broke off, or were unaware of one another for centuries, embraces *all* possibilities of time. We do not exist in the majority of these times; in some you exist, and not I; in others I, and not you; in others, both of us. In the present one, which a favorable fate has granted me, you have arrived at my house; in another, while crossing the garden, you found me dead; in still another, I utter these same words, but I am a mistake, a ghost." See Jorge Luis Borges, *Labyrinths: Selected Stories and Other Writings* (New York, 1964), 28.

11

Between What Is and
What If: Kevin Willmott's *CSA*

Thomas Prasch

The German philosopher G. W. F. Hegel insisted, in the introduction to his *Philosophy of History*, that necessity is one of the essential characteristics of history.[1] By this, he meant at least two things. First of all, this fit Hegel's understanding of history as directed, as having a clear design and aim. In Hegel's words, "the history of the World . . . has been a rational process; that the history in question has constituted the rational necessary course of the World-Spirit."[2] This is a conception that he shares with the Confederates of Willmott's film (as well as with the actual nineteenth-century Americans of whom they are a dark reflection), for whom such notions were crystallized in the idea of Manifest Destiny.[3] For Hegel, that history has a defined end made its particular unfolding inevitable, a "providentially determined process."[4] Second and somewhat more simple, Hegel's contention is that historical events are inevitable because they have already happened. You cannot change the past.

But the rest of us have always known better. And because we have always known better, the counterfactual history—the "what if" approach to the past—has its own long, rich history. From the territory of the personal (the remapping of a life around choices made or not made, the territory of second thoughts and regret) to the national/world stages (what if, indeed, as Willmott suggests in *CSA*, the South had won the Civil War?),[5] the counterfactual has provided a mechanism for exploring the meaning of the factual.

And, thus, alternative histories have long been a generic staple. Examples can be culled from high literature, ranging from Renaissance/Enlightenment utopian thought (More through Voltaire) to recent work (such as Philip Roth's recent *Plot against America*, 2004) to pulp fiction (all those sci-fi parallel universes, from Verne and Wells forward); in film, again high (say, the search for the fictive Balkan film pioneer that anchors Angelopoulos's *Ulysses' Gaze*, 1995; also, Woody Allen's *Zelig*, 1983) and low (*This Is Spinal Tap*, 1984, for example); and in television as well (all those parallel-universe episodes of *Star Trek* and *Twilight Zone*, as well as the conceptual root for whole series such as *Time Tunnel* and *Quantum Leap*).

The mockumentary, the genre to which Willmott's film belongs, has become so deeply established that it merits—and, indeed, has begun to develop—its own critical literature.[6] There is, in other words, for practically everyone but Hegel, always another way that history might have come out. And thinking through what might have been becomes a way of understanding what actually is. Or, as Willmott himself often says in discussions of *CSA*, the territory of the film lies between "what if" and "what is."[7]

Even some historians have begun to take the genre seriously.[8] Among historians, the new tendency to play the counterhistorical game has come against significant and long-established opposition. Niall Ferguson, covering the historiography in his introduction to *Virtual History*, summarizes the tradition of resistance to such exercises, noting that

> the attitude of generations of historians, for whom, in the dismissive phrase of E. H. Carr, "counterfactual" history is a mere "parlour game," a "red herring." . . . This hostility to counterfactual arguments has been and remains surprisingly widespread among professional historians. Indeed, E. P. Thompson has gone so far as to dismiss "counterfactual fictions" as mere "*Geschichtsswissenschlopff*, unhistorical shit."[9]

For Ferguson, such resistance can be explained by the commitment of such historians to one or another form of "determinism," which, because of the limiting take on historical causation, locks historians into an essentially predestined account of historical events and prevents them from playing out the possibilities of contingency in the form of alternative pasts.[10]

In Ferguson's account, deterministic versions of history can take a number of forms—he mentions religious, idealistic, and materialist variations, and his historiography tracks the anticounterfactual determinism through Augustine, Hegel, and Comte—but his particular target is clearly the Marxist English historians who dominated British historical studies in the postwar era (but have been in notable decline over the past two decades). Thus, Ferguson's enemies list begins with Carr: "Of all the English socialist historians, probably the least original thinker." It

Official seal of the Confederate States of America. *Courtesy of Kevin Willmott.*

continues to Thompson (and Christopher Hill by a light sideswipe): "By a not dissimilar route, E. P. Thompson also arrived back at the determinist position. . . . At root, it was just reheated Hegel." And it ends with a denunciation of the Gramsci-inspired "younger generation of Marxist historians."[11] For Ferguson, the failure of such historians was not just in their resistance to counterfactuals but also in their commitment to a Marxist agenda. Alternative history thus becomes a tactic to help consign Marx to the dustbin of history. That this cannot really explain the whole, not entirely Marxist profession's resistance to alternative histories is, for Ferguson, beside the point.

Ferguson and company have been, in turn, pilloried for their own political agendas. Tristram Hunt asserts,

Behind the light-hearted maybes lurk more uncomfortable historical and political agendas. The conservatives who contribute to this literature portray themselves as battling against the dominant but flawed ideologies of Marxist and Whig history. But "what if" history poses just as insidious a threat to present politics as it does to fuller understanding of the past. It is no surprise that progressives rarely involve themselves, since implicit in it is the contention that social structures and economic conditions do not matter.[12]

For Hunt and similar critics, the conservative-dominated counterfactual movement reinforces a general reaction against the social history of recent decades, reinserting more conventional historical explanations (the "great man" account of history, for example). Hunt's argument, however, works far better for historians engaged in prose experiments with counterfactualism—in addition to Ferguson, Hunt lists Conrad Black, whom Hunt notes is "a man facing a few counterfactuals of his own"; David Frum, "the former Bush speechwriter"; and John Adamson, "who indulges the dream of Cambridge dons down the centuries"[13]—and far less to filmmakers who have developed the mockumentary genre, many of whom, Willmott included, would seem firmly anchored in leftist politics and for whom the mockumentary form has provided a means to subvert dominant discourses.

But no such ideologically contentious account is really necessary to explain the historical profession's deep resistance to the counterfactual. Rather, the roots of this divide can be found in the process of the professionalization of history writing over the course of the last half of the nineteenth century.[14] In some fashion, in the pursuit of professionalization, historians had to escape the long shadow of Walter Scott, whose work had done so much earlier in the nineteenth century to inspire interest in Scottish history but who had accomplished that end in novels. To differentiate themselves from the Scott tradition, historians had to eschew fiction. It is for this end that German historian Leopold von Ranke's insistence on a source-based empirical history provided such a useful grounding.[15] Von Ranke's famous dictum, that history was "wie es eigentlich gewesen" (how it actually was), precluded exploration of how it actually was not.

And, indeed, it is in defense of such empiricism that Thompson penned his denunciation of "*Geschichtscheissenschlopff*, unhistorical shit." Examined in context—the passage occurs in the long essay that Thompson wrote denouncing Louis Althusser and his theoretical approach to historical subjects—Thompson's anger was prompted above all else by Althusser's dismissal of the empirical grounding of historical studies. Thompson harrumphs, "History (Althusser tells us) hardly exists other than . . . as the application of a theory . . . which does not exist in any real sense."[16] To this, Thompson's strikingly von Rankean response underlines the empirical ground of the discipline: "facts are *there*, inscribed in the historical record, with determinant properties."[17] And it is in precisely this context that Thompson goes on, denouncing a range of "theory" (from Althusser to sociologists to counterfactualists): "all of these theories hobble along programmed routes from one static category to the next. And all of them are *Geschichtenscheissenschlopff*, unhistorical shit."[18] Thompson, notably, accuses such approaches of exactly the same sort of programmatic determinism that Ferguson criticizes in Thompson and his fellow travelers.

But in the end, the theoretical arguments are beside the point, given that historians engage in counterfactuals pretty routinely, whatever their ostensible objections to the practice. Sometimes, this engagement can be subtle; as Geoffrey Eley and David Blackbourn have argued, historians' exploration of the *Sonderweg*, the "special path" of German history (specifically, the route that took Germany, as opposed to its also pretty anti-Semitic Depression-rocked neighbors, down the path to National Socialism) always implicitly measures German developments against an unexpressed norm,[19] which amounts to posing a counterfactual alternative to the "special path." More explicitly, as Ferguson himself notes, even his Marxist opponents routinely flirt with the counterfactual: Carr wondered what might have happened had Vladimir Lenin not died when he did, and E. J. Hobsbawm similarly speculated about a Soviet Union without Stalin.[20] Indeed, it is not difficult to find an American history textbook that poses precisely the counterfactual question that Willmott asks: what would happen if the South won the war? (before going on to assert that it could not possibly have done so).

This brings us back to the subject of Willmott's film. *CSA* is, to put it simply, a mockumentary that explores what might have been the course of American history had the South won the Civil War. But *CSA* is not, in fact, a simple film. What Willmott offers is a double-level mockumentary: a presumably straightforward British documentary about American history since the southern victory, framed as a presentation on CSA-controlled network television (complete with reiterated warnings that the network is "not responsible for the views expressed"). This allows for Willmott to play at multiple forms of parody.

Within the British "documentary," there is, most centrally, the parodying of classic documentary style, above all else targeting the Ken Burns–style, talking-head approach.[21] But then, embedded in it, in the clips and images used to illuminate the experts' outlines of this historical alternative world, there are, aside from the expected "archival" images and bits, parodies on Hollywood film styles, from the silent era forward. We begin with D. W. Griffith, of course; instead of *Birth of a Nation*, we get the great silent director's rather more comic *Hunt for Dishonest Abe*, about the manhunt for Abe Lincoln, seeking to escape the states in blackface. And this is followed with astute (and hilarious) parodies of later genre staples: the romanticized South (now North) of *Gone with the Wind*, the classic biopic,

Abraham Lincoln in blackface. *Courtesy of Kevin Willmott.*

the John Wayne–era war movie, the vintage musical, even reality television (a *Cops* parody called *Runaways*).

Beyond the parodies, there is the alternative history itself. Willmott's
film presents an imagined historical narrative that begins with southern
triumph and continues through a reframed postwar trajectory: the im-
position of slave systems in the North; Canada, haven for abolitionists,
repositioned as a key enemy as well as the new site for African American
cultural efflorescence, from blues and jazz to Presley; a twentieth-century
history remade by that fact, as by southern Manifest Destiny–fueled expansion both west and south (to create an American Western hemispheric
empire); the tensions and riots of the 1960s reconceptualized as guerrilla
war against a still slave-state America.

But, in addition to the film-in-a-film documentary, there is the frame.
The British documentary is broken by regular commercial breaks, re-
flecting the presumed norms of CSA-run television. In the parody commercials that fill those breaks, Willmott is at his wildest, imagining the
products and pitches that might thrive were slavery and the racist slogan-
eering that accompanies it still alive and well. As he puts it in his commentary to the film, "the commercials were used as a way to bring slavery
into the modern world, to make slavery real again."[22] Willmott is also at
his slyest here: there is more reality than we might think in the products

he chooses to promote, although it would give away his best and darkest point to say more than that. Suffice it to say that viewers should stay for the final credits and that there is less distance than we might imagine between the imagined racism of the Confederacy and the actual state of things in post–Civil War America.

But then, that there is less distance between those two, that in some significant ways the South did win the Civil War, is Willmott's sly central argument. As he himself puts it, commenting on the film, "obviously, they lost on the battlefield, but they won in their attempt to hold onto their way of life."[23] Or, as he also says, "by reversing the history, we see how the South won, by losing, how our sympathy for the Lost Cause . . . reduces our horror of slavery and makes the causes of the war suddenly change."[24] Given the current terms of American political power,[25] it is not an argument that can be readily dismissed. The tension that this southern victory, or at least half-victory, creates is one for the hearts of Americans, as Willmott suggests: "The struggle we've had in this country has always been, that there are moments when we're the U.S.A. and then we appear a bit more like the C.S.A."[26] By pushing a counterfactual that sees only the latter side, Willmott forces us to examine the fundamental character of American race relations.

So how do we evaluate *CSA* or, for that matter, any mockumentary? There are two key criteria: plausibility and utility. Plausibility addresses the likelihood of the proposed alternative history: is there any way this might have happened? Utility concerns the usefulness of the counterfactual as a means of understanding the factual, exploring dimensions of the real trajectory of history: how does this alternative history illuminate aspects of the actual? For both criteria, *CSA* gets high marks.

Consider plausibility first: could the South have won the Civil War? At several points, they nearly did. Willmott's particular version of this alternative posits European aid to the South, secured by Confederate diplomacy after key military victories. In fact, there was an active pro-southern diplomatic campaign and supporters for the southern cause abroad.[27] Willmott's case focuses principally on Judah Benjamin, the (Jewish) Confederate secretary of state, but Judah was not the only Confederate (indeed, interestingly, not even the only Confederate Jew) engaged in covert diplomacy abroad; Edwin De Leon was also active in courting European opinion on the Confederacy's behalf in the early years of the war.[28] In Victorian Britain, especially, where the Northern blockade of southern ports had devastating effects on cotton-starved British manufacturing districts, a range of pro-southern voices, from the hard-hit industrial North to the halls of Parliament, promoted British intervention on behalf of the southern cause.[29] The struggle even found echoes in professional anthropology, where it was precisely at this point, in 1863–1864, that the deeply racist polygenist argument, with its claims on behalf of African enslavement, split British anthropological societies and gained a voice in the London Anthropological Society.[30] And the *Trent* affair, in which U.S. naval forces seized Confederate diplomats from a British mail ship, provoked a major diplomatic crisis that came close to bringing the British into the war on the rebel side.[31]

And Willmott's conjectural postwar history rings true as well (or mostly true at any rate). Canada had provided haven for British Loyalists during the American Revolution,[32] for runaway slaves in the period leading up to the Civil War,[33] and for draft dodgers during the Vietnam War;[34] it is the logical site for flight in an imagined collapse of the North. To sustain slavery as a system, the Confederacy would indeed have had to extend it, and Willmott's conjectured fusion of northern slavery with the expansion of factory systems seems a sensible way to do that. Statements by Confederates, and the postwar history of southern voices in Congress, reinforce both the claims that Willmott makes for a Central/South American empire and for relative isolation from European fields of action.[35] Southern racial ideologies in particular make a conjunction of interests between a reconfigured CSA nation and either Nazi Germany or apartheid South Africa far more probable (or, in the South African case—since U.S. policy supported apartheid through most of the Cold War—simply more enduring). That none of this would prevent unresolved racial tensions from emerging a century later, in a somewhat different guise, seems likely as well. So sure, it could have happened.

Counterfactual Iwo Jima. *Courtesy of Kevin Willmott.*

But it did not. And therefore *CSA* is really only an interesting counterfactual, something more than mere parlor game, if this alternative history tells us something about ourselves, about the real history it replaces. And here Willmott's clearest argument is a bluntly simple one: that American black-white relations have been fundamentally, essentially shaped by a history founded on slavery; that whatever you might wish to say about state's rights or slavery's long-term economic nonviability, it is to keep their slaves that the South fought the war; and that, in reprisal against those now freed but still subjugated slaves, the racial policies of the late-nineteenth century and first half of the twentieth century (Jim Crow and the rest) were shaped.

And here Willmott's fight is with a historical memory that tends to forget and forgive, that prefers to evade the uncomfortable facts of slavery and postwar Jim Crow wherever possible, that would rather mention all this in passing before returning to the traditional triumphalist tone that has dominated in American historical narrative. As he notes in his own commentary on the film, "the film attempts to put slavery in the proper position in the American Civil War: front row, center stage."[36] As he further notes, "understanding slavery is something many Civil War lovers like to avoid, minimize, or even reject," and the focus of the film thus provides "a way to keep slavery center stage."[37] Willmott's fight is not just with historians, especially with the public school versions of American history but with a film history as well, far richer in the romanticization of a southern past than with clear grapplings with the history of slavery. This is a film history shaped, after all, by those two great landmarks: Griffith's celebration of the Klan as saviors of the South in *Birth of a Nation* ("It is like writing history with Lightning," as President Wilson famously said of it)[38] and the romantic vision of tragic southern subjugation, *Gone with the Wind*, both films every bit as counterfactual as Willmott's (although somehow they never get treated that way).

On top of the schoolroom history and the projected images of film, add in the forgiving celebration of pop-culture kitsch, from rebel flags to southern rock. And then top it all off with the southern-sympathizing patterns of denial that routinely figure in our Republican-dominated (and mostly southern Republican-dominated) political culture, determined to rewrite the Civil War as a struggle over "states' rights" rather than slavery and, in the contemporary realm, to declare the racial problems of America solved (see, for example, President Bush's remarks on the anniversary of the *Brown v. Board* decision in 2004)[39] while dismantling the government programs that contribute to solving them in fact (thus, the chipping away at affirmative action, national support for public education, the welfare system, etc.).[40] In all these respects, national memory seeks to erase the taint of slavery. Against all that, Willmott is determined that we remember it.

And in doing so, he plays fascinating games with the tangled tango of "what if" and "what is." For what is especially striking about the imagined history of Willmott's conjectural past is how much of it is, quite simply, true and how much more just barely not true. This is the calculated mechanics of what Willmott terms his "reverse history," keeping the artifacts but adjusting the narration to fit an altered view.[41] An exiled and aged Abe Lincoln, in Willmott's film, regrets having not dealt more directly with slavery during his presidency; the actual Lincoln was guilty of just such evasions, even if he did not live long enough to rue them.[42] The Manifest Destiny ideology that fueled westward expansion, that shaped the racial categories that accompanied it, and that featured mission schools for American Indians designed to both subjugate them and destroy their cultural roots is just as much a feature of actual American history as of Willmott's Confederate past.[43] As Willmott notes, "some history simply doesn't change. That was the point of the treatment of American Indians."[44] That is the point, too, of Willmott's joking ghettoization of American Jews on Long Island: "I used the Long Island joke as another example of how minorities are often placed in a certain section—'hood, reservation, or ghetto—where they could be controlled and manipulated."[45] Similar treatment of Asian minorities requires little adjustment between Willmott's counterfactual and the actual long record of discrimination.[46] As Willmott astutely points out, "extermination and genocide are the cousins of slavery."[47] American interference in Central and South American states may not have constituted full-scale imperial conquest, but actual American policy was not exactly hands-off. The racial violence of the 1960s might not have been revolutionary guerrilla actions intended to overthrow a slave system, but both revolutionary ideology and guerrilla tactics were part of the story.[48]

And because "what is" so thoroughly intertwines with the "what if" of Willmott's alternative history, *CSA* works to expose, through comic exaggeration, the critical real territory of unresolved racial tensions in America today, rooted in part in the failure to engage fully the historical terrain of slavery leading up to the Civil War and the postwar abandonment of Reconstruction's promise to bring freed slaves fully into the nation. As Willmott puts it, "there are all these connections to our lives today that I think the film opens up. It makes you see things that you see every day but you don't really think about the origins of."[49] For any who would doubt the relevance of this exploration, the images of the abandoned black population of New Orleans in the wake of Katrina provide ample evidence that the problem of race in America remains utterly unresolved.[50] In *CSA*, Willmott insists that we see what is at the root of that irresolution.

NOTES

1. This chapter extends on a paper delivered at the Film and History Conference, Dallas, Texas, November 2006; that paper in turn was developed from remarks made at a special showing of *CSA* at Washburn University, Topeka, January 27, 2006.

2. G. W. F. Hegel, *Philosophy of History*, trans. J. Sibree (New York: Dover, 1956), 10, and more generally, 9–14. Hegel reverts to the issue in the closing pages of *Phenomenology of Mind*, trans. J. B. Baillie (Atlantic Highlands, NJ: Humanities Press, 1967), 801, 807–8.

3. For a recent discussion of Manifest Destiny, well attuned to the way that the ideology played across the sectional divisions of the United States in the years leading up to the Civil War, see Anders Stephenson, *Manifest Destiny: American Expansionism and the Empire of Right* (New York: Hill & Wang, 1995), esp. chap. 6. See also, Frederick Merk, *Manifest Destiny and Mission in American History: A Reinterpretation* (New York: Knopf, 1969).

4. Hegel, *Philosophy of History*, 13.

5. And Willmott is hardly the first to make the suggestion. See, most obviously, MacKinley Kantor, *If the South Won the Civil War* (1961; rpt., New York: Macmillan / Forge Books, 2001). Two essays in Albert Castel's *Winning and Losing in the Civil War* (Columbia: University of South Carolina Press, 1996) play with the counterfactual case. Conservative commentator William S. Lind's suggestion, in 1999, that America would be better off (more moral, less dominated by the federal government, racially more at rest) under Confederate rule sparked significant controversy; see http://www.freecongress.org/commentaries/2003/030109WL .asp. Roger Ransom's *The Confederate States of America: What Might Have Been* (New York: Norton, 2005) appeared after the first festival showings of Willmott's film, as did Amanda Foreman's essay "The *Trent* Incident Leads to War" (which, like *CSA*, finds hope for the South in international intervention on their behalf), in Andrew Roberts, ed., *What Might Have Been: Imaginary History from Twelve Leading Historians* (London: Orion, 2005), 92–104. The *Trent* incident is again central in Robert Conroy's recent novelistic reimagining of the conflict (with Britain siding with the confederacy), *1862* (Novato, CA: Presidio Press, 2006).

6. See, for example, Craig Hight and Jane Roscoe, *Faking It: Mock-Documentary and the Subversion of Factuality* (Manchester: Manchester University Press, 2002), or the mockumentary filmography hosted by the library of the University of California, Berkeley, at http://www.lib.berkeley.edu/MRC/mockumentaries.html.

7. Comments at the Washburn University showing of *CSA*, January 2006; see also "The Reality of the Fiction," Kevin Willmott's commentary track to the DVD version of *CSA*.

8. See Roberts, *What Might Have Been*; Niall Ferguson, ed. *Virtual History: Alternatives and Counterfactuals* (New York: Basic Books, 1999).

9. Ferguson, *Virtual History*, 4–5. Ferguson mistranscribes Thompson: the word he used, in fact, was *Geschichtscheissenschlopff*. Following Ferguson's footnotes, the Thompson quotation is credited to E. P. Thompson, *The Poverty of Theory and Other Essays* (New York: Monthly Review Press, 1978), 300. In my own copy of *The Poverty of Theory*, however, the quotation appears on page 108.

Curiously, other sources follow Ferguson's pagination; for example, Barney Warf, "The Way It Wasn't: Alternative Histories, Contingent Geographies," in *Lost in Space: Geographies of Science Fiction*, ed. Rob Kitchin and James Kneale (New York: Continuum, 2005), 26; David Gilbert and David Lambert, "Counterfactual Geographies: Worlds That Might Have Been," at http://pure.rhul.ac.uk/portal /files/1196747/GilbertLambertcounterfacts.pdf, 9. It could be that there is another version of Thompson's book out there with fundamentally different pagination. It could also be, however, that the later articles are simply cribbing Ferguson's references. Since both works follow the same outlines—all citing Carr and Thompson before, like Ferguson, moving on to Michael Oakeshott—and since they all get the German wrong, it seems likely Ferguson is the real source for all the citations.

10. Ferguson, *Virtual History*, 5, but pretty much throughout the introduction. Following recent trendy borrowings from scientific thought, Ferguson's account of contingency nods to chaos theory; see 77ff.

11. Ferguson, *Virtual History*, 53, 55, 56.

12. Tristram Hunt, "Pasting over the Past," *Guardian*, April 7, 2004, at http:// www.guardian.co.uk/education/2004/apr/07/highereducation.news/print. Hunt, interestingly, cites the same passages of Thompson and Carr that everyone else uses.

13. Hunt, "Pasting over the Past." The wry note on Black refers to his conviction for mail fraud; although he was appointed to the House of Lords by Tony Blair, his position as press magnate doubtless makes him suspect in Hunt's eyes. Black's counterfactual experiment is "The Japanese Do Not Attack Pearl Harbor," in Roberts, *What Might Have Been*, 153–65. David Frum speculated about what would have happened if Al Gore had won the election in 2000 (Hunt's again wry comment: "I thought he did") in "The Chads Fall Off in Florida," another essay from *What Might Have Been*, and in a brief interlude in *Comeback: Conservatism That Can Win* (New York: Random House/Broadway Books, 2009), 8. John Adamson's alternative history of Britain without a civil war appears as chapter 1 in Ferguson's *Virtual History*.

14. For an excellent account of the English version of these developments, see Philippa Levine, *The Amateur and the Professional: Antiquarians, Historians, and Archaeologists in Victorian England, 1838–1886* (Cambridge: Cambridge University Press, 1986).

15. Von Ranke's writings on historical method have been recently collected in Georg G. Iggers, ed., *The Theory and Practice of History* (London: Routledge, 2010).

16. Thompson, *Poverty of Theory*, 14.

17. Thompson, *Poverty of Theory*, 28.

18. Thompson, *Poverty of Theory*, 108.

19. See David Blackbourn and Geoff Ely, *The Peculiarities of German History* (Oxford: Oxford University Press, 1984).

20. Ferguson, *Virtual History*, 55–56.

21. Willmott discusses his debt to Ken Burns in "The Reality of the Fiction."

22. Willmott, "The Reality of the Fiction."

23. Willmott quoted from "*CSA*: With the Filmmakers," bonus feature to the DVD version of *CSA*.

24. Willmott, "The Reality of the Fiction."

25. At least at the time of the film's making and the period of its theatrical release; the November 2006 elections, at least potentially, change the equation.

26. Willmott quoted from "*CSA*: With the Filmmakers."

27. See Charles M. Hubbard, *The Burden of Confederate Diplomacy* (Knoxville: University of Tennessee Press, 1998); D. P. Crook, *Diplomacy during the American Civil War* (New York: Wiley, 1975); and, specifically on diplomatic struggles by both sides to gain the support of France, Lynn M. Case and Warren F. Spencer, *The United States and France: Civil War Diplomacy* (Philadelphia: University of Pennsylvania Press, 1970).

28. On Judah Benjamin's diplomatic work, Willmott himself cites Eli Evans, *Judah P. Benjamin: The Jewish Confederate* (New York: Free Press, 1988); see Willmott, "The Reality of the Fiction." See also Robert N. Rosen, *The Jewish Confederates* (Columbia: University of South Carolina Press, 2000), esp. 79–80. Edwin De Leon's own account of his activities on behalf of the Confederate cause abroad, originally published as a series of newspaper articles in 1867–1868, has recently been collected (and augmented with some of De Leon's pamphlets of the time) in Edwin De Leon, *The Secret History of Confederate Diplomacy Abroad*, ed. William C. Davis (Lawrence: University of Kansas Press, 2005); see also Rosen, *The Jewish Confederates*, 155–58.

29. The British debate has been especially well covered in the historiography. See, for the political maneuvering, Howard Jones, *Union in Peril: The Crisis over the British Intervention in the Civil War* (Chapel Hill: University of North Carolina Press, 1992); for a close analysis of the public debate and its key actors, Richard Blackett, *Divided Hearts: Britain and the American Civil War* (Baton Rouge: Louisiana State University Press, 2001); and for an interesting explanation of the failure of intervention, Sheldon Vanauken, *The Glittering Illusion: English Sympathy for the Southern Confederacy* (Washington, DC: Regnery, 1989).

30. The classic instance is the presentation (and the debate it provoked, printed along with the essay) of James Hunt's "The Negro's Place in Nature," *Journal of the Anthropological Society of London* 2 (1864): xv–xvi.

31. The *Trent* affair is mentioned in all the works on the British response to the war mentioned in note 12; it comes up frequently in counterfactual accounts, including those in note 5; and it has been recently treated by historians in more detail, in Norman Ferris, *The Trent Affair: A Diplomatic Crisis* (Knoxville: University of Tennessee Press, 1977), and Gordon Warren, *Fountain of Discontent: The Trent Affair and Freedom of the Seas* (Boston: Northeastern University Press, 1981).

32. W. Stewart Wallace's classic account *The United Empire Loyalists: A Chronicle of the Great Migration* (1922; rpt., Toronto: University of Toronto Press, 1972) still serves to sketch the basic dimensions of the Loyalist diaspora after the American Revolution.

33. See Robin Winks, *The Blacks in Canada: A History* (Montreal: McGill/Queen's University Press, 1971), chap. 6. See also Willmott, "The Reality of the Fiction."

34. A recent account can be found in John Hagan, *Northern Passage: American Vietnam War Resisters in Canada* (Cambridge, MA: Harvard University Press, 2001).

35. Particularly useful in this respect is Robert E. May, *The Southern Dream of a Caribbean Empire 1854–1861* (1973; rev. ed., Gainesville: University Press of Florida, 2002). See also Reginald Horsman, *Race and Manifest Destiny: The Origins*

of American Racial Anglo-Saxonism (Cambridge, MA: Harvard University Press, 1981), with particular attention to the proposals of Matthew Maury, 280–81.

36. Willmott, "The Reality of the Fiction."

37. Willmott, "The Reality of the Fiction."

38. For this quotation, as well as evaluation of the debates about it (and the conclusion that indeed Wilson likely said it), see Richard Schickel, *D. W. Griffith: Am American Life* (New York: Simon & Schuster, 1984), 268–70 and 619 n. 5.

39. President Bush's remarks appear at http://www.whitehouse.gov/news /releases/2004/05/20040517-4.html. Note in particular how Bush, who grew up in a Texas that still segregated its schools, declares of the battle against racial inequality: "We tend to think of this as the distant drama of another country."

40. For a handy summary, see "The Demise of Affirmative Action," in Terry H. Anderson, *The Pursuit of Fairness* (New York: Oxford University Press, 2000), chap. 5.

41. Willmott uses the term in "The Reality of the Fiction." His first example— the famous painting of the surrender of Appomattox, where the image is used but the narration is simply reversed—covers the creation of counterfactuals, but the implications become more complex when the "what if" and the "what is" more closely coincide, as with, say, Manifest Destiny.

42. The racial ideas of Lincoln have long fueled discussion and debate among historians. For a recent survey (and continuation of the debates), see Brian R. Dirck and Allen C. Guelzo, eds., *Lincoln Emancipated: The President and the Politics of Race* (DeKalb: Northern Illinois University Press, 2007). For Willmott's own quite interesting discussion of Lincoln as a "good" but not "perfect" man, conflicted in his approach to slavery especially early in his presidency, see his comments in both "The Reality of the Fiction" and "*CSA:* With the Filmmakers."

43. On Manifest Destiny, see note 3. On the assimilationist politics of mission schools for Native Americans, see David Wallace Adams, *Education for Extinction: American Indians and the Boarding School Experiment* (Lawrence: University Press of Kansas, 1995); Michael Coleman, *American Indian Children at School, 1850–1930* (Jackson: University Press of Mississippi, 1993); and Paul Francis Prucha, *American Indian Policy in Crisis: Christian Reformers and the Indian, 1865–1900* (Norman: University of Oklahoma Press, 1975).

44. Willmott, "The Reality of the Fiction."

45. Willmott, "The Reality of the Fiction." The actual anti-Semitism of southern racial ideology is well documented, ironically, in Rosen, *Jewish Confederates.*

46. See, for example, Angelo Ancheta, *Race, Rights, and the Asian American Experience* (New Brunswick, NJ: Rutgers University Press, 1998).

47. Willmott, "The Reality of the Fiction."

48. For a recent overview, see Jeffrey O. G. Ogbar, *Black Power: Radical Politics and African American Identity* (Baltimore: Johns Hopkins University Press, 2004).

49. Willmott quoted in "*CSA:* With the Filmmakers."

50. Willmott himself makes the Katrina connection as well in "The Reality of the Fiction."

12

The "Serious" Mockumentary: The Trivialization of Disaster? The Case of Peter Watkins

James M. Welsh

As the mockumentary has taken its place in the public consciousness, filmmakers, fans, journalists, and academics—the clever, earnest, and trendy alike—have attempted to define its parameters. A complicated and sometimes contradictory genre, it encompasses the parody and the fake, the gentle wit of Christopher Guest and the biting political sarcasm of Michael Moore, the "comic" and the "serious." While there is certainly much to explore in those films that engage in overt "mocking" of their subjects, such as Guest's *Best in Show* (2000) or Larry Charles's controversial *Borat: Cultural Learnings of America for Make Benefit Glorious Nation of Kazakhstan* (2006), it is often the "serious" mockumentary—with its portrayal of false or "alternate" history—that presents audiences and scholars with the genre's most compelling challenges. Its appropriation of the documentary format asks us to consider not only the filmmaker's overt narrative commentary but also our understandings of the documentary form itself.

This contradictory notion of the "serious mockumentary" involves some key definitive questions: What, for example, constitutes a documentary film? What are the limits of the documentary genre? What are the basic expectations for such films? Truth? Newsreel accuracy? Authenticity? Objectivity? If the intention is not to "mock" the true or the authentic, by what logic could the work be called a "mockumentary"? In a contorted form, when does a documentary become something else again?

During the 1950s in Britain, the documentary film turned experimental, when filmmakers Ken Russell, Kevin Brownlow, and Peter Watkins all began testing the limits of the genre. But the BBC had strict guidelines establishing limits and constraints on the documentary genre. Peter Watkins got his first assignment at BBC on the basis of his brilliant amateur faux documentary *The Forgotten Faces* (1961), which purportedly "documented" the Hungarian rebellion of 1956 but in fact was shot in county Kent, south of London. Watkins had never set foot in Budapest, but he had carefully studied photographs of the rebellion, and media "experts" were fooled by his work, which seemed "authentic." This creative experimentalism carried forward to the two films that Watkins directed for BBC, *Culloden* (1964) and *The War Game* (1965), the latter of which ultimately earned an Academy Award for Best Documentary in 1966, even though the event "documented" was entirely speculative, a nuclear attack on county Kent in England that had never occurred. Should there be ethical concerns about "documenting" the imaginary?

Consider, therefore, a film that portrays the possible consequences of a nuclear attack that never occurred: should such a film be considered a "documentary" if it is "documenting" merely the hypothetical, even though it may be filmed in effectively convincing cinema verité, "documentary" style? *The War Game*,[1] directed by Peter Watkins, was destined to become the most controversial film ever made in Britain to that point; it was banned from being broadcast by the BBC, and the banning was debated in Parliament and in the editorial pages of newspapers throughout the United Kingdom for well over a year, until, finally, the BBC relented and agreed to permit the film's release for art house cinemas only, though it was still considered too "horrific" for telecasting.

The "horrific" nature of *The War Game* was inextricably tied to its documentary style and its (implied) factuality. Prior cinematic depictions of nuclear war and its aftermath had been deliberately, even ostentatiously, abstract. Stanley Kramer's all-star *On the Beach* (1959) used empty streets and abandoned buildings to suggest the extinction of the human race, while *Panic in the Year Zero* (1962) and *Dr. Strangelove* (1964) used stock footage of mushroom clouds to suggest the obliteration of, respectively, Los Angeles and the entire civilized world. *Fail-Safe* (1964) presented its twin nuclear attacks on Moscow and New York in a form that was more intimately framed yet still emotionally detached. The attack on Moscow, narrated on speakerphone by the American ambassador, ends in midsentence with a high-pitched scream: the sound of the phone being melted as the nuclear fireball engulfs it. Brief scenes depicting New Yorkers going about their business on a clear fall day represent the last moments of peace in the city. At the moment the bombs detonate, each one ends in a freeze-frame.[2] *The War Game* allows no such comfortable detachment from

Scenes such as this shocked audiences of *The War Game. Pathe Contemporary Film, courtesy of Photofest.*

the immediate aftereffects of a nuclear-tipped missile. Watkins's cameras place the viewer on the ground and in the moment, amid flames, rubble, and shattered lives. Dazed, burnt, begrimed survivors stagger past the camera, buffeted by the hundred-mile-per-hour winds of a firestorm. Death occurs in full view of the camera and is marked not by a blinding flash or a freeze-frame but by the effects of heat stroke and asphyxiation.

The broadcasting ban remained in effect for more than twenty years, and by the time that it was lifted, *The War Game* had been eclipsed by later (and even more horrendous) end-of-civilization-as-we-know-it productions. The BBC's *Threads* (1984), directed by Mick Jackson, depicted the rapid disintegration of normal life in Sheffield during the aftermath of a nuclear attack. It followed two films made for American television the previous year: Lynne Littmann's *Testament*, set in a fictional suburb of San Francisco, and Nicholas Meyer's *The Day After*, set in the university town of Lawrence, Kansas. All three films, products of the renewed Cold War anxieties of the early 1980s, presented themselves as dramas, with "typical" individuals and families acting as viewpoint characters. They abandoned Watkins's use of a dispassionate narrative voice and his presentation of the figures on screen as generic humans, "this woman" or "this man," rather than as individuals with histories and personalities.

The grim horror of Watkins's imagery. *Pathe Contemporary Film, courtesy of Photofest.*

At the same time, however, all three films offer their audiences a vision that is Watkins's writ large. They, like *The War Game*, chronicle—matter-of-factly and in horrific detail—a bleached and broken postbomb world, defined by chaos, despair, and pain. "Britain Can Take It!" propaganda films proclaimed during the Blitz of 1940–1941. *The War Game*, like this trio of films, documented the aftermath of imagined Cold War "blitzes" to argue that, in the age of nuclear weapons, those who expressed such optimistic sentiments were merely deluding themselves.

But no one to my knowledge has ever referred to any of these films as a "serious mockumentary"—at least not until the advent of postmodern reflexivity, where the label "mockumentary" grew in descriptive breadth and was applied retroactively to not only parody but fakes and speculative history as well. But does this label represent a trivialization of those fearful speculations? For that is what Mick Jackson's *Threads* is about, taking the speculative thesis of *The War Game* one step beyond and speculating in more detail than what Watkins imagined about an uncivilized world deprived of all the advantages of modern science and technology.

The framework of the nuclear documentary (to describe the genre more accurately) was invented by Peter Watkins, who worked for the BBC and served an apprenticeship there before being handed his first project,

Culloden (1964), a historical documentary about the last battle fought on British soil, in the Highlands of Scotland in 1745. The success of *Culloden* enabled Watkins to make *The War Game* (the dream project of his youth), and the success of *The War Game* encouraged Watkins to make another hypothetical "documentary" (not really a "mockumentary"), which depicted Vietnam War protesters rounded up and put into detention camps in the California desert, where they were tried, brutalized, and then conveniently murdered by right-minded reactionaries empowered by the 1950 Internal Security Act, the so-called McCarren Act, which was in fact repealed shortly after the film's release in 1971. This was an entirely fictive scenario, shot convincingly in faux documentary style, using nonprofessional actors, revolutionary youngsters, and their elders. The events depicted *might* have happened had the war in Southeast Asia spiraled out of control; but, of course, nothing *in fact* like this ever occurred. Critics, both left and right, excoriated *Punishment Park* (1971), the only film that Watkins completed in the United States, but given our understanding of the budding genre at the time, none would have strained its boundaries so far as to call it a "mockumentary."

Rediscovering the film nearly thirty-five years later, Stuart Klawans wrote in *The Nation*, "In the depths of the Nixon era, Watkins set out to make a fiction film set in an America just slightly worse than reality" and, in doing so, made a film that, now, in the context of the abstracted "war on terror," might have been "snatched from today's awful reality."[3] This "fake documentary" was judged too brutal for mass consumption and was quickly withdrawn from the movie marketplace. Klawans found three justifications for the rerelease of *Punishment Park* on DVD by New Yorker Films in 2005: (1) its "absolute accuracy about the political divisions of the time," since the improvised speeches of the nonprofessional "actors" (dissidents, right-leaning tribunal members, National Guardsmen, and police) "reflected their actual beliefs" and hostilities; (2) the director's "astounding mimicry of television news coverage and BBC special reports. Few people had used this strategy before him; none since have done it better"; and (3) Guantánamo or Abu Ghraib: "It took thirty-four years, but the near future of Watkins's movie has now become our present."

Punishment Park is a fictional film shot in "realistic," newsreel documentary style; it is a false "documentary" set in the "near future." It is part of a strand in American culture—novels such as Jack London's *The Iron Heel* (1908), Sinclair Lewis's *It Can't Happen Here* (1935), and Robert A. Heinlein's *If This Goes On* (1940) and feature films such as *Gabriel over the White House* (1933) and *Keeper of the Flame* (1942)—that sees democracy as fragile and totalitarianism only a crisis away. It takes the dramatized "Communist takeovers" staged in the 1950s in towns such as Mosinee, Wisconsin, and inverts them.[4] The "takeovers" were political theater staged by the right to call attention to the "Red Menace" and the need for a strong government and vigilant citizens. *Punishment Park*, in contrast, is a call for citizens to be vigilant *against* a too-strong government more threatening to civil liberties than any communist enemy. To call it a "mockumentary" would be to trivialize its power, sense, and meaning; it would also be an insult to the filmmaker who put his career in jeopardy by making it. Watkins's next four films were to be made in exile, in Scandinavia, since there was no work for him in England. In his hands, whatever the stock—silver nitrate, celluloid, even videotape—would become volatile and explosive! The director developed a reputation of being difficult to work with, but, in fact, his methods of filmmaking were too forthright, direct, probing, and honest. This became true even in tolerant Sweden, where he made a documentary about teenage suicide called *The '70s People* (1975), which was critical of Swedish family culture and society.

As his award-winning amateur film *The Forgotten Faces* (1961) demonstrates, Peter Watkins began his "documentary" career through historical illusion and trickery. The success of his amateur film about the fall of Budapest during the ill-fated Hungarian Revolution of 1956 got Watkins hired at the BBC. Head of documentaries Huw Wheldon assigned Watkins to work with producer Stephen Hearst on a film titled *The Life and Times of Marshal Tito*. Watkins was cooperative and was then given full rein on a historical "documentary" that would dramatize the rebellion of the Highland Scots in support of Charles Edward Stuart (known as "The Young Pretender," or Bonnie Prince Charlie), who returned from exile in 1745 to raise an army that would place his father ("The Old Pretender," son of the long-deposed King James II) on the throne of the United Kingdom. The 1745 rebellion, initially successful, ended in 1746 when the rebel army was crushed by royal forces at Culloden Moor, in the hills above Inverness, Scotland.

The Highlanders loyal to Charles Edward Stuart (portrayed by Watkins as a thoughtless and indecisive fool) were seriously mismatched against a well-armed and effectively disciplined British army, led by a "conquering hero": the Duke of Cumberland, third son of King George II, whose praises are not exactly sung in this iconoclastic filmed treatment. In telling the story of the battle, Watkins depends to a degree on the "expert" commentary of Andrew Henderson, the eighteenth-century biographer of Cumberland. Watkins placed an actor representing Andrew Henderson on the battlefield as an on-camera commentator, reading from his "official" *History of the Rebellion*, published in 1753, as if he were an "embedded" reporter.[5] Watkins himself also provides a parallel off-camera commentary in his own voice to punctuate and chasten the "official" version from Andrew Henderson, drawing on the work of modern historian John Prebble, author of *Culloden* (1961).

The structure of Watkins's *Culloden*, with its mingling of re-creation, newsreel-style camera work, and commentary written after the fact by historians, evokes the American television series *You Are There*. Produced by the CBS network's news division, *You Are There* featured half-hour reconstructions of pivotal moments in history, as "reported" by CBS news correspondents. Television reporters in modern dress, playing themselves, conducted interviews with actors playing recognizable historical figures and "man in the street" figures who (also in period costume and character) commented on the action. *You Are There* focused on presenting a scrupulously "objective" version of history in which all sides were given equal time and reported facts, rather than drawing interpretive conclusions. Watkins's film, however, had a distinct point of view. Ultimately, *Culloden* is an antiwar film expressing outrage over the horrors of modern warfare and then the so-called pacification of the Highlands, resulting in what the Watkins narrator explains can only be described as a conscious policy of genocide. Nearly one hundred people were "butchered or maimed on the road to Inverness," the Watkins narrator explains, "whether or not they had taken part in the battle."

Between *Forgotten Faces* and *Culloden*, Watkins develops a more highly stylized documentary method. The strength of the earlier film is its careful set decoration and its apparent cinema verité style. In *Culloden*, Watkins sacrifices some of this intense "realism" by inserting the anachronistic Henderson as embedded reporter, who functions rather like Derek Jacobi's Chorus in Kenneth Branagh's 1989 film adaptation of Shakespeare's *Henry V*. Curiously, however (and I wish I could explain this better for my own satisfaction), the choric intrusion somehow does not destroy the "realistic" effect.

Watkins used exactly the same anachronistic device thirty-five years later in his film about the Paris Commune, titled *La Commune (Paris 1871)*, released at the Toronto Film Festival September 7, 2001. Against a background of fighting involving radical Republicans and Socialists against the Versailles-influenced National Assembly during the Franco-Prussian War, the film alternates between two embedded television journalists who are there to report the action. The problem, of course, is that the action is set in the year 1871. Perhaps a larger problem is that in this later film, the reporting goes on for nearly six hours. The reporters represent two media sources: one "official" ("Versailles TV," presumably the French national network), the other a low-budget guerrilla operation called "Commune TV." The contention eventually led to the slaughter of some twenty-five thousand "anarchists and innocent citizens alike," according to *Variety* reviewer Eddie Cockrell, who headlined his review of the experimental documentary in very extravagant terms: "white-knuckle thriller, history lesson, polemical mass-media critique, genre-bending docudrama."[6] In Toronto, the film was shown on one day, with a fifteen-minute intermission two hours into the show. At the Smithsonian in Washington, DC, it was presented in two parts over two weekends. After the film surfaced, Cockrell's enthusiasm was not sufficient to generate a popular audience for Watkins's 345-minute history lesson.

And yet, Peter Watkins has experienced something of a renaissance, as his work has been "rediscovered." In a feature appropriately titled "The Troublemaker," Paul Arthur brought attention to Watkins in *Film Comment*, the superslick, trendy organ of the Lincoln Center Film Society, calling Watkins "the Nostradamus of the postwar cinema," whose "dozen prickly, often incendiary fact-fiction hybrids" are for the most part unavailable to general viewers, in any format."[7] Watkins is gifted, that fact is indisputable, and about as innovative a documentary filmmaker as ever lived. But his gifts have been compromised by his temperamental inability to work smoothly with projects that he cannot utterly control. His rage against corporate control goes back to the flare-up over *The War Game*, a film that won the BBC an Academy Award that one needn't expect to see on display at the corporate headquarters at White City outside London.

The nearest approach that Watkins had to a studio film was *Privilege* (1967), funded by a London branch of Universal Studios, concerning a pop star manipulated into serving the agenda of a cynical right-wing government in power. His most well-crafted films—*Gladiators* (1969), a feature film for Sandrews, and *Edvard Munch* (1974), a television film released successfully as a feature film for art house audiences—were funded and shot in Scandinavia. With *Munch*, a complex psychological portrait of the expressionist painter best known for *The Scream*, Watkins went to an opposite extreme from the compact forty-seven-minute shock approach of *The War Game*. *Munch* was originally three hours long, though New Yorker Films released a shorter version for art house screenings. *The Journey* (1987), Watkins's epic remake of *The War Game*, ran to an impossible fourteen and a half hours of screen time. The idea, apparently, was that it could be screened an hour at a time over a fifteen-week semester, supposing that anyone would want to spend half a year examining the thoughts and frustrations of alienated filmmaker Peter Watkins. The film breaks down interestingly enough into multiple documentaries covering the development of the atom bomb, for example, the "White Train," and hours of discussions with "concerned" citizens (cf. *La Commune*). But nothing, really, is "mocked" by the treatment, save audiences' faith in what is real. Peter Watkins is to Christopher Guest or Michael Moore as Bertrand Russell is to Walt Disney or Oliver Hardy.

The disaster of *The War Game*—little to mock. *Pathe Contemporary Film, courtesy of Photofest.*

Throughout his career, Watkins has always been on the defensive, as if craving controversy and misfortune. After fighting what he called the "official" story for forty years, Peter Watkins finally "threw in the towel," according to Gayle MacDonald of the Toronto *Globe and Mail*.[8] Watkins had moved to Hamilton, Ontario, from Lithuania in 2002, accepting Canada as his home after a lifetime of (self-imposed) exile from his native Britain. After a retrospective of the director's work was mounted in his honor at the Cinematheque Ontario, Watkins became upset by a piece written for *The Globe and Mail* by John Bentley Mays, who called Watkins "one of the most extraordinary film artists of the late 20th Century" but added that the director's "very bleak, stark world-view" was "a problem worth noting, and arguing about."[9]

The oversensitive Watkins went ballistic after reading the piece and responded with a seven-page open letter announcing that he was "throwing in the towel" after four decades because he could no longer tolerate "the new era of (media) McCarthyism."[10] Watkins also refused to attend the concluding event of the Cinematheque tribute in his honor on March 8 and even heaped criticism on the Canadian Broadcasting Corporation, which had in fact been helpful to Watkins and permitted him to use its editing facilities during the 1980s, when Watkins struggled to complete his fourteen-and-a-half-hour epic *The Journey*. The outburst was irrational but not for Watkins, who had been nurturing a persecution complex for decades.[11]

John Bentley Mays, the journalist who triggered this incredible display of self-pity and outrage by suggesting that the director's "world-view" was more "simple and simplistic than his art at its best," found Watkins's "decision to commit hari-kari in our midst 'very distressing.'"[12] Liberal filmgoers were also distressed, since this was a truly talented though tempestuous artist who usually asked incisively probing questions but, unfortunately, had a low tolerance for criticism. In comparison to Peter Watkins, the far more famous Michael Moore is something of a pussycat.

Suppose, then, that Peter Watkins has "thrown in the towel." He will still leave behind a filmography that is consistently innovative, although sometimes puzzling and peculiar. The term *mockumentary* is in many ways too limited to describe *The War Game* or *Punishment Park*, his two speculative essay films dealing with the "near future" (though in both instances, a future that was never realized in quite the way Watkins imagined it might be). The "mockumentary" label might have some resonance, however, if applied to his historical reconstructions of the past, *Culloden* (his first feature film) and *La Commune* (his last). Both films depend on anachronistic gimmicks. In *Culloden*, Watkins broke with an otherwise uncompromisingly "realistic" treatment to place a historian on the battlefield to literally walk the audience through the battle. This imitative "See It Now" approach did not so much "mock" the treatment but, rather, enhanced it. In *La Commune*, however, the gimmick is far more intrusive, as multiple "embedded" television reporters cover an insurrection. The complication, of course, is that the insurrection takes place in 1871, fracturing credulity. The film, as described by *The Columbia Journalism Review*, "tells the story of the people's uprising that followed France's defeat in the Franco-Prussian war." While "anarchy and poverty reigned in the French capital, a group of workers and radical intellectuals set up a socialist regime that lasted for two months, until government troops, exiled to Versailles, conquered Paris and massacred more than 20,000 people involved with [this] utopian experiment."[13]

This was a "documentary" mannerism that Watkins had used before, in *Punishment Park*, in *Gladiators*, and in his Swedish videoplay, *The Trap* (1975). One significant difference, however, was that all of the earlier films just mentioned were set in the "near" future, not in the past. Another problem in *La Commune* is that the film is three to six times longer than the earlier examples and the anachronism is correspondingly more irritating, more insistent, and more shrill. In the case of the "Versailles TV" coverage, Watkins mocks the excesses of establishment network or cable television coverage. It is intended "to be a parody of mainstream news channels," with a cartoon, aristocratic anchor, accompanied by a "screaming pundit . . . arguing the loyalist position."[14] Loyal viewers of Fox Television News would recognize the setup.

But does the fact that *La Commune* mocks mainstream media television coverage make the film a "mockumentary"? Watkins has consistently criticized what he considers to be corrupt television and news-gathering practices, and he rejects the myth of "objectivity" that others believe should govern journalists and documentary filmmakers. Before the premiere of *La Commune* at the Musée d'Orsay in Paris, Watkins told *The Guardian* newspaper on February 25, 2000, that he believed "that had TV taken an alternative direction during the 1960s and 1970s and worked in a more open way, global society today would be vastly more humane and just."[15] Watkins believes that there has been an "accumulation of global media power with no accountability that is not only not being challenged but is not even being debated."[16] In a world of media "fakes"—false objectivity and artificial authority—what is the distance between "news" and "speculative history"? Do the boundaries of the "serious" mockumentary bleed into the reality of contemporary documentaries? Or do both undo each other? As the "fake" documentary undoes its "real" counterpart, does the too-often falsity of the "real" leave the "serious" mockumentary without a worthy target? Comic parody will always have its object—an ignorant society makes fun of what it does not understand and an anxious society laughs at what it most fears. (Witness, for example, the popularity of Kubrick's *Dr. Strangelove* in comparison to *The War Game*.) But if parody mocks in ways that obscure understanding, it is unaffordable. Similarly, if the "serious" mockumentary trivializes disaster—from the crisis of media ethics to the crisis of war—it, too, poses risks that are unaffordable.

NOTES

1. There has been a gradual resurgence of interest in the films of Peter Watkins (born Norbiton, Surrey, October 29, 1936): His American film *Punishment Park* (1971) was released on DVD by New Yorker Films in late 2005, and his Academy Award winner *The War Game* was released by New Yorker Films in July of 2006 on a DVD package that included his first professional film, *Culloden* (1964). For a complete annotated listing of his films to the late 1980s and a fully documented account of *The War Game* controversy in Britain, see J. M. Welsh, *Peter Watkins: A Guide to References and Resources* (Boston: Hall, 1986). The first career survey of the director's work was Joseph A. Gomez's *Peter Watkins*, published in the Twayne Series on Film Directors (Boston: Twayne, 1979).

2. See, for example, Kim Newman, *Apocalypse Movies: End of the World Cinema* (New York: St. Martin's Griffin, 2000), 147–62.

3. Stuart Klawans, "The Best Intentions," *The Nation*, December 12, 2005, 44.

4. Richard M. Fried, *The Russians Are Coming! The Russians Are Coming! Pageant Try and Patriotism in Cold-War America* (New York: Oxford University Press, 1998), 67–86.

5. This explanatory device is parodied in *Monty Python and the Holy Grail* (1975), where a historian in modern dress appears in the midst of the action (set in 982 AD) to comment on it. When he is slain by a passing knight, policemen in modern dress arrive to investigate the crime, and the movie ends with them arresting Arthur, Lancelot, Bedivere, and dozens of extras. The arrests take place during preparations for battle that are (unlike most of the rest of the film) shot with a distinctly Watkins-esque realism.

6. Eddie Cockrell, *"La Commune (Paris 1871),"* *Variety*, October 8–14, 2001, 64.

7. Paul Arthur, "The Troublemaker," *Film Comment* 40, no. 3 (2004): 58–65.

8. Gayle MacDonald, "Watkins Throws in the Towel," *The Globe and Mail*, March 9, 2004, R3.

9. MacDonald, "Watkins Throws in the Towel."

10. MacDonald, "Watkins Throws in the Towel."

11. See James M. Welsh, "The Modern Apocalypse: *The War Game*," *Journal of Popular Film and Television* 11, no. 1 (1983): 25–41.

12. MacDonald, "Watkins Throws in the Towel."

13. Gal Beckerman, *"Cri de Coeur*: The Revolution *Will* Be Televised," *Columbia Journalism Review* (September/October 2003): 55–56.

14. Beckerman, *"Cri de Coeur,"* 56.

15. Peter Lennon, "Hate and War," *The Guardian*, February 25, 2000, 2–3.

16. Lennon, "Hate and War."

13

The Making of
It Happened Here

Kevin Brownlow

The other day, I saw a prestigious Italian documentary called *La Grande
Storia*, about Nazi propaganda. RAI-TV researchers had made an
amazing discovery; in the archives of the *Reichsfilmintendant*, Fritz Hip-
pler, they had found a film made by the Germans to convince the occu-
pied territories that they had invaded England. It was called *The Conquest
of London* and it was made in 1941. When a friend sent me a tape, I eagerly
ran down to these remarkable images. I was amazed—they were so familiar. They were familiar, in fact, for I had shot them. I don't mean that I was
a *Wehrmacht* cameraman. I mean that I had been behind the 16 mm Bell &
Howell camera that had photographed these images of German soldiers
marching through London. In the 1960s, I had made what would now
be called a mockumentary, and the Italian television people had stolen
my footage, and in one of the most barefaced acts of pilfering I have ever
encountered, they had stripped off the soundtrack and put on their own.

I suppose I should have been angry. But I couldn't help feeling a certain
satisfaction. If that footage looked convincing enough to fool a hall full of
experts (the film was shown to a gathering of historians and researchers),
then we'd done rather well.

Mockumentary? No one had thought of the name in those days. It
was politely referred to as "history fiction." I didn't regard it as that. I

thought it a perfectly legitimate exercise to reveal a sober truth through a startling setting.

After the war, when the ghastly truth came out, you kept hearing people say, "It couldn't happen here." My father had witnessed British troops in action in Ireland in the Troubles, and after hearing about the Black and Tans, I knew that the Germans had no copyright on barbaric behavior.

When I first got the idea for *It Happened Here*, I was an office boy, just out of school at seventeen. I was carrying cans to a laboratory in Soho, when a black Citroen screeched to a halt beside me, two men jumped out and ran into a delicatessen, and one shouted back to the driver in German. It had all the hallmarks of a Gestapo raid from a war film, but it was happening in sunny, somnolent London. I had been reading Orwell's *1984* and was an admirer of John Wyndham's *The Kraken Wakes*, and I saw an exciting film in the story of what might have happened had the Germans won the war. However, office boys earning four pounds ten shillings a week were not encouraged to put their fantasies onto celluloid. I wanted to direct films, but the average age of film directors was fifty-seven. I could hardly be expected to wait another forty years; why not make the film myself? When I told my parents about my plans, my mother tried to discourage me. She was usually my strongest supporter, but I could see her point. "What about the big scenes?" she asked. "How on earth would you tackle, say, a Nazi rally in Trafalgar Square?" The moment she said that, I could see it in my mind's eye. I decided to tackle that scene as a priority.

I know now why they choose boys of my age for the army. They lack imagination. They will kill other young men without qualms. If you had asked me to list the drawbacks to staging a Nazi rally, I could not have done so. I just saw it as a mountain peak to be tackled, and once conquered, producers would form a queue outside my door with offers of finance. and I wouldn't have to bother with the rest of the picture.

I was now eighteen and it was 1956. I had already made one film, based on a Guy de Maupassant story, and although it had taken months to complete, it had brought me some small notoriety. I involved the same people and staged my Nazi rally. It was filmed on a rainy Sunday morning, and only a handful of people turned up. Far from reproducing the terrifying might of *Triumph of the Will*, the little group at the base of Nelson's Column looked as humble as a group of street cleaners. Almost before I had seen the rushes, I knew I had to retake it. I had spent what little money I had, but this was beyond humiliation. I borrowed heavily and staged it again, and this time I struck the spark of publicity. I never noticed them and cannot imagine how they knew what was taking place, but there were professional photographers from the glossy Continental magazines in Trafalgar Square that morning. Suddenly, I was big news.

The *Daily Express* interviewed me and prompted a protest from the Ministry of Works—it would never have issued a permit had it known what would take place.

I considered giving up after the first session; no one would have noticed. But abandoning the project now was out of the question. Everywhere I went, people asked me how the film was progressing. Every spare minute I thought about it. And now I had been promoted into the cutting rooms; as a trainee assistant editor, I was earning six pounds ten a week and had access to proper editing equipment. I reverted to simpler scenes. There were picturesque bomb sites in Soho, and I exploited these for stereotyped scenes of occupation, and when a display of German aircraft—Heinkels, Dorniers, and Messerschmitts—was mounted on Horse Guards Parade, I managed to sneak my actors in Luftwaffe uniform in front of a backdrop I could never have afforded to stage myself. But the actors got fed up with the long gaps between sessions and drifted away, and I was left with sequences I could not use.

Despite my shambolic organization and amateurish direction, I saw myself as the second Orson Welles. Thus, you will appreciate why I never wrote a script. Oh, I wrote an outline, a synopsis, but it covered no more than the first three reels. Had I written a complete script, I would have been faced with the limitations of my film, and worse, I would realize that it would never match *Citizen Kane*. But for a few delicious months, I fooled myself and those around me.

Scene still from *It Happened Here. Courtesy of Kevin Brownlow.*

One Saturday, I went down to the Portobello Road market where I had been told that a trader dealt in World War II *materiel*. While I was buying some German helmets, I asked the man if he knew of any collectors of this sort of stuff. "Well, there's one there." He pointed to a young man who resembled an art student. He said that his name was Andrew Mollo, he was sixteen, and he was an art student because he had been slung out of school.

I decided to ensnare him with an amazing piece of intelligence I had only just acquired. "Did you know there was a Russian family in Kensington who has a fantastic collection of German military stuff?"

"I think that's us," he said diffidently. And when I accompanied him home, I realized how right he was. He lived in a magnificent Kensington house, which later became the Moroccan Embassy. On the top floor lived the father, Eugene, a Russian veteran of the Red and the White armies, a man of immense knowledge who became my mentor and who collected Russian military items. On the next floor lived John, whose interest was French military history; on the next lived Boris, with his English collection; and on the first floor was Andrew, his room painted red, white, and black and his Third Reich items impressively displayed. I thought at first he was a Nazi, but I was being simplistic. A man can be fascinated by a subject without submitting to it. Take me as an example; a fervent anti-Nazi, I was making a military film about World War II, yet I was a convinced pacifist.

I had to have access to Andrew's collection, and so I offered him the instantly created post of art director. Mollo agreed. "I always wanted to put the collection to a creative use." Now it was my turn to impress him. I invited him to my place to look at the footage so far shot. Andrew, who loved the cinema, had never heard of amateur films, and when he saw my rushes, he was appalled. He was never someone to disguise his feelings. "Everything is incorrect," he said. I was outraged. Two years younger than me, and he sets himself up as an expert! "What do you mean, incorrect?" Andrew explained that the story was the wildest fiction. If it was to work, people had to be convinced by what they saw. It all had to be authentic. This was the first time that I had heard the word used in association with the cinema. I was used to British war films, which were about as authentic as Woolworth wine.

He told me about Erich von Stroheim. ("Hey, I'm supposed to be the film historian," I thought.) Stroheim was fanatical about authenticity, and the results showed in his masterpieces *The Merry Widow*, *The Wedding March*, and *Queen Kelly*. Emissaries were sent from Germany and Austria to discuss military matters with the great man. Little did they know that he had never been the Austrian cavalry officer he claimed; he was merely the son of a Jewish hatter from Gleiwitz. Oh, and a genius.

Andrew and I held our first session together just fifty years ago. We staged a brief scene in a bomb-battered back street of London, using an authentic Mercedes car and original *Wehrmacht* uniforms. The scene wasn't exceptional, but it looked completely different from anything else I had shot. For the first time, a scene for *It Happened Here* looked convincing.

Had I been left to my own devices, I would probably have produced just another British war film. Andrew soon taught me how thin and inaccurate these were, with their stiff upper lips and comic derision for the enemy. And I soon realized how phony they looked, with their inappropriate studio lighting and male-model actors.

With hindsight, I suppose the film was a sort of exercise in nostalgia. I was born in 1938, and my earliest memories were of the war, as were those of Andrew, born in 1940. The adults did a wonderful job of keeping the fear from us; as a result, the dogfights, doodlebugs, and military maneuvers were enormously entertaining. But one subject was never discussed: the Nazis. It was a subject avoided as strenuously as pornography to the Victorians. Something forbidden is always more enticing. My obsession with the Third Reich began in those far-off days and continues to the present.

People would try to find fault with the film before it was even made, but the beauty of a film far from completion was that one could defend it from every angle: "Ah, but are you going to include—?" "Yes, of course." (Hasty mental note!) When it came to the politics, I was on less-than-sure ground because I knew nothing about Nazism. I had battered my way through *Mein Kampf,* as well as the *Communist Manifesto,* but both were so badly written and such heavy going that I got little out of them. I learned more from arguments with my Marxist friends.

Whatever the drawbacks of *It Happened Here* may be—and they are many—it has one shining virtue. It is the only feature film produced since 1933 that attempts to set forth what National Socialism stands for. I don't believe that you could find even a German film that goes so far. We in England were never told what we were fighting for, apart from obvious clichés such as Freedom, and despite Frank Capra, I don't believe that the Americans were told either. We were certainly not told what we were fighting against, except Evil and Brutality.

We both read voraciously about the period and talked to men who had served in armies both allied and enemy. Occasionally, we learned facts that had not reached the public domain.

The scales were removed from my eyes one day when Andrew told me that someone had borrowed a swastika flag for a party. Why would anyone want a swastika flag for a party? Well, we had been invited, so along we went. It was April 20, a significant date: Hitler's birthday. A large number of men turned up, most of them with Nazi badges in their lapels. So the party was a Nazi party! I approached the host and said that I had always wanted to put this question to someone of his beliefs: how did he justify the camps?

"Oh, that's simple," he replied.

> In the last war, internment camps were built to house enemies of the state. We had them; ours were in the Isle of Man. The Germans had them, too. Now, the majority of those opposing National Socialism were, naturally enough, Jews. So more and more Jews were put inside. The internment camps, the concentration camps, began to fill up. Now, the Jews are a filthy race and they brought with them lice and disease. A camp built for 8,000 had perhaps 25,000 in it. Disease spread. Now what would you do with 25,000 diseased people? Turn them loose on the population? No, you'd exterminate them. It's the kindest thing to do.

Once I had heard that, I realized that Nazism was a disease—a disease of the mind. And you couldn't invent dialogue for such people unless you believed as they did. So we brought some of these men into the film. We couldn't use that quote, since it hardly fitted the circumstances, but what our tame Nazis said in front of our camera was disturbing enough. This marked the coming of age of *It Happened Here*.

By this time, I had found the leading actress—the Irish wife of a film collector friend—and we had embarked on further difficult scenes, such as the Germans marching through London—the very shots that appeared in that Italian documentary. I had become an editor, and my assistant was a Territorial Army reservist. He promised me fifty men for a weekend session. When the day came, they evidently found it impossible to get up. I was left in the lurch, staring at goose-stepping pigeons and wondering whether there was some way I could use those. When we came to try again, we made sure that we had plenty of men to march through Parliament Square. By a strange coincidence, a film unit was shooting a scene from *Day of the Triffids* on the other side of the square, and our production manager roared up in his car, saying "I think I've run over a triffid!" We had loudspeakers and playback equipment to broadcast German marches, to keep everyone in step—and round the corner came a group of *Bundeswehr* officers on leave from their Panzers at the Castlemartin training grounds in Wales. Most had had combat experience in the *Wehrmacht* or Hitler Youth; they were fascinated by our platoon of infantry and, to Andrew's satisfaction, pronounced them "absolutely correct." They stayed with us the rest of the day.

We got reactions much stranger than that. A woman approached one of our German officers with a cup of tea, and as I was thinking what a nice British touch, she threw it all over him. The police received calls that the British National Socialist Party had mobilized when our riot bus roared through Notting Hill Gate—and Colin Jordan and his Nazis, whose head-quarters were in the next street, tried to follow us, but we shook them off.

Much of this ended up in the papers. Despite all the publicity, offers of finance came there none. One French woman briefly raised our spirits, but she turned out to be a con artist. Andrew went into the film industry as a result of *It Happened Here.* He worked as an assistant director for Woodfall on *A Taste of Honey* and met Tony Richardson. When he heard about our film, Richardson asked to see a sample. "If you can do the film for £3,000," he said, "we will find the money."

And so we became semiprofessional. We switched to 35 mm, proved that we could blow up the 16 mm material that we had shot so far, and set out to finish the film as fast as we could.

Nonetheless, we were soon hard up for film stock. At the National Film Theatre, at a showing of a Stroheim film, I met Stanley Kubrick. He expressed interest in our film, for he had started in much the same way. "My biggest problem was raw stock," he said. "How are you doing for 35 mm film?"

"Pretty badly."

"Well, here's what you do. Call my secretary Monday and I'll arrange for you to have the short ends from *Dr. Strangelove.*" He was as good as his word, and although I was terrified that we would find Peter Sellers coming through in double exposure, everything was fine.

The picture had its premiere at the London Film Festival in 1964 at a packed house at the two thousand–seat Odeon, Leicester Square. Colin Jordan and his Nazis attended but were as quiet as mice, perhaps because of the policemen seated behind them. The reaction was everything we had hoped for. One of our coworkers, Peter Watkins, was inspired to make a film about what might happen if we lost the next war, a mocku-mentary to end them all, *The War Game* (1966).

It seemed as if a dazzling career awaited us. But then we made mistake number 1. We were dazzled by an offer from United Artists to distribute the film around the world. We should have settled for a more modest dis-tributor, for United Artists proved the worst choice we could have made. It delayed the release for two years, by which time its novelty value had faded and Peter Watkins's far more alarming film had appeared. It in-sisted on the sequence with the real Nazis being censored before it would release the picture. And despite its immediate financial success, United handled the film in such a way that we made no money, although I have no doubt whatsoever that it did.

And the hoo-ha in the press led some to believe that if we used real Nazis, we must be sympathizers. (People are very simplistic when it comes to films.) I didn't help myself by appearing on (black and white) television in dark clothing, which made me look like a Blackshirt. Thus, we were not

Filmmaker Kevin Brownlow. *Courtesy of Kevin Brownlow.*

exactly submerged by offers. In fact, the only firm offer that I can remember resulting from *It Happened Here* was second unit on *The Viking Queen*. But, oh my friends, what an adventure! Making a film is like going to war; making this one was like being a general. A strange comment from a pacifist, but when we were blowing up farmhouses, driving a forty-seven-ton Jagd Panther tank, or filming the surrender of an SS brigade, we were conscious of the supreme privilege of reliving history. We fired the authentic weapons; the extras wore the original uniforms; and some of the men we had corralled had actual experience of what we were re-creating.

Working with Andrew was an unforgettable experience. He might have been difficult to deal with—you could never foretell his reactions—but he was able to conjure up uniforms and *materiel* as if by magic. He didn't seem to need money. He would depart for Germany and return with an estate car packed with *Wehrmacht* uniforms, acquired in bulk from the air-raid shelters in Dusseldorf. He spotted a German army *Kubelwagen* on the streets of Kensington and persuaded the Polish owners to let us use it. He stopped me time and again from drifting into "film" direction—the sort of clichéd scene that could only exist in a movie. And if we were held up by a modern obstruction in the middle of shot, he would take a camouflage net and disguise it in five minutes flat. He has since worked on such major films as *The Pianist* and *Downfall,* and I regret that in making *It Happened Here*, I might have prevented him—prevented both of us—from a productive career as professional film directors.

Yet do I regret making the film? Not for one moment. But as for those larcenous TV people in Italy—is there a lawyer out there?

Epilogue: Mockumentaries Meet New Media

Spencer Schaffner

In 2009, the South African hip-hop group Die Antwoord released its online music video "Enter the Ninja," and it quickly went viral. The five-and-a-half-minute video, directed by South African cinematographer Rob Malpage, garnered millions of views on a range of video-hosting sites, including YouTube, where the most-watched version of the video has (as this chapter goes to press) more than ten million views. As "Enter the Ninja" climbed to the top of "most watched" lists at sites such as the Viral Video Chart (viralvideochart.unrulymedia.com), music critics began debating the authenticity of this gritty and bizarre act out of South Africa.[1] Die Antwoord's interactive website, www.dieantwoord.com, offered few clear answers. At the site, users can view a five-minute-and-eighteen-second documentary-style video interview with the group's lead singers, peruse photos of the band members (taken by photographer Ross Garrett), listen to the group's music, follow Die Antwoord on Twitter, and link to a profile page for the band on Facebook. In combination, all of these materials made it increasingly clear to savvy viewers that the members of Die Antwoord were carefully positioning themselves among hoax, spoof, parody, forgery, mockumentary, and the real thing.[2] This rich assemblage of online materials—websites, Twitter feeds, Facebook profiles, photos, text, music, and mockumentary-style video—is becoming the face of mockumentary online.

In this, the final chapter in *Too Bold for the Box Office: The Mockumentary from Big Screen to Small*, I discuss various examples of web mockumentaries, including my own experiences creating two web mockumentary projects: 9interviews.com and "The Urban Literacy Center Manifesto" site. I begin by describing several web mockumentary projects, showing how they include significant connections to and departures from the tradition of mockumentary films. As networked assemblages of digital texts and materials, online mockumentary projects continue to do much of the same rhetorical work of mockumentary films. For instance, web mockumentary projects use, explore, and question genre conventions, and these new web mockumentaries foreground how textual authenticity is established (and undermined). At the same time, the move to the networked environment of the web has brought with it certain noticeable changes from film mockumentaries. One change that I discuss is the commodification of mockumentaries online for use in corporate marketing campaigns. In addition, the position of what was the *viewer* of mockumentaries has shifted to more of a *user* position, with the users of web mockumentaries playing active roles in examining and discovering various elements of a mockumentary. Web mockumentary projects still reward the skepticism of savvy users, are often critical, and blur distinctions among categories such as hoax, parody, forgery, and satire; but web mockumentaries do so through much more diverse textual arrays than their filmic counterparts.

The Die Antwoord homepage (http://www.dieantwoord.com). Lead singers Ninja (Watkin Tudor Jones) at left and ¥o-Landi Vi$$er (Yolandi Visser) at right. Gray text at left indicates links to areas of the site.

WEB MOCKUMENTARIES

Mockumentary videos have proliferated online in recent years. While my focus is on complex web mockumentary projects, it is worth noting that many web mockumentaries are quite simple. This places many on-line mockumentaries in the tradition established by films such as Orson Welles's *Citizen Kane*, Woody Allen's *Zelig*, Larry Charles's *Borat: Cultural Learnings of America for Make Benefit Glorious Nation of Kazakhstan*, and the Guest oeuvre. Some of the more recent and popular examples of web mockumentary videos include but are not limited to Jordan Bellamy's "David Crowder*Band Rockumentary: Shred On, Buddy," a musical-subculture mockumentary; the series "In the Mix," which is a spoof about a London rap group; the "O-Cast," a farcical account of Greek gods living in Manhattan; and "Pretty, the Series," which deals with pageant culture. Topically as well as structurally, many of these online video projects align themselves in particular with the well-known Christopher Guest oeuvre. This is to say that web mockumentary videos appropriate the more typified conventions of documentary filmmaking (interviews with subjects and experts, voiceover, handheld camera work, and so on) to examine artists (frequently musicians) and subcultures. As one would expect, these web mockumentary videos are typically shorter than full-scale film mockumentaries, while several web mockumentaries take the form of serials in the mode of popular mockumentary-style situation comedies, such as *The Office*.

Discussions of new media forms online typically rely on Jay David Bolter and Richard Grusin's book-length study of new media titled *Remediation: Understanding New Media*.[3] This book deals with a range of new media forms, but it is worth noting that Bolter and Grusin's concept of remediation was first worked out in discussions of the relationships between film and interactive CD-ROMs. In an article published in the journal *Configurations* in 1996, Bolter and Grusin suggest that "remnants of old media" come together in assemblages of new media.[4] In reference to film versions of classic works produced in Hollywood in the 1990s, they write, "With reuse comes a necessary redefinition, but there may be no conscious interplay between media. The interplay happens, if at all, only for the reader or viewer who happens to know both versions and can compare them."[5] We see this kind of reuse and redefinition very clearly in the case of web mockumentary videos of the kind I have just described, as such videos are not so much new or innovative from a cinematic perspective, when compared with their film counterparts, as much as they are remediations of traditional mockumentary films placed in the differently networked environment of the web. Viewers of web mockumentaries can embed these new media objects on their blogs or web pages, comment on the videos, and post their own response videos via a video-sharing site such as YouTube. Online mockumentary videos, then, take advantage of some of the additional affordances of the web (interactivity, hypertext networks, multimodality) while remaining legible as mockumentaries in the filmic tradition I have referred to.

Some web mockumentaries are much more ambitious. These are multigeneric web mockumentary projects, and as networked media assemblages, they go several steps further in terms of what Bolter and Grusin call "redefinition." These are online mockumentary projects that feature traditional forms of mockumentary video embedded in an array of other texts, feeds, and online genres. In these projects, the typical goals of a mockumentary (i.e., being funny while questioning such things as genre conventions and authenticity) are accomplished not only through film but in many related and linked genres as well. Web mockumentary projects form what Clay Spinuzzi and Mark Zachry have referred to as genre ecologies[6] and others have described as "genre systems."[7] Genre ecologies and systems are enmeshed networks of texts that coordinate messages using different genres that each bring variable forms of content, messages, and valences. In the case of web mockumentary projects, these networks of texts and genres form ecologies and systems that involve such things as forged and simulated documents, photos, written materials, videos, and performances. This wide array ultimately magnifies, triangulates, and intensifies the claims to authenticity that a mockumentary can make while exploring what constitutes "real" documentation in more traditional and generically singular mockumentary videos and films.

Take, for instance, the mockumentary project released online in 2004 by the carmaker Volvo. The project was centered on an eight-minute mockumentary video titled "The Mystery of Dalarö," but that video was also accompanied by a television commercial and a spoof website (www .carlossoto.com). The mockumentary video, which is internally credited to Carlos Soto but was later revealed to be the work of Spike Jonze,[8] purports to be about a village near Stockholm, Sweden, where thirty-two people spontaneously decided to purchase the same new model of Volvo on the same day. While the film presents itself as an unbiased inquiry into this consumer coincidence, it was in fact part of an elaborate, multipart marketing campaign. In this instance, the mockumentary has been appropriated for the purposes of advertising. "The Mystery of Dalarö" is a traditional mockumentary in terms of its form—it involves voiceover narration, interviews with couples and individuals staged in authentic-looking domestic environments, and handheld camera work that, as Pat Cooper and Ken Dancyger remark, both "evokes realism and pokes fun at it."[9] However, what makes the Volvo mockumentary somewhat more complicated than traditional mockumentary videos is that it was promoted via planted participants in various online chat rooms[10] and via messages sent to mobile phones. Teasers for the video went to "mobile phones [while] driving traffic to Volvo's Web site via an email link where the full 'documentary' could be viewed and more details about the new car could be accessed."[11] By using chat rooms and mobile phones to promote intrigue about the event the video purported to document, Volvo's advertisers extended the reach of the authenticating mechanisms found in the video mockumentary itself.

The Die Antwoord web mockumentary project is even more elaborate.[12] Spearheaded by performance artists Watkin Tudor Jones (stage name "Ninja") and Yolandi Visser (written "¥o-Landi Vi$$er" on the group's website), who have worked on previous performance-based projects such as MaxNormal.TV and the Constructus Corporation, the authenticity of Die Antwoord is constructed via the group's recorded performances, in still images of the band, via music videos, on Twitter and Facebook, in a short mockumentary video interview, via other in-character interviews posted online, and in live performances. Similar to the spoof band Spinal Tap, which was "featured" in *This Is Spinal Tap* and which subsequently performed live, Die Antwoord also performs live. In a further layering of representations, snippets of those live performances have been uploaded to video-sharing sites such as YouTube where they continue to produce and reproduce the group's self-representations.

The Die Antwoord website authenticates the band's reality.

The Die Antwoord web mockumentary project is worked out across a broad spectrum of genres, all functioning as different windows on what is ultimately represented as a consistent image of the band. That consistency lends itself to a sense that the band is "real," authenticating Die Antwoord from multiple angles. Actions such as deft profile creation on Facebook and in-character tweeting via Twitter help to substantiate the band members as authentic speakers of a South Africanized hip-hop dialect while building a fan base and generating traffic to Die Antwoord's other online materials. On Twitter, followers read tweets such as "O MY GWWW-WWAAAAAAAD-'DEM GOLD COAST PRAWNS WAS PUMPIN OFF THEIR FOKKEN TENTACLES YESTERDAY INSIDE ANOTHER FOK-KEN . . . "[13] and "N to da moerefokken Z homeboy!"[14] Tweets such as these—and Die Antwoord has released a steady stream of such content online—provide a view of the band as linguistically legitimate, and that view is consistent with the numerous video interviews with the band available on video-sharing sites such as YouTube. These multiple media-based angles on the band validate the "realness" of Die Antwoord.

With that said, the goal of a mockumentary is not the same as that of a forgery: where forgeries aim to dupe naive readers and consumers of texts into thinking a fake is legitimate, mockumentaries reward savvy viewers who crack the code of the simulation. Web mockumentaries, then, ostensibly work only to authenticate their objects of study (here it is the hip-hop act that is Die Antwoord) while calling into question the very mechanisms through which such authentications are accomplished. In the more long-standing genre of mockumentary film, the objectivity of documentary films is the focus of the scrutiny. In web mockumentaries, a much broader array of texts is questioned. Photography, web design, tweeting—all of this is foregrounded by Die Antwoord as susceptible to manipulation and falsification. Mockumentaries prompt viewers to question while being entertained, and Die Antwoord accomplishes this work in multiple ways online.

What this means for the status of "the mockumentary," then, is that the transition to the web has multiplied the number of channels that are used to represent an inauthentic subject as authentic *and* that are critically examined. Die Antwoord is, in my reading of its work, directly questioning the use of sites such as Twitter and Facebook to create what appear to be static and real identities that are then used by performers and other public celebrities to establish, maintain, and generate cultural capital. Because web mockumentaries are no longer bound by the constraints and affordances of film, they are able to ultimately question much more than the genre of the documentary film. The broad spectrum of texts put to use by Die Antwoord, for instance, becomes its own objects of study. In the following section, I go on to discuss how the web mockumentaries I have created attempt to further this critical agenda.

9INTERVIEWS.COM AND THE
URBAN LITERACY CENTER MANIFESTO

One of the more compelling things about mockumentary films is that, while being funny, they are also incisively *critical* in orientation. Mockumentaries such as *This Is Spinal Tap* (1984) are known and appreciated for their humor, but *This Is Spinal Tap* is also an inquiry into and critique of fan culture, the recording industry, and the spectacle of celebrity. The mockumentary film *The Confederate States of America* (2004), by Kevin Willmott, is an even more powerful example of the mockumentary format being put to use for critical examination—this time of racism, American culture, political ideology, commodity culture, constructions of history, and the genre of documentary film itself. *Zelig* (1983), Woody Allen's farcical history about a character who is discovered to have participated in a range of important historical events, also balances humor with an interrogation of what are typically represented as complete and totalizing historical accounts. Similarly, Christopher Guest's *For Your Consideration* (2006) is a funny *and* thoughtful critique of Hollywood culture. These goals of questioning and interrogating what is known, accepted, and un-questioned have long been a centerpiece of mockumentary film, and as such, I see them as readily compatible with the main goals of academic scholarship.[15] What would it mean, I have asked, to import procedures from critical mockumentary filmmaking into the creation of online projects about academia and the creation of academic knowledge?

My first foray into web mockumentary projects, then, involved a collaborative project titled 9interviews.com.[16] Anchoring the site are nine mockumentary-style videos of job interviews with PhD candidates in the disciplines of English, cultural studies, ethnography, and speech and hearing sciences. While each video interview is different, our intention in making the project was for the videos as a whole to critically examine such things as the use and abuse of academic jargon, the genre of the "project pitch" in face-to-face interviews, specialization in academic research, and the interview process itself. The actors (interviewers and interviewees) improvised around basic themes to create the raw footage for the interviews, which was then edited down to vignettes of two to five minutes.[17] In an effort to lend the project some credibility, we bundled the videos with a credits page (several of the actors assumed pseudonyms), offered a page of "links about the job market," and established the faux production company Perkle Productions. Our intention in surrounding the videos with other texts was to authenticate the videos and provide genuinely useful materials to potential viewers. We attempted to strike a balance wherein we questioned some aspects of the academic job market while providing modest forms of assistance to potential job seekers.

To be perfectly clear, our goals were quite the opposite from the Volvo mockumentary project. Whereas Volvo appropriated the mockumentary to increase its brand awareness while telling an entertaining story, we developed this web mockumentary because it allowed us to document, make light of, and critique an emotionally and intellectually bankrupt economic arrangement.

After several months of work, we released 9interviews.com in anticipation of the 2004–2005 meeting of the Modern Language Association, a well-established event for many academic job interviews. We also promoted the site by posting about it in an array of online fora. Unique visitors to the site were soon in the thousands, and those users helped circulate links to the site. In subsequent years, traffic to the site has remained quite steady, with peaks coming around the time of the association meeting.

Four years later, in 2008, I published a second web mockumentary project, this one with a more varied array of coordinating elements and diminished reliance of video. Where the 9interviews.com project is primarily centered on the nine mock interviews, the Urban Literacy Center Manifesto site relies on a range of elements, including photos, text, links, video, and the design of the site itself. The project, which is published in the peer-reviewed online journal *Kairos: A Journal of Rhetoric, Technology, and Pedagogy*, focuses on what I, posing as "the curator," present as a found manifesto written on twenty-nine pieces of cardboard that were taped to an abandoned building in downtown Champaign, Illinois.[18] The cardboard manifesto makes several points, but its main message is that abandoned city buildings should be converted into politically radical literacy centers. These new centers are imagined as sites where what the manifesto refers to as "IMMINENT ACTION!" can take place.

Visitors to the site can explore the hyperbolic messages of the manifesto in several ways: via photographs of the original handwritten cardboard texts, in the form of a transcript, and by listening to a recorded reading of the text (playable as an embedded .wav file). However, this is not to say that the content of the manifesto is the only intended message in the Urban Literacy Center Manifesto site. As the undisclosed author of the manifesto, I was over the top in my claims, but in my role of curator, I am much more reserved. By presenting myself as merely the curator of the manifesto, I purposively distance myself from its claims while questioning why curation is not a mainstay of more academic disciplines. In disciplines of art and design, it is common for scholars to curate exhibits and for this work to count as scholarship, but selecting and arranging materials is not universally valued in the academy. With that said, the project also aims to question what could be called the academic appropriation of the "original" manifesto for purposes of academic discussion. The Urban Literacy Center Manifesto site, then, aims to encourage visitors to

The Urban Literacy Center, with the original cardboard manifesto.

think about what constitutes academic appropriation and how so-called research discoveries become the commodities trafficked in by researchers like me. Like some of the more critical mockumentaries discussed earlier, I created the multiple parts of this mockumentary project to develop various forms of critique through a range of channels and types of texts.

The use of multiple types of texts in a single web mockumentary means that one can enhance, explore, and at times undermine authenticity from multiple angles at once. Mockumentaries are not only about their subject matter but about how knowledge is produced. The Urban Literacy Center Manifesto site includes, for example, a mockumentary-style video interview titled "3 min video interview w/the curator." In this mockumentary-style interview with "Spencer Schaffner, assistant professor of English," I offer an academic, reserved perspective on the manifesto. Where the manifesto itself is volatile, emphatic, and deliberately impractical in its call to refurbish the "hollow centers" of urban life, the "interview" addresses practical questions, is largely descriptive, and ultimately focuses more on the text of the manifesto itself than on what that document tries to accomplish. The inclusion of the mockumentary-style "interview with an expert" functions as an internal reference to the genre of the mockumentary. This is to say that the interview is intended as a clue that the site is part spoof. Roughly a minute into the interview, I pose an internal contradiction by claiming that the manifesto is a "protest on a very small, vernacular scale. It's not a website. It's not a documentary film." Of course, the Urban Literacy Center Manifesto *is* a website, and it *uses* documentary film. At this point, the project gives itself away as a convoluted mixture of "real" and "fake."

What I have found most promising in my work with the mockumentary as a form, in both 9interviews.com and the Urban Literacy Center Manifesto site, is a growing understanding that the so-called spoof text at the center of a mockumentary—in *This Is Spinal Tap*, the spoof is Spinal Tap the band; in Die Antwoord's work, the spoof is also the band—is not deprived of all meaning simply by nature of being featured in a mockumentary. The handwritten manifesto that I composed, revised, handwrote on individual sheets of cardboard, and then taped to an abandoned city building in Champaign, Illinois, is not somehow invalidated because it is featured in an online mockumentary. This manifesto is deeply enveloped in a larger project about its so-called discovery, but like Die Antwoord's live performances, the manifesto is no less a "real" piece of writing. Mockumentaries prompt us to question how we know what we know, but that knowledge is not then entirely undermined. Familiar genres, like the documentary film, are certainly questioned. But this is not to say that mockumentaries traffic entirely in sham objects. What web mockumentaries presume to document can be as substantial and meaningful as the objects of study featured in more seemingly authentic investigations.

CONCLUSION

The Internet has become home to an array of fake home pages, digitally altered images, and even phishing scams, so it is no surprise that mockumentaries have proliferated in this digital environment as well. Web mockumentaries do much of the same critical and satirical work as their film counterparts while employing more widely distributed sets of texts and activities. This is to say that the web mockumentary projects that I have discussed accomplish similar things as their film counterparts while no longer being bound exclusively by the constraints and affordances of film.

One way of seeing the 1984 release of the film *This Is Spinal Tap* is as part of a public campaign for critical media awareness. This campaign could be said to have been initiated by Orson Welles, taken up by Woody Allen, and later developed by Kevin Willmott. This public campaign for critical media awareness challenges the viewers of mockumentaries to question how the genre conventions of documentary film contribute to and detract from what we know. The web mockumentaries that I have discussed further this campaign by prompting the consumers of web mockumentaries to question how multiple media forms interact online to convey a message. Web mockumentaries make it apparent that the look, feel, and design of a site are not necessarily valid indicators of authenticity. Similarly, photos can be digitally altered, videos staged and edited to enhance their authenticity, Twitter feeds strategically scripted, and assemblages of multiple texts designed to complement one another in a persuasive array. Web mockumentaries extend, then, the campaign for critical media awareness established by mockumentary film in numerous ways. With that said, though, web mockumentaries still entertain and, as I have attempted to show, present interesting materials in compelling ways.

NOTES

1. Ryan Dombal, "Who the Hell Are Die Antwoord?" *Pitchfork*, 2010, pitchfork.com/features/articles/7766-die-antwoord; Jaimie Hodgson, "Die Antwoord and 'Zef'—South Africa's Biggest Non-existent Scene," *NME Online Magazine*, 2010, http://www.nme.com/blog/index.php?blog=15&title=die_antwoord_and_zef_sooth_ifricah_s_mos&more=1&c=1&tb=1&pb=1.

2. The antics and costuming of Die Antwoord's lead singers, Ninja (Watkin Tudor Jones) and ¥o-Landi Vi$$er (Yolandi Visser), are immediately reminiscent of performance artists such as Leslie Hall (http://www.lesliehall.com) and Nikki S. Lee (http://www.tonkonow.com/lee.html). Jones, Visser, Hall, and Lee are similar in creating personas that critically examine the legibility of such constructs as class, race, and identity in popular culture.

3. Jay David Bolter and Richard Grusin, *Remediation: Understanding New Media* (Cambridge, MA: MIT Press, 2000).

4. Jay David Bolter and Richard Grusin, "Remediation," *Configurations* 4, no. 3 (1996): 311–58.

5. Bolter and Grusin, "Remediation," 339.

6. Clay Spinuzzi and Mark Zachry, "Genre Ecologies: An Open-System Approach to Understanding and Constructing Documentation," *Journal of Computer Documentation* 24, no. 3 (2000): 169–81.

7. Christine Tardy, "A Genre System View of the Funding of Academic Research," *Written Communication* 20, no. 1 (2003): 7–36; Charles Bazerman, "What Is Not Institutionally Visible Does Not Count: The Problem of Making Activity Assessable, Accountable, and Plannable," in *Writing Selves/Writing Societies: Research from Activity Perspectives*, ed. Charles Bazerman and David Russell (Fort Collins, CO: WAC Clearinghouse and Mind, Culture, and Activity, 2002).

8. Jennifer Whitehead, "Spike Jonze Unveiled as Man Behind Spoof Volvo Film," *Media Week*, 2003, http://www.mediaweek.co.uk/news/205625/Spike-Jonze-unveiled-man-behind-spoof-Volvo-film.

9. Pat Cooper and Ken Dancyger, *Writing the Short Film* (Burlington, MA: Elsevier, 2005).

10. Jean Halliday, "Volvo Goes Viral with European-Targeted Web 'Mockumentary,'" http://www.fordforums.com/f667/volvo-goes-viral-european-targeted-web-mockumentary-63871.

11. Nicola Keay, "Sybase 365 is a One-Stop-Shop for Advertising and Media Agencies, Such as Ourselves, Who Work with Clients Requiring Local and International Mobile Campaigns," 2011, http://www.sybase.com/detail?id=1050120.

12. It is worth noting that online mockumentary projects such as Volvo's "The Mystery of Dalarö" and Die Antwoord are not without precedent on the Internet. On the contrary, simulations of many kinds have proliferated online. Sites such as http://www.martinlutherking.org, which is titled "Martin Luther King Jr.— A True Historical Examination," and the Dihydrogen Monoxide site (http://www.dhmo.org) are two of the more well-known examples of online simulations. These are "fake" websites, for lack of a more nuanced term. Martinlutherking .org is a white supremacist site posing as a pro-King, informative site about the civil rights movement. The Dihydrogen Monoxide site appears at first glance be a scientific website about "the controversy surrounding dihydrogen monoxide"— while a closer examination reveals that the seemingly dangerous substance in question is merely water (H_2O). The site, then, functions as a spoof of what might be termed "environmental cause sites" (such as websites about global warming and CO_2 emissions) and in so being can be seen as advocating for an increased awareness of scientific concepts. In both these examples, of which there are many more, the design of a certain genre of website—the informative dot-org or the scientific cause site—is simulated to dupe viewers long enough to get a certain message across.

13. January 24, 2011.

14. January 19, 2011.

15. Thomas Doherty, "The Sincerest Form of Flattery: A Brief History of the Mockumentary," *Cineaste* 28, no. 4 (2003): 22–24.

16. Brandy Parris and Spencer Schaffner, 2004, 9interviews.com.

17. The video files found at 9interviews.com were not originally posted to YouTube, which was not yet established in 2004. Subsequently, in 2010, the videos were moved to the YouTube site. As a result, view counts on the individual videos do not reflect the full traffic each video has had.

18. Spencer Schaffner, "Urban Literacy Center Manifesto," *Kairos: A Journal of Rhetoric, Technology, and Pedagogy* 12, no. 3 (2008), http://www.technorhetoric .net/12.3/topoi/schaffner.

Selected Filmography

Addio zio Tom (see *Goodbye Uncle Tom*)

An Affair of Love (*Une liaison pornographique*) (2000)—two anonymous characters meet to share sexual fantasies. (France) Frederic Fonteyne

AFR (2007)—the fictional killing of the Danish prime minister by his secret gay lover. (Denmark) Morten Hartz Kaplers

An Alan Smithee Film—Burn Hollywood Burn (1998)—after his blockbuster is horribly edited against his wishes, a filmmaker runs off with his failed debut film, threatening to burn it. (USA) Arthur Hiller, Alan Smithee

Alien Abduction: Incident in Lake County (1998)—experts debate footage showing a family abducted by aliens. (USA) Dean Alioto

All You Need Is Brains (2009)—a mockumentary about the parody rock group the Zombeatles, who inhabit a zombie universe. (USA) Doug Gordon

Alternative 3 (1977)—a political conspiracy to establish a settlement on Mars is uncovered. (UK) Christopher Miles

American Zombie (2007)—a documentary project about an undead community living in Los Angeles. (USA/South Korea) Grace Lee

Andalucia: un siglo de fascinacion (1996)—a series of seven episodes in the last one hundred years of Andalusian history, creating and revising Andalusian national identity. (Spain) Basilio Martin Patino

. . . and I was born to sweet delight! (*. . . Va man dar khoshbakhti-e shirin be donya amadam!*) (2000)—the story of a lonely man who films his daily life with an 8 mm camera and his lonely neighbor who talks about his daily life on tape. (Iran) Kiarash Anvari

The Appleby Sensation (1997)—a British documentary film crew attempts to un-cover the truth about why a California yuppie couple's first child is born with a New York accent. (USA) Aaron Orullian

Bad News Tour (1982)—a rockumentary produced by a bumbling BBC crew trying to cover a struggling British heavy metal band as it heads out on tour. (UK) (Bob Spiers, BBC)

Beefcake (1999)—homage to the muscle magazines of the 1940s–1960s. (Canada/ UK/France) Thom Fitzgerald

Behind the Mask: The Rise of Leslie Vernon (2005)—a film crew follows Leslie Ver-non, a serial killer in training. (USA) Tom McLoughlin

Believe (2007)—a trailer-park-to-riches comic parody of multilevel marketing and the ethics of sudden success. (USA) T. Justin Ross

Best in Show (2000)—mock docusoap of competitors in a dog show. (USA) Chris-topher Guest

Bigger Than Tina (1999)—examines the ambition of a wildly untalented Melbourne singer-songwriter, trying to make the big time. (Australia) Neil Foley

The Big Tease (1999)—a flamboyant Scottish hairdresser mistakes an invitation to attend a Hollywood stylist contest for an invitation to compete. (UK/USA) Kevin Allen

The Blair Witch Project (1999)—three student filmmakers vanish while making a documentary on a local urban legend—only their horrific footage is found. (USA) Daniel Myrick, Eduardo Sanchez

Bob Roberts (1992)—satiric profile of a corrupt American right-wing folksinger turned politician. (USA/UK) Tim Robbins

Borat: Cultural Learnings of America for Make Benefit Glorious Nation of Kazakhstan (2006)—a Kazakh documentary filmmaker attempts to understand American culture as he travels the country. (USA) Larry Charles

Born in the Wrong Body (*Geboren in een verkeerd lichaam*) (1995)—a Dutch white het-erosexual man discovers that he is actually a member of an African tribe, and he undergoes behavioral training, therapy, and physical reconfiguration in his quest for "racial reassignment." (Netherlands) Arjan Ederveen

Bottomfeeders (2001)—a political campaign volunteer uses Spam to make a point and upsets the political system. (USA) Brian Price

Boyz Unlimited (1999)—a televised boy band spoof series. (UK) Liddy Oldroyd

Brass Eye (1997)—a series of seven documentary television episodes that satirize the media and its responses to various crimes and social ills. (UK) Michael Cumming

Brothers of the Head (2005)—the tragic biography of conjoined-twin punk rock stars. (UK) Keith Fulton, Louis Pepe

Brüno (2009)—Gay Austrian fashion guru brings his show to America. (USA) Larry Charles

The Buried Secret of M. Night Shyamalan (2004)—a documentarian discovers that the acclaimed director's supernatural films are autobiographical. (USA) Na-thaniel Kahn

The Burkittsville 7 (2000)—a companion piece to *The Blair Witch Project* in which an archivist revisits the story of a hermit thought to have murdered seven children. (USA) Ben Rock

Bye Bye Belgium (2006)—a fake television special report that Flanders has left the Belgian kingdom. (Belgium) Isabelle Christiaens, Philippe Dutilleul

The Calcium Kid (2004)—an unknown London fighter fights for the world championship. (UK) Alex De Rakoff

The Canadian Conspiracy (1985)—exposes a Canadian plan to subvert the United States by taking over its media. (Canada) Robert Boyd

Cannibal Holocaust (1980)—discovery of horrific footage captured by a film crew searching for cannibals. (Italy) Ruggero Deodato

CB4 (1993)—a rockumentary parody that follows the story of CB4, a fictional rap group that is loosely based on NWA and 2 Live Crew. (USA) Tamra Davis

C'est arrivé près de chez vous (see *Man Bites Dog*)

Children of the Revolution (1996)—Stalin's love child with a young Australian woman brings Australia to the brink of war. (Australia) Peter Duncan

Close Up (Nema-ye Nazdik) (1990)—depiction of the real-life trial of a con man impersonating filmmaker Mohsen Makhmalbaf, featuring the people involved, playing themselves. (Iran) Abbas Kiarostami

Cloverfield (2008)—a monster attack in New York is documented by a small group of friends using a handheld camera; the film is portrayed as footage classified by the U.S. military. (USA) Matt Reeves

CNNNN: Chaser Non-stop News Network (2002–2003)—a ten-episode satire of global news corporations. (Australia) Bradley Howard

Comic Book: The Movie (2004)—a documentary filmmaker and comic book fan attempt to right the unfaithful film adaptation of his favorite character, set to the backdrop of the 2002 San Diego Comic-Con. (USA) Mark Hamill

The Compleat Al (1985)—mockumentary about the career of musical parody star Weird Al Yankovic. (USA) Jay Levey, Robert K. Weiss

Confetti (2006)—British mockumentary about a fashion magazine wedding competition. (UK) Debbie Isitt

Conspiracy '58 (2002)—Short film that claims that the 1958 FIFA World Cup in Sweden never occurred but was staged as a Cold War strategy. (Sweden) Johan Lofstedt

Contest Searchlight (2002)—a parody of the contest and documentary series *Project Greenlight*. (USA) John Fortenberry

CSA: The Confederate States of America (2004)—an alternate history in which the Confederates won the American Civil War. (USA) Kevin Willmott

Culloden (1964)—a BBC report of the battle from 1746, presented as if cameras had been there to film it. (UK) Peter Watkins

The Cup (2008)—television series centering on the exploits of a minor junior-league soccer team. (UK) Matt Lipsey

Curse of the Blair Witch (1999)—promo for *The Blair Witch Project*. (USA) Daniel Myrick, Eduardo Sanchez

Da Ali G Show (2003–2004)—Sacha Baron Cohen portrays unorthodox journalists who conduct farcical interviews. (USA/UK) Sacha Baron Cohen

Da Hip Hop Witch (2000)—a hip-hop parody of *The Blair Witch Project*. (USA) Dale Resteghini

Dadetown (1996)—a small town's prosperous paper clip manufacturer closes, and a yuppie-staffed computer division takes over. (USA) Russ Hexter

The Daily Show (1996)—America's top fake news show, hosted by Jon Stewart. (USA) Chuck O'Neil, David Wain, Andy Barsh, Scott Preston, Christian Santiago

La Dame Aux Gladiolas (1979)—mock biography of Dame Edna, a character played by Barry Humphries. (UK)

Dark Side of the Moon (Opération lune) (2002)—uncovers the CIA's falsification of the *Apollo 11* moon landing. (France) William Karl

David Holzman's Diary (1967)—a young filmmaker tries to capture the reality of his life on film, in the form of a fake documentary. (USA) Jim McBride

The Day Britain Stopped (2003)—detailing a series of events leading from a nationwide train strike in the midst of winter, forcing all Britain's motorways to become gridlocked; the lack of employees able to make it to work in turn leads to two aircraft colliding over London. (UK) Gabriel Range

The Day Today (1994)—a spoof of British news broadcasting, featuring send-ups of hard-hitting journalism, sports news, and "vox pops." (UK) Andrew Gillman

Death of a President (2006)—an investigative documentary examines the as-yet unsolved assassination of President George W. Bush. (UK) Gabriel Range

The Delicate Art of Parking (2003)—a filmmaker makes an exposé of parking enforcement officers. (Canada) Trent Carlson

Diary of the Dead (2008)—film students encounter real-life zombies while making a horror film. (USA) George A. Romero

Dill Scallion (1999)—the success and failure of a Texas bus driver turned country singer. (USA) Jordan Brady

The Disappearance of Kevin Johnson (1995)—investigating the disappearance of a Hollywood filmmaker. (USA/UK) Francis Megahy

District 9 (2009)—set in Johannesburg, South Africa, aliens are forced to live in a militarized ghetto. (USA) Neill Blomkamp

Dog Bites Man (2006)—follows the misadventures of a struggling news team as it travels around the country producing news segments. (USA) Dan Mazer

Dot (2002)—the rise and fall of a dotcom. (USA) Simeon Schnapper, Brett Singer

Drop Dead Gorgeous (1999)—behind-the-scenes look at a teenage beauty pageant. (USA/Germany) Michael Patrick Jann

Elvis Meets Nixon (1997)—a mockumentary of Elvis's real-life trip to the White House to become a federal marshal under the Drug Enforcement Administration. (USA) Allan Arkush

Endsville (2000)—a religious cult in Endsville, New York, believes that the world is coming to an end as the result of a giant flood. (USA) Steven Cantor

Enlightenment Guaranteed (1999)—two very different brothers travel from Germany to Japan to stay at a Zen monastery. (Germany) Doris Dörrie

The Entertainer (1999)—tells the story of would-be comic Trevor Evans and his bid for stardom. (UK) John Arnold

Ever Since the World Ended (2001)—after a plague wipes out all but 186 people in San Francisco, two of them set out to make a documentary on their survival. (USA) Calum Grant, Joshua Atesh Litle

F for Fake (Vérités et mensonges) (1975)—Orson Welles's essay on art and filmmaking. (France) Orson Welles

Faces of Death (1978)—real accident footage mixed with mock deaths provides illustration for a coroner's display of "faces of death." (USA) John Alan Schwartz

The Falls (1980)—the world has been affected by a mysterious occurrence called "the Violent Unknown Event," which causes unexplained phenomena, such as immortality. (UK) Peter Greenaway

Fandom: A True Film (2004)—a blend of documentary and mockumentary footage that tells the story of an obsessed fan who travels to meet Natalie Portman and loses his mind along the way. (USA) Nicholas Tucker

Fear of a Black Hat (1993)—an academic filmmaker chronicles the rise and fall of the controversial hip-hop band NWH. (USA/UK) Rusty Cundieff

The Festival (2005)—a young director goes to a prestigious film festival to gain a distribution deal. (Canada) Phil Price

Final Cut (1998)—after the funeral of a filmmaker, his friends gather to watch his last project, consisting of secret videos of all their greatest sins. (UK) Dominic Anciano, Ray Burdis

First on the Moon (*Первые на Луне*, or *Pervye na Lune*) (2005)—a mockumentary about the first Russian space voyage, supposedly accomplished in 1938. Mixes archival footage and fake KGB materials. (Russia) Aleksei Fedorchenko

Fishing with John (1991–1998)—musician John Lurie knows nothing about fishing but takes friends on fishing trips to exotic locations anyway. (USA) John Lurie

The 5th Quadrant (2002)—a mock reality series on the paranormal. (Canada) Lee Smart, Bruce Pirrie

500 Bus Stops (1997)—a four-episode BBC mockumentary on the life and career of a boring, untalented singer/songwriter. (UK) Willy Smax

The Forbidden Quest (1993)—in 1931, an Irish filmmaker catches up with J. C. Sullivan, the carpenter and last surviving crew member of the *Hollandia*, a Norse ship that sailed in 1905 to Antarctica. (Netherlands) Peter Delpeut

Forgotten Silver (1995)—a New Zealand filmmaker is rediscovered from the ranks of the obscure and celebrated for his achievements. (New Zealand) Costa Botes, Peter Jackson

From the Journals of Jean Seberg (1996)—faux documentary on the life of actress Jean Seberg. (USA) Mark Rappaport

Fubar (2002)—exploring the lives and friendship of two "headbangers," from youth to adulthood and all the beer in between. (Canada) Michael Dowse

F**kland (2000)—video diary of a magician from Buenos Aires who plans to impregnate British women there to populate the islands with children belonging to both cultures. (Argentina) Jose Luis Marques

Full Frontal (2002)—seven men and women in the hours before they are all brought together at a friend's birthday party. (USA) Steven Soderbergh

Gamers: The Movie (2006)—an award-winning mockumentary about players trying to set a world record for playing a Dungeons and Dragons–like game, cast with 1980s film stars. (USA)

The Games (1998)—mock docusoap on the administration of the 2002 Sydney Olympic Games. (Australia) Christopher Folino

Get Ready to Be Boyzvoiced (2000)—a film following fictional Norwegian boy band Boyzvoice. (Norway) Espen Eckbo, Henrik Elvestad

Ghostwatch (1992)—the live television investigation gone wrong of the "most haunted house in Britain." (UK) Lesley Manning

Goodbye Uncle Tom (*Addio zio Tom*) (1971)—documentary filmmakers go back in time to the pre–Civil War American South to film the slave trade. (Italy) Gualtiero Jacopetti, Franco Prosperi.

G-SALE (2003)—a mockumentary about garage sale fanatics. (USA) Randy Nargi

Guns on the Clackamas: A Documentary (1995)—a group of filmmakers tries to film a Western, but cast members keep dying unexpectedly. (USA) Bill Plympton

Guy (1997)—the relationship between a filmmaker and her subject, as she seeks to film an ordinary life. (UK/Germany/USA) Michael Lindsay-Hogg

Happy Birthday, Mr. Mograbi (*Yom Huledet Same'ach Mar Mograbi*) (1999)—a filmmaker assigned to cover Israel's fiftieth-birthday celebration faces his own birthday as well. (Israel/France) Avi Mograbi

Hard Core Logo (1997)—a Canadian punk band self-destructs on its reunion tour. (Canada) Bruce McDonald

The Hellstrom Chronicle (1971)—originally promoted as a science fiction film, a scientist outlines the path of insects taking over the earth. (USA) Walon Green, Ed Spiegel

The History of White People in America (1985)—examination of white middle-class Americans. (USA) Harry Shearer

The History of White People in America: Volume II (1986)—more episodes from this series. (USA) Harry Shearer

Hollywood Mortuary (1998)—when the greatest Hollywood makeup artist of the twentieth century finds himself aging and unable to get work, he goes to work at a mortuary and learns to raise the dead to garner attention. (USA) Ron Ford

How to Irritate People (1968)—John Cleese offers instruction on how to irritate friends, family, and workmates. (UK) Ian Fordyce

Human Remains (2000)—dysfunctional British couples discuss their lives together. (UK) Matt Lipsey

Las Hurdes (see *Land without Bread*)

Husbands and Wives (1992)—the romantic relationships between New York couples. (USA) Woody Allen

I Am a Purifier! (2002)—tells the story of a young prostitute's adaptation to her life. (Iran) Kiarash Anvari

Idioterne (see *The Idiots*)

The Idiots (*Idioterne*) (1998)—middle-class cult groupies who feign mental retardation for the shock value of their behavior. (Denmark) Lars Von Trier

Igazi Mao, Az (see *Mao, the Real Man*)

Incident at Loch Ness (2004)—the tale of all hell breaking loose as famous filmmaker Werner Herzog attempts to make a documentary about the Nessie myth while a documentary about his life is being filmed and a pigheaded producer tries his damndest to make Herzog's film a mindless high-grossing blockbuster. (UK) Zak Penn

The Independent (2000)—an independent film producer searches for funding for his next film. (USA) Stephen Kessler

In Smog and Thunder: The Great War of the Californias (2003)—documentary about a fictional civil war in California. (USA) Sean Meredith

Interview with the Assassin (2002)—an ex-marine claims to be the second shooter in the Kennedy assassination. (USA) Neil Burger

It Happened Here (1966)—Nazi Germany successfully invades and occupies Great Britain during World War II. (UK) Kevin Brownlow

It's All Gone Pete Tong (2004)—biography of a DJ who loses his hearing. (UK/Canada) Michael Dowse

Jackie's Back! (1999)—the story of the comeback concert of a 1960s and 1970s rhythm-and-blues diva. (USA) Robert Townsend

Jeffrey Archer: The Truth (2002)—the long-suppressed story of Archer's life and loves. (UK) Guy Jenkin

Jimmy MacDonald's Canada: The Lost Episodes (2005)—a "lost" Canadian public affairs series. (Canada) Grieg Diamond

Kath and Kim (2002–2007)—television series in which a mother and daughter negotiate suburban life and love. (Australia) Gina Riley, Jane Turner

The Keith Barret Show (2004)—chat show host interviews celebrity couples in the hope of finding the secret to a successful marriage. (UK) Tony Dow

Kenny (2006)—an Australian everyman who delivers and cleans toilets. (Australia) Clayton Jacobson

Kevin Turvey—The Man behind the Green Door (1982)—a week in the life of an investigative reporter. (UK) Colin Gilbert

King of Chaos (1998)—a journalist investigates the suspicious death of a media magnate. (UK) Bryn Higgins

Kombi Nation (2003)—a camera crew follows four young New Zealanders on a tour of Europe. (New Zealand) Grant Lahood

Konspiration 58 (see *Conspiracy '58*)

Land without Bread (*Las Hurdes*) (1933)—the poverty of Spanish peasants under Franco. (Spain) Luis Bunuel

Larry David: Curb Your Enthusiasm (1999)—Larry is approached by HBO about having his own hour-long special. (USA) Robert B. Weide

The Last Broadcast (1998)—an investigation into the murder of the makers of a cable access show. (USA) Stefan Avalos, Lance Weiler

The Last Polka (1984)—the last concert of the Shmenge Brothers, a Leutonian Polka duet whose characters were first developed on Second City Television. (Canada) John Blanchard

The Left Side of the Fridge (*La Moitié gauche du frigo*) (2000)—a filmmaker captures his roommate's fruitless search for work on film. (Canada) Philippe Falardeau

The Legend of Boggy Creek (1972)—accounts of encounters with an Arkansas Sasquatch. (USA) Charles B. Pierce

Une liaison pornographique (see *An Affair of Love*)

Life beyond the Box: Margo (2003)—the biography of the character, Margo Ledbetter, from *The Good Life*. (UK) Margie Kinmonth

Life beyond the Box: Norman Stanley Fletcher (2003)—the biography of Britain's best-loved con artist. (UK) Kim Flitcroft

Lisa Picard Is Famous (aka *Famous*) (2000)—a documentarian follows an actress looking for fame. (USA) Griffin Dunne

Living with the Fosters (2002)—a reporter follows a survivalist family preparing for Y2K. (USA) Joe Schanderson

LolliLove (2004)—a story about a husband and wife who form a charity to give each homeless person a lollipop with a cheery slogan on the wrapper but who are really only serving themselves. (USA) Jenna Fischer

Look around You (2002–2005)—a parody of educational television (season 1) and documentary about "the world and future of science and technology" (season 2), set roughly twenty-five years before the actual release dates. (UK) Tim Kirkby

Love Mussel (2001)—upheaval in a small town enjoying an unexpected economic boom. (New Zealand) Michael Hurst

L7: The Beauty Process (1998)—the trials and tribulations of a punk band in a pop music market. (USA) Krist Novoselic

Made in Secret: The Story of the East Van Porn Collective (2005)—a fictional documentary about an anarcho-feminist porn collective. (Canada) One Tiny Whale

The Magician (2005)—an Australian mockumentary following the works of a hit man in Melbourne. (Australia) Scott Ryan

The Making of . . . And God Spoke (1993)—the disastrous production of an epic biblical film. (USA) Arthur Borman

Man Bites Dog (*C'est arrivé près de chez vous*) (1992)—a film crew profiles the daily life of an assassin. (Belgium) Remy Belvaux, Andre Bonzel

Man of the Year (1995)—biography of a gay male pinup model. (USA) Dirk Shafer

Man with a Plan (1996)—the political career of a Vermont dairy farmer. (USA) John O'Brien

Mao, the Real Man (*Igazi Mao, Az*) (1995)—a mock documentary on the life of Chairman Mao. (Hungary) Szlveszter Siklosi

Marion and Geoff (2000–2003)—the video diary of a Welsh cab driver, as he tells the story of his failed marriage. (UK) Hugo Blick

The Mating Habits of the Earthbound Human (1999)—an alien anthropologist looks at human courtship. (USA) Jeff Abugov

Medusa: Dare to be Truthful (1992)—parody of Madonna rockumentary. (USA) Julie Brown, John Fortenberry

A Mighty Wind (2003)—three groups of 1960s folksingers join together for a tribute concert. (USA) Christopher Guest

Mike Bassett: England Manager (2001)—the fortunes of the English football manager at the World Cup. (UK) Steve Barron

Il Mistero di Lovecraft—Road to L. (2005)—an Italian horror mockumentary about H. P. Lovecraft coming to Italy in 1926. (Italy) Federico Grecco, Roberto Leggio

Modern Family (2009–2011)—television series that takes a satirical look at the trials and tribulations of three families. (USA) Michael Spiller, Jason Winer, et al.

La Moitié gauche du frigo (see *The Left Side of the Fridge*)

Morris: A Life with Bells On (2009)—follows the efforts of an avant-garde Morris dancing team as it attempts to evolve its art form. (UK) Lucy Akhurst

Muffin Man (2003)—the downfall of the human race, largely due to overeating. (USA) Jessica Eisner

My Brother's Light (2002)—the real story behind the filming of the independent film *The After School Special*. (USA) Rocco Pucillo, Michael Wolinski

My Little Eye (2002)—an Internet webcast that is a horror version of *Big Brother*. (UK/USA) Marc Evans

Nailing Vienna (2002)—the home movie of three petty criminals trying to make a film. (UK) Jonathan English

The Naked Brothers Band (2007–2009)—stars two real-life brothers and their real-life friends in a teenage fantasy of a world-famous kid rock band, with cameras following the band members everywhere they go. (USA) Polly Draper, Melanie Mayron, Jonathan Judge

Nema-ye Nazdik (see *Close Up*)

Neurosia—Fifty Years of Perversion (1995)—while hosting a tribute to himself, a gay filmmaker is murdered. (Germany) Rosa von Praunheim

9interviews.com (2004)—lampoons the academic conference interview experience.

No Burgers for Bigfoot (2007)—spoofs amateur filmmaking, as the director and cast search for Bigfoot. (USA) Jonathan Grant, Josh McKarnie

No Lies (1973)—in the style of direct cinema, a student filmmaker strips away the defenses of his subject, and she reveals the story of her rape. (USA) Mitchell Block

The Nominees (*We Can Be Heroes*) (2005)—an Australian TV mockumentary about five fictitious candidates nominated for the prestigious Australian of the Year Award. (Australia) Matthew Saville

Norbert Smith: A Life (1989)—charts the life and career of an aging British thespian. (UK) Geoff Posner

Normal Ormal: A Very Political Turtle (1998)—takes aim at conservative British politicians, through the life and career of an ambitious right-wing member of their ranks. (UK) Metin Huseyin

Nothing So Strange (2002)—the conspiracy surrounding the assassination of Bill Gates. (USA) Brian Flemming

The Office (2001–2002)—mock docusoap focusing on the relationships among British workmates. (UK) Ricky Gervais, Stephen Merchant

The Office (U.S.) (2005–)—a U.S. send-up of office life, modeled after the British series. (USA) Paul Feig, Ken Kwapis, Greg Daniels, Ken Whittingham

Oil Storm (2005)—a fictional documentary involving increased oil prices and a hurricane similar to Hurricane Katrina. (UK/USA) James Erskine

The Old Negro Space Program (2003)—on the fictional NASSA, or Negro American Space Society of Astronauts, lampooning far-reaching racial segregation in the United States. (USA) Andy Bobrow

Omar Gatlato (1976)—male posturing and alienation in Algerian society. (Algeria) Merzak Allouache

On Edge (2001)—a professor profiles figure-skating competitors in Southern California. (USA) Karl Slovin

The Onion News Network (2007, 2011)—a parody television news program, begun in 2007 and relaunched in 2011. (USA) J. J. Adler, Will Graham

Operation Good Guys (1997–2000)—a British satire of an incompetent police force, often seen as a precursor to *The Office*. (UK) Dominic Anciano, Hugo Blick, Ray Burdis

Opération lune (see *Dark Side of the Moon*)

Otaku no video (1991)—a look at Japanese anime fandom, featuring an average person who slowly becomes a fanatic. (Japan) Takeshi Mori

Parks and Recreation (2009–)—chronicles officials in an Indiana town as they pursue random projects to enhance their community. (USA) Greg Daniels, Michael Shur

Paths to Freedom (2000)—follows two characters recently released from Dublin prison. (Ireland) Ian Fitzgibbon

People like Us (1999)—a BBC reporter covers the everyday lives of different professionals. (UK) John Morton, Willy Smax

Pervye na Lune (see *First on the Moon*)

Pilot Season (2004)—spoofs the classic prime-time television series format. (USA) Sam Seder

Posh Nosh (2003)—a parody of network cooking shows. (UK) Chris Langham

Prehistoric Park (2006)—a six-episode mockumentary that depicts a hypothetical scenario whereby a time machine is used to create a wildlife park. (UK) Nigel Marven

The Proper Care and Feeding of an American Messiah (2006)—an unemployed blue-collar man believes himself to be a fourth-generation messiah and attempts to determine his purpose. (USA) Chris Hansen

The Protagonists (1998)—an Italian movie crew goes to London to film a documentary on a murder. (Italy) Luca Guadagnino

Punishment Park (1971)—a BBC crew captures footage of a brutal penal system designed to deal with U.S. dissidents. (UK) Peter Watkins

Rain of Madness (2008)—mock on the making of the film *Tropic Thunder* (2008), parodying *Hearts of Darkness: A Filmmakers Apocalypse* (1991) on the making of *Apocalypse Now*. (USA) Justin Theroux, Steve Coogan

Rain without Thunder (1992)—a journalist covers a court case in a future America where abortion is outlawed. (USA) Gary Bennett

Real Life (1979)—a Hollywood filmmaker tries to capture a year in the life of a typical American family. (USA) Albert Brooks

Real Stories (2006)—satirical Australian television series that parodies current affairs shows. (Australia) Hamish Blake, Andy Lee

Real Time: Siege at Lucas Street Market (2001)—armed robbers seeking drug money attempt to hold up a convenience store, and the ensuing action is captured on security and police footage. (USA) Max Allan Collins

REC (2007)—a Spanish horror mockumentary about a news crew that, while making an episode of its TV show, runs into a mysterious and deadly infection. (Spain) Jaume Balaguero, Paco Plaza

Red File 66-095: Strawberry Estates (1997)—researchers investigate supernatural incidents in an insane asylum. (USA) Ron Bonk

Reno 911! (2003–2009)—Comedy Central parody of *COPS* about an inept police force in Reno, Nevada. (USA) Michael Patrick Jann, Robert Ben Garant, Brad Abrams, Thomas Lennon

The Return of Bruno (1988)—musical biography promo for a 1980s album by Bruce Willis. (USA) James Yukich

The Return of Spinal Tap (*A Spinal Tap Reunion: The 25th Anniversary London Sell-Out*) (1993)—sequel to *This is Spinal Tap*. (USA) Jim Di Bergi

R2-D2: Beneath the Dome (2001)—biography of the *Star Wars* robot character. (USA) Don Bies, Spencer Susser

R2PC: Road to Park City (2000)—a naive filmmaker sets out to make a feature film that will screen at the Sundance Film Festival. (USA) Bret Stern

Ruins (1999)—Mayan and Aztec objects are decontextualized, placed in museums, and become indistinguishable from their forged counterparts; as commentary on the colonial project, real and fake become indistinguishable. (USA) Jesse Lerner

The Rutles—All You Need is Cash (1978)—parody of the Beatles. (USA/UK) Eric Idle, Gary Weis

Rutles 2: Can't Buy Me Lunch (2002)—sequel to *The Rutles.* (UK) Eric Idle

The Sasquatch Hunters (1997)—a group of researchers encounter Sasquatch while investigating strange bones. (USA) Fred Tepper

Screwed in Tallinn (*Torsk på Tallinn*) (1999)—a busload of single Swedish men embark on a trip to Tallinn. (Sweden/Estonia) Tomas Alfredson

September Tapes (2001)—based on "found" documentary footage left by the filmmakers who have disappeared while making a film about their search for Osama bin Laden in the wake of the September 11 attacks. (USA) Christian Johnston

Series 7: The Contenders (2001)—a reality game show where contestants hunt one another. (USA) Daniel Minahan

A Set of Six (1990)—a set of six short films that follow sextuplets after they have a falling out on their birthday. (UK) John Stroud

Shadow of the Blair Witch (2000)—promo for the sequel to *The Blair Witch Project.* (USA) Ben Rock.

Shakespeare In . . . and Out (1999)—an aspiring Shakespearean actor sets out to play Othello but ends up making porn. (USA) Peter Shushtan

Showboy (2002)—a network employee being profiled by a BBC film crew is sacked and goes to Las Vegas to pursue his dream of dancing in a Vegas show. (USA) Lindy Heymann, Christian Taylor

Sidewalks of New York (2001)—six Manhattanites struggle to find romance. (USA) Edward Burns

Six Days in Roswell (1998)—an amateur ufologist visits the fiftieth-anniversary celebrations of the Roswell UFO landing. (USA) Timothy B. Johnson

Skull Island: A Natural History (2005)—a history of King Kong's island home. (USA) Michael Pellerin

Slaves of Hollywood (1999)—the competition among assistants in Hollywood. (USA) Terry Keefe, Michael Wechsler

A Small Summer Party (2001)—a television comedy spin-off of Marion and Geoff. (UK) Hugo Blick

Smallpox 2002: Silent Weapon (2002)—a docudrama that reports on an attack made by terrorists using the disease of smallpox to attack the world. (UK) Daniel Percival

Smashey and Nicey: The End of an Era (1994)—two British disc jockeys present their life stories. (UK) Daniel Kleinman

Sonovovitch (1975)—follows a fictitious Soviet ballet star, Vladimir Sonovovitch, as he defects while on tour to the West. (Canada) Miriam Adams

Space Odyssey: Voyage to the Planets (2004)—docudrama about a manned voyage through the Solar System. (UK) Joe Ahearne

Special Bulletin (1983)—television news coverage of a nuclear terrorist event. (USA) Edward Zwick

Spice World (1997)—a false documentary on the lives of the popular group the Spice Girls. (UK) Bob Spiers

The St. Francisville Experiment (2000)—four filmmakers spend the night in a haunted mansion. (USA) Ted Nicolaou

Stardom (2000)—the career of a supermodel. (France/Canada) Denys Arcand

Sto je Iva snimila (see *What Iva Recorded*)

Summer Heights High (2005)—an Australian TV mockumentary about three fictitious characters at a public high school; the show's creator, actor Chris Lilley, plays all three protagonists, and two of the characters in this series are previously featured in two of Chris Lilley's past television shows, including *We Can Be Heroes*. (Australia) Chris Lilley

Supervolcano (2005)—a docudrama about the eruption of a Yellowstone volcano. (UK) Tony Mitchell

Surf's Up (2007)—a behind-the-scenes look at the annual Penguin World Surfing Championship (animated). (USA) Ash Brannon, Chris Buck

Sweet and Lowdown (1999)—biopic of fictional jazz guitarist. (USA) Woody Allen

Swimsuit: The Movie (1997)—parody of making of *Sports Illustrated* swimsuit edition. (USA) Vic Davis

The Swiss Spaghetti Harvest (1957)—considered by many to be the original mockumentary, a BBC April Fool's Day news hoax that followed Swiss workers as they harvested the spring spaghetti crop. (UK) BBC

Take the Money and Run (1969)—the career of a failed criminal. (USA) Woody Allen

Talking to Americans (2001)—a comic look at Americans' near ignorance of Canada. (Canada) Geoff D'Eon

Tanner '88 (1988)—the failed campaign of an American presidential candidate. (USA) Robert Altman, Garry Trudeau

Tanner on Tanner (2004)—the sequel to the 1988 series, focusing on the onetime candidate's filmmaker daughter. (USA) Robert Altman, Garry Trudeau

Ted (1998)—black comedy about the Unabomber and his friends. (USA) Gary Ellenberg

That Peter Kay Thing (2000)—a series of six documentaries featuring such venues as a men's club, bingo hall, service station, and ice cream van. (UK) Andrew Gillman

That's Adequate (1989)—the head of a Hollywood movie studio rips off other studios' hit movies. (USA) Harry Hurwitz

They Shoot Movies, Don't They? (1998)—the desperate last acts of a first-time director trying to secure funding for his feature film. (USA) Frank Gallagher

The Thin Pink Line (1998)—a film crew try to save the life of a gay death row inmate. (USA) Joe Dietl, Michael Irpino

This Is Spinal Tap (1984)—classic mock documentary about the career of a British band. (USA) Rob Reiner

To Die For (1995)—the murderous ambitions of a television personality. (UK/USA) Gus Van Sant

Torsk på Tallinn (see *Screwed in Tallinn*)

Total Drama Island (2007–2008)—a Canadian TV mockumentary of reality shows about a group of teens competing for $10,000. (Canada) Todd Kauffman, Mark Thornton

The Tournament (2005)—a small Canadian town's peewee hockey team gears up for its tournament. (Canada) Bruce McDonald, Peter Svatek

Trailer Park Boys (2001)—follows Julian, Ricky, and Bubbles as they commit crimes and hatch crack-pot schemes to make money, most of which are illegal and often involve growing marijuana. (Canada) Mike Clattenburg

Tribulation 99: Alien Anomalies under America (1992)—in the year 1000, aliens flee their dying planet and take refuge under the earth's surface. (USA) Craig Baldwin

Tristram Shandy: A Cock and Bull Story (2005)—a director attempts to adapt a fictitious autobiography, in which the narrator keeps interrupting the action. (UK) Michael Winterbottom

20 Dates (1998)—a filmmaker explores the "reality" of love in Los Angeles. (USA) Myles Berkowitz

2gether: The Series (2000)—the trials and troubles of a fictional boy band in the music business. (Canada/USA) John Pozer, Robert Ginty, Paul Lazarus, Gilbert M. Shilton

Unauthorized Biography (*Milo—Death of a Supermodel*) (1997)—biography of a fictional model. (USA) Andrea Black, Russell Firestone

Unmade Beds (1997)—nine months in the romantic lives of four New Yorkers. (France/UK/USA) Nicholas Barker

The Urban Literacy Center Manifesto (2007)—a manifesto tacked to an abandoned building attempts to turn passersby into literacy activists.

. . . Va man dar khoshbakhti-e shirin be donya amadam! (see *. . . and I was born to sweet delight!*)

Vérités et mensonges (see *F for Fake*)

Vertical Features Remake (1978)—the academic debate over the reconstruction of visual research. (UK) Peter Greenaway

Waiting for Guffman (1996)—mock docusoap about the production of a small-town musical. (USA) Christopher Guest

The War Effort (2003)—a documentary film crew follows the lives of several self-proclaimed patriots who enter a radio contest during the war on terrorism. (USA) Bob Cesca

The War Game (1966)—a fictional worst-case-scenario docudrama about nuclear war and its aftermath in and around a typical English city. (UK) Peter Watkins

War of the Worlds (1938)—infamous fake news radio broadcast that inspired panic in pre–World War II America. (USA) Orson Welles

The Watermelon Woman (1996)—a young female African American filmmaker searches for the story of a black actress in the 1930s known as the Watermelon Woman. (USA) Cheryl Dunye

Wayne Anderson: Singer of Songs (2005)—seven-part documentary look at an ordinary man who dreams of breaking into the music scene. (New Zealand) Glenn Elliott

We Can Be Heroes (see *The Nominees*)

Welcome to Hollywood (1998)—a documentary maker tries to make a star out of an aspiring actor. (USA) Tony Marks, Adam Rifkin

What Iva Recorded (*Sto je Iva snimila*) (2005)—a teenager's record of a family dinner. (Croatia) Tomislav Radic

Where Are the Bredstix? (1999)—a rockumentary that follows the band the Bread-stix through rock, country, rap, a failed attempt at techno, and, ultimately, its mysterious disappearance. (USA) Matthew Tobey

Where's Marlowe? (1999)—a two-man film crew attempts to document life in the office of a private investigator. (USA) Daniel Pyne

Who's the Caboose? (1997)—New York actors compete in Los Angeles for television roles. (USA) Sam Seder

The Wicksboro Incident (2003)—two filmmakers uncover evidence of an alien inva-sion. (USA) Richard Lowry

Without Warning (1994)—television news coverage of evidence of extraterrestrial contact with Earth. (USA) Robert Iscove

The Work and the Story (2003)—the man who pioneered "Mormon cinema" is dead, and three young Mormon filmmakers compete to take his place. (USA) Nathan Smith Jones

Yacht Rock (2005–2008)—a mockumentary series on adult contemporary music during the late 1970s and early 1980s. (USA) J. D. Ryznar

Yom Huledet Same'ach Mar Mograbi (see *Happy Birthday, Mr. Mograbi*)

Zelig (1983)—the biography of a chameleon-like man who can look and act like whomever he is around, set in the 1920s. (USA) Woody Allen

Zero Day (2003)—the video diary of two students who declare "war" on their high school. (USA) Ben Coccio

Index

About the Contributors

Heather Merle Benbow is a senior lecturer in German and co-convenor of European studies at the University of Melbourne, Australia. She has published on German and European literature, film, and the history of ideas in the modern era. Her monograph *Beginnings of Modern Gendered Discourse in Late Eighteenth-Century Germany: Literary, Philosophical, and Popular Portrayals of Female Orality* appeared in 2010. She is particularly interested in intercultural issues and national identity in German culture and their intersection with gender identity. Currently, she is working on a monograph on the portrayal of Turkish women in German popular culture.

Kevin Brownlow is a historian, preservationist, and filmmaker. His childhood memories of the V-I bombings led him to create the alternate history film *It Happened Here* (1966; with Andrew Mollo) and later write the book *How It Happened Here* (1968), on the film's making. His first book, *The Parade's Gone By*, has long been considered one of the key texts in silent film scholarship. Throughout his career, he has published several other books, including *The War, the West, and the Wilderness* (1979), *Hollywood, the Pioneers* (1979), *Behind the Mask of Innocence* (1992), *Mary Pickford Rediscovered* (1999), and *Winstanley, Warts and All* (2009). His early solo film credits include Tony Richardson's *The Charge of the Light Brigade*, 1968),

Winstanley (1978), and a thirteen-year restoration of Abel Gance's *Napoleon* (1927). With his producing partners David Gill and Patrick Stanley, he has presented several noted television series and documentaries, including *Hollywood* (1980), *The Unknown Chaplin* (1983), *Buster Keaton: A Hard Act to Follow* (1987), *Cinema Europe* (1996), *Lon Chaney: A Thousand Faces* (2000), *Cecil B. DeMille: An American Epic* (2004), *Garbo* (2005), along with several others. In 2010, Brownlow received an Academy Honorary Award at the Second Annual Governors Awards for his contributions to the study of silent film.

Chris Hansen is an award-winning filmmaker and director of the film and digital media program at Baylor University. He holds an MFA in script and screenwriting. His first feature, *The Proper Care and Feeding of an American Messiah,* screened in twenty national and international film festivals, including AFI's Dallas International Film Festival and the Virginia Film Festival, and his second feature, *Endings,* won awards at festivals including Trail Dance International (Best Screenplay), Atlanta Underground (Best Director), and Southern Winds (Best Dramatic Feature). In addition to his film work, he edited the book *Ruminations, Peregrinations, and Regenerations: A Critical Approach to "Doctor Who"*; contributed the opening chapter "From Tekken to Kill Bill: The Future of Narrative Storytelling?" to Craig Detweiler's collection *Halos and Avatars: Playing Video Games with God*; and has written about independent filmmaking for *Reel Indies* magazine.

Craig Hight is a senior lecturer with the screen and media studies department at the University of Waikato. His research interests focus on documentary theory, including aspects of the production, construction, and reception of documentary hybrids and the relationship of digital media technologies to documentary practice. With Dr. Jane Roscoe, he cowrote *Faking It: Mock-Documentary and the Subversion of Factuality* (2001) and recently completed a book on television mockumentary series, titled *Television Mockumentary: Reflexivity, Satire and a Call for Play* (2010). His current research focuses on the relationships between digital media technologies and documentary practice, especially the variety of factors shaping online documentary cultures.

Linda Kornasky is a professor of English and the coordinator of the gender studies program at Angelo State University in San Angelo, Texas. She has published articles on American popular culture in *Popular Culture Review* and elsewhere, focusing on issues of regional, ethnic, and gendered identity. In 2008, she published an essay examining Polish American characters in popular American regional fiction (*Maine's Place in the En-*

vironmental Imagination, edited by Michael D. Burke). And more recently, her study of sexuality in American literary naturalism from the 1890s to the present appeared as a chapter in *The Oxford Handbook of American Literary Naturalism*, edited by Keith Newlin (2011).

Jerome Kuehl is an independent television producer whose principal but not exclusive interest is in visual history. He was historical adviser to the twenty-six-part 1964 BBC production *The Great War* and was associate producer of *The World at War*, the twenty-six-part series made by Thames Television in the 1970s, which set new standards for accuracy and authenticity in the use of film archives. He was head of general studies at the United Kingdom's National Film School from 1979 to 1981. In the 1980s, he was director of Open Media, whose productions included the much-praised late-night, live, open-ended *After Dark*. In the 1990s, he was a writer and consultant to the twenty-four-part CNN production *The Cold War*. In 2001, he wrote and coproduced the four-part *La Grande Aventure de la Presse Filmée* (The Great Adventure of Newsreels) for France 3. Jerome is part owner of *History Today*, a monthly magazine for historically minded nonspecialist readers. He is also the recipient of a lifetime achievement award by FOCAL International, the Federation of Commercial Audiovisual Libraries. He is currently working on a television history of the United Nations as a political-military alliance during the Second World War.

Thomas Prasch is professor and chair of the department of history, Washburn University. He received his PhD from Indiana University, writing a dissertation on working-class subjects in Victorian photography. He served as film review editor for the *American Historical Review*, 1995–2004, and since 2001 has edited a biannual selection of film reviews for *Kansas History*. Recent publications include "Behind the Veil: Forms of Transgression in Ken Russell's *Salome's Last Dance*," in *Ken Russell: Re-viewing England's Last Mannerist*, edited by Kevin M. Flanagan (2009); "Eating the World: London in 1851," in *Victorian Literature and Culture* (2008); entries on London 1862, Calcutta 1883–1884, and London 1886 in *Encyclopedia of World Fairs and Exhibitions*, edited by John Findling and Kimberley Pelle (2008); and "Mirror Images: John Thomson's Photographs of East Asia," in *Century of Travels in China: Critical Essays on Travel Writing from the 1840s to the 1940s*, edited by Douglas Kerr and Julia Kuehn (2007).

Eve Allegra Raimon is professor of arts and humanities at the University of Southern Maine. Her book *The "Tragic Mulatta" Revisited: Race and Nationalism in Nineteenth Century Antislavery Fiction* was published in 2004.

She also coedited the collection *Harriet Wilson's New England: Race, Writing and Region*, published in 2007, which includes a forward by Henry Louis Gates Jr. Professor Raimon teaches in American studies, focusing on ethnic and gender studies as well as critical race theory. Her research interests intersect American studies and cultural studies. She also teaches in the MA program in American and New England culture and in the women and gender studies program. Other publication topics include the rhetoric of higher education curricular reform, the political history of U.S. miscegenation, and the interdisciplinary teaching of race. Her current project is *Beyond the Black Heritage Trail: Race, Place, and Public Memory*, with Cassandra Jackson, associate professor at the College of New Jersey. Professor Raimon received her PhD in English and American literature from Brandeis University in 1995.

Gary D. Rhodes currently serves as codirector of film studies at the Queen's University in Belfast, Northern Ireland. He is the author of such books as *Lugosi* (1997), *White Zombie: Anatomy of a Horror Film* (2002), and *The Perils of Moviegoing in America* (2012), as well as the editor of such anthologies as *Horror at the Drive-In* (2001) and *Edgar G. Ulmer: Detour on Poverty Row* (2008). Rhodes is also the writer-director of such documentary films as *Lugosi: Hollywood's Dracula* (1997), *Chair* (2000), and *Banned in Oklahoma* (2004). Currently, he is at work on a history of the American horror film to 1915.

Spencer Schaffner earned his PhD in language and rhetoric from the University of Washington and is currently associate professor of English at the University of Illinois, Urbana-Champaign, where he teaches courses for the Illinois Informatics Institute, the Odyssey Project, and the Center for Writing Studies. Spencer has published in such journals as *Discourse and Society*, *Ethos*, *American Literary History*, and the *Journal of Sport and Social Issues*. He is also the author of *Binocular Vision: The Politics of Representation in Birdwatching Field Guides* (2011). Spencer's interest in web mockumentaries has led him to create two online mockumentary projects: 9interviews.com, an online mockumentary about the academic job market; and "The Urban Literacy Manifesto," a scholarly mockumentary project.

John C. Tibbetts is an associate professor of film at the University of Kansas. His eighteen published books include, most recently, *Schumann: A Chorus of Voices* (2010) and *All My Loving? The Films of Tony Palmer* (2009). Other books include *The American Theatrical Film* (1985), *Dvorak in America* (1993), *Encyclopedia of Novels into Film* (2002), and *Composers in the*

Movies (2005). His articles on film, literature, painting, theater, and music have appeared in *Notes, Film Comment, Opera News, Historical Journal of Film Radio and Television,* and *Literature/Film Quarterly.* He has worked as a broadcaster for National Public Radio, the Christian Science Monitor Radio Network, Voice of America, and CBS television. Both of his radio series, *The World of Robert Schumann* and *Piano Portraits,* have been heard worldwide on the WFMT broadcast network and National Public Radio. He was recently awarded the 2008 Kansas governor's Arts in Education Award. His latest book is *The Gothic Imagination: Conversations about Science Fiction, Fantasy, and Horror in the Media* (2011).

A. Bowdoin Van Riper is a historian who specializes in depictions of science and technology in popular culture. His publications include *Science and Popular Culture: A Reference Guide* (2002), *Imagining Flight: Aviation and the Popular Imagination* (2003), *Rockets and Missiles: The Life Story of a Technology* (2004; reprint, 2007), and *A Biographical Encyclopedia of Scientists and Inventors in American Film and Television* (2011). He was guest editor, with Cynthia J. Miller, of a special two-issue themed volume of *Film & History* ("Images of Science and Technology in Film," spring/fall 2010); and the editor of *Learning from Mickey, Donald, and Walt: Essays on Disney's Edutainment Films* (2011). He is currently at work on two collections coedited with Cynthia J. Miller: *Undead in the West: Vampires, Zombies, Mummies, and Ghosts on the Cinematic Frontier* and *Cadets, Rangers, and Junior Space Men: Televised "Rocketman" Series of the 1950s and Their Fans.*

Robert G. Weiner is associate humanities librarian at Texas Tech University, where he serves as the liaison for the College of Visual and Performing Arts and film studies. He is the coeditor of *From the Arthouse to the Grindhouse* (2010), *James Bond in World and Popular Culture* (2010), *Cinema Inferno* (2010), and *In the Peanut Gallery with Mystery Science Theater 3000* (2011). Rob's writing has appeared in *The Landscape of the Hollywood Western* (2006), *The Gospel according to Superheroes* (2006), *Gotham City: 14 Miles* (2010), and *Routledge History of the Holocaust* (2011), as well as in *Shofar, Texas Library Journal,* and *The International Journal of Comic Art.* He is the author of *Marvel Graphic Novels: An Annotated Guide* (2007) and coauthor of the *The Grateful Dead and the Deadheads: An Annotated Bibliography* (1997). He is the editor of *Perspectives on the Grateful Dead* (1999), *Captain America and the Struggle of the Superhero* (2009), and *Graphic Novels in Libraries and Archives* (2010). Rob also serves on the editorial board for the *Journal of Graphic Novels and Comics.* He was featured as music historian in the film *Lubbock Lights* (2005) and has appeared on the nationally broadcast television program *Biography.*

Jim Welsh (James Michael Welsh) was educated in Bloomington, Indiana, and Lawrence, Kansas, majoring in English and history at Indiana University and specializing in textual criticism and cinema studies at the University of Kansas. He founded the Literature / Film Association and was editor in chief of *Literature/Film Quarterly* for more than thirty years. His recent books include *The Encyclopedia of Novels into Film* (2nd ed. rev., 2005), coauthored with John C. Tibbetts; *The Literature/Film Reader: Issues in Adaptation* (2007), coedited with Peter Lev; *"No Country for Old Men": From Novel to Film* (2009), coedited with Rick Wallach and Lynnea King; *The Pedagogy of Adaptation* (2010), coedited with Laurence Raw and Dennis Cutchins; and *The Francis Ford Coppola Encyclopedia* (2010), coauthored with Gene D. Phillips and Rodney Hill.

Scott Wilson is a senior lecturer in film history, film theory, and cultural studies in the Department of Performing and Screen Arts at Unitec, Institute of Technology in Auckland, New Zealand. Scott had worked extensively in the music industry, both locally and internationally, before moving toward an academic career. Having previously taught at the University of Auckland and at Victoria, University of Wellington, Scott combines his continuing interests in popular culture with his love of cinema theory and critical and cultural studies. Scott has published on areas as diverse as album cover design, nostalgia in national cinema, and the hermeneutics of road safety advertising. His first book, *The Politics of Insects: David Cronenberg's Cinema of Confrontation* (2011), is now available.

About the Editor

Cynthia J. Miller is a cultural anthropologist specializing in popular culture and visual media. She is film review editor of *Film & History: An Interdisciplinary Journal of Film and Television Studies* and serves as president of the Literature/Film Association, as well as on the editorial advisory board for *The Encyclopedia of Women and Popular Culture*. Cynthia has written and spoken extensively on the B-movie and Western film genres, and her writing has appeared in a range of journals and volumes across the disciplines, including *Film & History, Women's Studies Quarterly, Human Organization, Anthropologica, Social Justice, The Journal of Popular Film and Television, Contexts: Understanding People in Their Social Worlds, The Historical Journal of Film, Radio, and Television, Post Script*, and *Kansas Quarterly*. Cynthia has also served as guest editor for *Film & History* and *Post Script: Essays in Film and the Humanities*. She is currently coediting two anthologies with A. Bowdoin Van Riper: *Cadets, Rangers, and Junior Space Men: Televised "Rocketman" Series of the 1950s and Their Fans* and *Undead in the West: Vampires, Zombies, Mummies, and Ghosts on the Cinematic Frontier*.